Praise for
Living on Purpose

For too many individuals, knowing God's will seems a far-off, mysterious, difficult to understand process. In the pages of *Living on Purpose*, author Barry Ham brings clarity to the believer who seeks to better grasp God's purpose for their life.

Living on Purpose is an excellent, thought-provoking, God-loving, and think-activating book to help you in your quest to find and follow God's direction for your life.

JOSH D. MCDOWELL
Author and speaker

Watching the Summer and Winter Olympics always stirs my patriotic spirit. Watching the Paralympics hits all my emotional and motivational chords. Watching athletes competing in spite of their physical and mental limitations is humbling and makes me appreciate the fierce capacity in the human spirit to "live life with a purpose."

Barry has created a great blueprint for examining the areas of life where focused intentionality is necessary. No matter your age or station in life, this is a valuable read. For those already "laser focused with purpose" it can function like a meat cutter "steeling" his knife's edge for razor sharpness. For those drifting and meandering through life, it can be a GPS to help identify markers and get you focused on a destination. And the last chapter is a wonderful "jump starter" for clearing the fog and finding determination to make the rest of your journey "purpose focused."

DON NEEDHAM
Pastor of Seniors at Woodmen Valley Chapel
Colorado Springs, CO

I have read several books on mission, purpose, calling, etc. I believe that Dr. Barry Ham's *Living on Purpose* is the most practical book on this subject I have read. It not only speaks to the reality of purpose in the life of believers, but it provides practical steps to consider in living the reality that God designed us for a purpose.

Today, many of us are living life through our own efforts and abilities. We work hard, have families and friends, and have many distractions intended to entertain us. This routine of life often leaves us frustrated, wanting more, and seeking authentic purpose in life. We end up asking ourselves, "Do I have a purpose here on earth?" This question is complex and may be considered too big to answer or even understand. Dr. Barry Ham presents a compelling discussion that details how God designed us to live life with purpose. *Living on Purpose* presents practical actions designed to help us purposefully live in relationship with God, others, and ourselves. Living with such intent leads to a legacy that reflects a life lived on purpose.

Dr. Sarah Scherling, EdD
Vice President of Academic Administration
College of Adult and Graduate Studies
Colorado Christian University

Life can be hectic and demanding, but there are really just two overarching callings that should govern all we do: love God and love others. Barry Ham has shown us how an unwavering commitment to those two tasks can help everything in our lives fall beautifully into place.

Jim Daly
President of Focus on the Family

Living on Purpose takes you on a journey to building the life you were created to live. This book gently sets you back on track in your relationships, work, finances, health, decision making, and goals for life. I thoroughly enjoyed reading it and am going through sections of it a second time.

Chuck Hagele, MBA, CPC
Executive Director of Project Patch

As a "visual learner," Barry Ham has written a sort of "user's manual" on living life with purpose! In a compelling way, he shares his personal story and practical examples that reveal how we can grab life and live it to the fullest! *Living on Purpose* will be a resource for anyone needing to get back on the path of their designed purpose in life and for anyone who wants to explore tried and tested ways to find their purpose in life.

MARK TEDDER
Director of Worship Planet

Seriously, another book on living a purposeful life? Honestly, I've read many. But this one made me uncomfortable, as it caused me to think and rethink about who and what matter most in this life. I needed the recalibration. You might as well. In his typical warm, engaging, and humorous style, Barry helps us to live life as it's intended to be lived.

WADE BROWN
Executive Director of PastorServe

"Why are we here?" is a mountain of a question. For many of us, its terrain is so massive and steep that we turn away from any semblance of an attempt to explore the answers, much less live them out. In *Living on Purpose*, Dr. Barry Ham not only winsomely invites us on the journey, but with wisdom gleaned from many years as a teacher and counselor—as well as a fellow human being—he also provides us with biblical guidance and practical footholds for the climb. I've known Barry for many years, and he authentically models what he says in these pages. I'm grateful for such a roadmap that beckons us with the Life-giving invitation to embrace fully the reality that we've been created by God with loving intentionality.

MATT HEARD
Founder of *THRIVE* and author of *Life with a Capital L: Embracing Your God-Given Humanity*

Dr. Barry Ham has done a most practical, comprehensive, and inspiring pursuit of *Living On Purpose*. Barry is like the wise sage who has *really* been there, done it. He calls the reader out of the masses and upward toward the tightrope of greater possibilities for an abundant life that promises to outlive us; a spiritual and relational legacy. Throughout each chapter, Barry stands on solid footing using Biblical truths, tried and true life experiences, and an easy conversational style that offers an uplifting voice high above the crowd. As he was with me, let Barry be your guide and there's more than a chance that together you will get to the other side!

JEFF KOZYRA,
Restoration pastor, New Life Church,
Colorado Springs, CO.

Living
on
Purpose

DESTINY IMAGE BOOKS BY BARRY HAM

Unstuck

God Understands Divorce

Living on Purpose

KNOWING GOD'S DESIGN FOR YOUR LIFE

BARRY D. HAM PH.D.

DESTINY IMAGE® PUBLISHERS, INC.

P.O. Box 310, Shippensburg, PA 17257-0310

"Promoting Inspired Lives."

This book and all other Destiny Image and Destiny Image Fiction books are available at Christian bookstores and distributors worldwide.

Cover design by Eileen Rockwell
Interior design by Terry Clifton

For more information on foreign distributors, call 717-532-3040.

Or reach us on the Internet: www.destinyimage.com.

ISBN 13 TP: 978-0-7684-1728-9
ISBN 13 EBook: 978-0-7684-1729-6
ISBN 13 HC: 978-0-7684-1730-2
ISBN 13 LP: 978-0-7684-1731-9

For Worldwide Distribution, Printed in the U.S.A.

1 2 3 4 5 6 / 20 19 18 17

This book is dedicated:

First, to our children and their spouses. It is the longing of my heart that you would intimately embrace the heart and the desires of the Living God to live fully the life for which He has created you.

Second, to our young granddaughter Launa, who I pray will grasp the concepts of this book from an early age. If you do, the Lord will use you in powerful and significant ways.

Third, to my cousin Diana Pilcher, who never ceases to amaze me with her determined faithfulness to overcome the challenging obstacles of this world in order to live out every single day that God has entrusted to her. Thank you for your continued inspiration to purposefully live life!

Fourth, to all those who truly long to know why they are here, the purposes for which they were created, and the destiny to which they have been called. *"Ask and it will be given to you; seek and you will find; knock and the door will be opened to you"* (Matt. 7:7).

Acknowledgments

While it might be easy to assume that a book travels from the author's thoughts to paper (or computer keyboard) in a straight or direct line, it is actually quite a bit more circuitous than that. In the case of this book, it began to percolate some 30 years ago following life-changing events and intense soul searching. It then was tucked away in the crevices of my brain for numerous years. It came to the forefront about 15 years ago and then once again was shelved for a few years as attention was given to writing some other pressing materials. But finally it has made it to these pages. Yet, even then, it wasn't without the thoughts, support, and assistance from others to whom I am most grateful.

I will never forget the lengthy, transparent, and gut wrenchingly honest conversations that took place with my friend of over 45 years, Mark Berrier, as I began this journey in the mid-1990s. Thanks, Mark, for your commitment to faithful, caring, and genuine relationship. *"Faithful are the wounds of a friend..."* (Prov. 27:6).

In every book project with which I have been involved, the humble, servant-hearted guidance of author and friend Paul Batura has been invaluable. Thanks, Paul, for your attention to making time with people a priority.

Once again, the folks at Destiny Image have been phenomenal. I appreciate the commitment to excellence with which each member of the team pursues his or her piece of the process. Ranging from publicist Sierra White to production project manager John Martin, and all those in between, know that your desire to glorify God with the best product possible does not escape notice. Thank you to editor Jennifer Janechek for your tireless eyes that peruse each word and thought in a manuscript to catch mistakes, ask questions, and clarify my thoughts. My eyeballs would cross if I did what you do on a daily basis. But I'm glad that you do it!

Brad Herman, while you are also a part of that team, I want to express my gratefulness to you separately. You have been the agent and the person with whom I have been privileged to work these past couple of years. You have been everything from a sounding board to a source of creative thought. You have indulged my obsessiveness with particular details while never wavering in your willingness to "give it to me straight" as we have thrown around ideas. But even beyond that, through our regular phone conversations and e-mails, you have become a trusted friend. Thank you.

Once again, I would not be able to produce what I do were it not for the constant support and love of my wife and best friend, Andee. Whether you are reading the first drafts that come out of the printer, correcting my initial typos, or giving me insights as to ways that I can make concepts more digestible, you are beyond the best! I could not have a better partner in life. Thank you does not begin to adequately express that—but, thank you!

Finally, I have been able to pen these pages only because of the grace that God Almighty has extended me to do so. Without His love, forgiveness, and willingness to use the rants and musings of a decidedly flawed individual, it would not be possible. It is to Your glory that I commit the words in this book!

Contents

Foreword

"Purpose." How do we know it? Is it predetermined long before we are ever here, or is it just something that happens to us?

While I have been involved in the world of broadcasting for more than 50 years, I didn't get here by design—at least not my own, but by a broken finger. It was 1967, and I was 12 years old and playing little league baseball. Now, looking back, I don't know that I was endowed with any particular talent for the sport, yet I was pretty convinced that major league baseball should draft me right out of junior high school. I was sure that I would be a valuable asset to them. I was playing catcher when, about halfway through the season, a foul tip hit and broke my right index finger. With my season over, I was invited up to the local radio station broadcast booth to help with the coverage of the little league games. While it might be surprising that a radio station would cover youth sports, you have to remember that this was Hope, Arkansas. As it turned out, I did OK at this job and before long was hosting my own youth show and even helping out with the news.

Did God cause the broken finger so that I would enter the broadcast field and experience all that would follow, or did He simply use the situation, as it happened, to my advantage? Was I pursuing my passion, or was God awakening a passion within me that I didn't even know I had? These are all good questions.

When I was ten years old, my grandma would take me to the vacation Bible school summer program. It was during this time that I realized that Jesus, the Son of the Almighty God, wanted to have a relationship with me. That seemed pretty clear as I made my decision to follow Him, and I have never looked back. But again, did God cause me to attend that vacation Bible school so that I would accept Him, or did He use the fact that I was there to lead me into a relationship with Him?

Again, good questions. But someone else might ask, "Does it even matter whether or not I fully understand the cause and effect of circumstances that seemed to have shaped the course of my life?

In the pages of *Living on Purpose,* you will find answers to some of these very questions, but more importantly, you will find reasons for your purpose and purpose for your journey.

You see, our existence here on this earth, yours and mine, is not an accident. Our Creator had very specific things in mind when He placed us here. And at one time or another, most of us ask ourselves, "OK, why am I here? What is my existence all about?" Those are some of the very reasons that Barry wrote this book—so that you don't have to wonder and wander; so that you don't have to guess, but you can clearly know God's purposes for your life.

During the 19th century, it was the custom of the young Native American Dakota men, especially during puberty, to seek contact with the Divine power. A young man would leave the camp and find a secluded spot where he could concentrate alone. He would spend days without food, drink, or sleep—begging and imploring the Divine to give him some kind of direct revelation. In order to convince the gods of his sincerity, he might gash his arms with a knife or even cut off a finger. He was desperate for some kind of vision where an animal or some other phenomenon would speak to him, giving him specific direction for his life as an adult.

I am grateful, and you probably are too, that we don't have to go to such extreme measures to know God's purpose and direction for our lives. It is my hope and prayer that the pages of this book will encourage and enlighten you as you strive to be "living on purpose."

—Governor Mike Huckabee

Chapter One

What, Where, Why?—An Introduction to God's Reasons

"The purposes of a man's heart are deep waters,
but a man of understanding draws them out."
—PROVERBS 20:5

What? Where? When? Why? These are the logical questions that begin this book. What is the meaning of life? Where am I going? When will it all make sense? Why am I here? My suspicion is that if you are reading these words, then you are asking these questions, which have preoccupied the great thinkers and philosophers of the ages and millions of other people.

I remember sitting in a graduate course decades ago with Dr. Jim Snyder. He would come to class and talk about his hour-long drive from the mountains to the university that he made every day. As he described the music he listened to and the sandwich he ate on the drive in, he would wax philosophical, asking, "Are we just on a mud-ball flying through space?"

As much as I enjoyed Dr. Snyder's counseling classes, I also realized that his question was genuine—and that he had no earthly idea as to the answer. And yet, he was not much different from the vast majority of people who travel on this "mud-ball." How we live life is not determined by our level of education, our financial status, or our physical appearance. We all, universally, at one time or another, unless our thinking processes are completely rusted, have wondered: "Where did man come from?" "Why was I born?" "What am I supposed to do?" And the list goes on.

I don't believe for a moment that it is an accident that we ask these questions. I wholeheartedly believe that those deep longings to know and understand are a part of our psychological and emotional DNA. They have been wired into us at the core of who we are. But I am getting a little ahead of myself.

~~~

As a university professor myself, I frequently tell my students that they are the exception. Exception? The exception to most of the population. By that I mean—they are thinkers. Now perhaps I should clarify. While it would be nice to believe that all college and university students are thinkers, I'm afraid that is not necessarily the case. You see, the vast majority of students who enter the post-secondary educational world do so for one of two reasons: either 1) they have chosen a career path that they desire to pursue, or 2) they are "supposed to." Supposed to what? Supposed to go to college.

Time and time again I find myself in conversations with students, counseling clients, or just friends in casual chit-chat. What I repeatedly discover is that most of them haven't given a great deal of thought to what this mud-ball's journey through space is all about. Well, that is not completely true. In one of their soul-searching philosophical moments, perhaps during a high school biology course, they privately wondered, "Hmm, I wonder what life is all about?" But it may have seemed like a topic that was too overwhelming, too big to grasp, and kind of hurt their head to think about. So, they pulled their head back below the clouds and rejoined the masses that simply went on with their lives.

I think that some feel that contemplating and asking life's hard questions isn't necessarily rewarding. Instead, they believe they will get smacked down for thinking outside of the box. I picture the "whack-a-mole" game at the arcade. When the mole pops up, you quickly whack him with your mallet. People who dare to think risk a similar response. It would seem that most people are content to adhere to the following life script: a) spend your elementary years watching cartoons and playing make-believe games with your friends; b) try not to stand out too much during middle school in order to make it to high school in one piece; c) don't say anything that will make you unpopular and do your best to get OK grades in high school so you can get into college; d) go to college so you can get a diploma in order to get a job; e) get a job in your chosen field in order to make a living; f) get married so that you will have a companion and so that you can have kids (though in this age it doesn't always seem to be in that order); g) build a life creating the 2.5 kids, obtaining the dog and cat, buying the brick house with the two-car garage, and taking the annual vacation; h) regularly invest in your 401(k) plan so that you can retire as soon as possible from that job that you only slightly enjoy (and that is on a good day); i) retire and become a couch potato, a snowbird, or a perpetual RV traveler so that you can…well; j) wait for life to end.

OK, I know I haven't painted this life in the best of lights, but I can't tell you the number of individuals, ages 65, 75, or 85 with whom I have spoken who have described their life in similar terms. When

I asked them if they were satisfied with their last three quarters of a century, their reply, far too often, is, "No." If I then pursue questioning, "Then why did you do it this way?" the response is often, "Because that is what I thought I was supposed to do." In other words, they had followed the pattern handed down by their parents, allowed themselves to be influenced by the pursuits of their friends, or got caught in the flow of the society and culture—chasing dreams of money and success as presented throughout the media. They didn't do too much thinking—they just followed.

Back to my university students. While some of my students haven't been out of high school long, I have many who are adults who have been in the workforce, experiencing more of life, before stepping out of that flow to re-enter school. They have thought this decision through, at least a little bit, though they still may not have a clear picture of what life is about.

So, we have to begin to ask ourselves some challenging questions. Well, I guess we don't actually have to. But if we don't want to wake up at 75 years of age and find ourselves thinking, "Oops, I missed it. I missed the opportunity of this thing called 'life,'" then some questions are in order. Some of these questions I have mentioned above. Others may include the following: "Do I find myself simply trying to get through life as painlessly as possible so that I can then retire? Because surely that is when I will begin to enjoy life." "Do I get up and go through the routines of the day just so that I can get up and do it again tomorrow?" "Is all that I have to look forward to in life summed up in 'acquire some stuff, have a little bit of fun, and then die'?" "Do I endeavor to stay busy so that I don't have to think about it all?" As one song sung by Peggy Lee so clearly expresses:

Is that all there is?
Is that all there is?
If that's all there is, my friends,
Then let's keep dancing.

Let's break out the booze and have a ball
If that's all there is.[1]

One author asked the questions like this: "Is there an intelligence behind the origin of the universe? Is there a purpose for its existence, and our individual lives? Or is the universe simply an accident, something that emerged out of nothing? Perhaps simply one of an infinite number of universes that somehow arose from pre-existing quantum laws?"[2]

Questions, questions, questions! But are there any answers? It is my confident and convinced position that there are. And that is what this book is truly about. I don't believe for one minute that we are an accident condemned to wander about aimlessly, filling our time with busyness until this life is over and we draw our final breath. Every fiber in my being wants to scream out to a lost and dying world— "We were created and placed here with purpose and for a purpose. And you are not abandoned to guessing what it is!"

Beginning Point

"Living life without purpose is like embarking across the ocean without a destination in mind, compass or any other navigational equipment. It might be enjoyable for the first few days or weeks, but when water and food rations run low, the Dramamine pills run out, and you are totally lost with no idea which way is the quickest to land, things get drastic fast. We wouldn't think of taking a risky voyage like this, but somehow we end up sailing through life without a clue as to where we are going or what it will take to get there."[3]

Does that sound familiar? Have you been going through life doing what you're "supposed to do," following the latest trends of the culture, endeavoring to keep up—and you're not even sure with what? If that describes you, I get it. It once described me as well.

The question was driven home for me over 30 years ago. I was a relatively young husband with two children. I lived in a decent suburban neighborhood and was serving in a local church ministry. However, some developments in life had occurred that were unraveling my core. No, it wasn't any single traumatic event such as a tragic accident or death. It actually was a slowly developing disillusionment—a disillusionment with people. "Wait—with people? I thought you said you were in ministry. Doesn't that involve people?" Oh yes—very much so. Maybe too much so. As I worked with people, I guess I expected them to grow and behave and treat each other with love and kindness. Along with that, I'm sure that I put too much confidence in them, expecting them to meet my needs for validation. I mean, if they grew in their relationships and their love of God, then that must mean I was doing a good job. But if they weren't, then I felt like a failure. And if my success depended on their responses, then I guess I was a failure. Much like in the song lyrics from earlier, I began to ask myself, "Is this it? Is this all there is?" Those questions began my journey into purpose.

Now the easiest thing to do would have been to bury my head in the sand and just try to pedal faster. I mean for many people, busyness helps them avoid deeper thought and reflection. Or perhaps I could find a new career field that offered more excitement. But I knew deep down inside that any of those efforts would have the same effect on me as getting on a glamorous cruise ship with no destination. So, I took the risk and began to ask myself hard questions—really hard questions: "What am I supposed to be doing?" No—deeper. "Do I even want to do ministry anymore?" No—deeper. "Do I even want to serve God?" Getting closer. "Do I even want to believe in God?" Keep going. "Does God even exist?" There we go. It doesn't get much more foundational than that.

But with that question came a flood of other related thoughts: "If He doesn't exist, then I really am aimlessly wandering on a mudball flying through space. Now what?" And that is where I began my search—a desperate search. I had to know the answer to this question before there could be any other questions. Skipping over this because it made my brain hurt would have been akin to my saying, "It is too much work to figure out a destination for my trip—let's just get on the ship, or the car, or the airplane." Because if there is no destination, then even the mode of transportation is inconsequential.

In my search, I read and read and read. I spoke to and interviewed scholars and then read some more. I read everything I could get my hands on—from philosophy to archeological data. Now this book is not meant to be an apologetic (defensive) work about God, but a book about *purpose*. However, I will share with you that there was an overwhelming amount of rational, thoughtful evidence that more than supported a belief in the existence of God. A couple of examples of this would be *Evidence That Demands a Verdict* and *More Evidence That Demands a Verdict*, both by Josh McDowell.[4] These have since been updated to *The New Evidence That Demands a Verdict*.[5] McDowell's books played a significant role in my journey. A few other scholarly authors whose works I would recommend would be Ravi Zacharias, Lee Strobel, Norman Geisler, and Frank Turek. But know that there are countless others. Needless to say, these few sentences here don't even begin to summarize the vast amounts of material that I consumed in my quest to answer that one simple question: "Does God exist?" But for the purposes (no pun intended) of this book, know that the answer I arrived at was a resounding yes! This is a huge, essential question that is foundational to all others. And my one-paragraph description is not meant to trivialize this issue in any way. If you haven't answered this question for yourself, I would encourage you to check out some of the many resources available.

Now that I had answered the bottom-line core question regarding the existence of God, the follow-up questions were, "Well then, if He exists, how do I know what He wants me to do? What does He expect of me? I am still flying on a mud-ball through space—now what?"

Again, my quest for answers took me from the depths of archaeology to the heights of scientific probability. I examined the texts of various religions, studying them through the lens of rational evidence. Am I saying that God can be boiled down to hard measureable facts and that there is no need for faith? Certainly not. But all of creation screams that the Creator is not the Master of chaos but of order. It is possible to arrive at our faith from a place of reason. We are even encouraged in First Peter 3:15 to be prepared to explain to others the reason for our hope (see 1 Pet. 3:15). It is not a blind, stumbling-in-the-dark hope. It is a rational, thoughtful hope. God provides us clear reasons to believe—if we will look for them.

Just one example of this would be the prophecies in the Bible regarding the coming of the Messiah. With enormous detail, the prophet Isaiah foretold numerous aspects of Jesus' life and death 700 years before He walked on this planet.[6] King David wrote about details of the Messiah in the Psalms, including His not remaining in the grave, nearly 1,000 years before Jesus' life. When all the various prophecies are taken into account, probability researchers have calculated that the chances of these prophecies just happening to come true on their own is one-in-one vigintillion. For those of you who know me and hear me use my own word concoctions such as scrillion or gazillion, which mean, essentially, "a whole big gob," this word *vigintillion* is actually a real number. It is a 1 with 63 zeros after it. What does that mean in laymen's terms? That the chances of these prophecies of Scripture coming true apart from God's intervention is virtually impossible. Now I would remind you that this is simply one of an overwhelming wealth of evidences.

So, again for the sake of brevity, but at the unintended risk of oversimplifying, I concluded that the Scriptures of the Bible are the truths and instructions of God for mankind. But now the questions get more interesting. We have established what I would call the two foundational truths: God is, and the Bible is His revealed Word for man. However, many may arrive at this point of acceptance without having searched to get here. They have not been on a quest that led them to these foundational pillars, yet they accept that the pillars are true. Then they may ask, "So what?" Seventy-five percent of the population in the United States believe there is a God, and the vast majority of those claim to believe that the Bible is true. However, if you were to ask many of them to tell you something about the Bible, they would be at a loss for words. After stammering for a bit, they might say, "Well, I think it says that God helps those who help themselves," or "God wants everyone to be happy," or "Spare the rod, spoil the child," or any number of other homespun nuggets that get attributed to the Bible, even though they are actually not from God's Word. You see, the reality is, reading the Bible requires time and effort—both of which are in short supply at the end of a day. Yet, I would contend that this time and effort is both necessary and well spent if we want to grasp the concept of purpose.

~~~

In 1975, I bought a new car—a Ford Maverick. OK, not the smartest purchase I ever made—especially when you consider (get ready to groan, guys) that I traded in my 1965 Mustang for it. After driving the Maverick for a number of years, I decided that the engine needed to be rebuilt. At that stage of my life, I enjoyed working on cars, and I decided to rebuild the engine myself. So, what do you think I did? If you said, "I imagine that you got a hacksaw and a blowtorch and dismantled the car, laying the cut-up pieces all over the driveway and staring at them." Hmm—well, that would not be correct. While I could have approached it this way, the result would not have been a rebuilt engine. No, what I did was I purchased a 1975 Ford Maverick engine manual. I read it thoroughly, some sections more than once, so that I could properly take everything apart, replace the parts that needed replacing, have parts machined that required it, and properly put it all back together—with the end result being, I hoped, that the engine would run again, and run well. I carefully followed each step, paying close attention to the instruction manual's details. As a result, the car started up and ran well.

But what would you have thought of my adventure if I told you that instead of reading the manual I bought cute pictures to hang in my garage that said things like "Just drive your car fast and feel the wind in your hair," or "Cars are for taking you places, so enjoy the ride"? You might scratch your head and ask, "What do those things have to do with fixing the car?" They don't have anything to do with it, but I like the quotes and hanging them on my garage wall is a whole lot easier than reading the manual. Now, I recognize that the scenario I have just presented is absurd. You can't rebuild an engine that way. And you can't live a life that way. Yet, on a daily basis, I see people trying.

~~~

Back to my foundational truths: God is, and the Bible is His instruction guide. God is, and He created this earth and every living thing on it. He made you and me. The psalmist writes *"For you created my inmost being; you knit me together in my mother's womb"* (Ps. 139:13). He goes on to write: *"...All the days ordained for me were written in your book before one of them came to be"* (Ps. 139:16). God knows us—I mean, He really knows us. He designed the earth and the people on it with a knowledge and understanding of how it and we all work. In the same way that Ford designed and built my car, God designed and built mankind and specifically—you and me. So, shouldn't I spend time in His instruction manual if I want to understand what life is all about? Wouldn't it make sense to consult my Creator if I want to know why He put me here? Of course it would. But for so many people, their understanding of life comes from pithy sayings on Facebook or cute framed crocheted quotes purchased in gift boutiques. Hardly authoritative sources on life. While I understand that Facebook doesn't require me to think a lot, and while I certainly like some of the sayings more than what God's Word may ask of me, perhaps I need to figure out what I really want to know.

I have one shot at this life. I am on earth for a brief moment on the time continuum. So what do I want to do with it? Honestly, my choice becomes about whether I want to simply exist or whether I want to really live to its fullest, the life I have been granted. Author Bruce Waltke writes, "In our culture we consider someone uneducated to be foolish, but the Hebrew concept of the fool was not an ignorant individual, but a person who has the truth and simply does nothing with it."[7] What do you want to do with it?

The Big Picture

Approximately twenty years ago, I moved to Colorado. I bought a piece of property and within a couple of years had a house built. Construction began on the house in about March and the move happened in October of that same year. But here is the amazing thing—the house was actually built before March. You see, it was built in the mind of the home builder.

Months before the foundation was poured, the architect had drawn the plans. These plans were drawn in consultation with the engineer to make sure that everything was as it needed to be. In other words, supporting walls and pillars had to be in the correct places structurally if the house was to stand firm; windows needed to be located in places that were accessible for opening and closing; correct drain systems had to be buried underground; appropriately angled roof trusses had to be constructed; and so on, with dozens of details.

But what if, even though the blueprints had been completed, when the materials were delivered to the construction site, the framers took all of the lumber and simply nailed the boards together in such a way that they were end to end and stretched three miles? In other words, they built the house as though it was just one long piece of wood. Ridiculous, right? Or what if all the shingles for the roof were placed on the ground and the concrete for the foundation was poured on top of those shingles? That wouldn't make a lick of sense. If I wanted to live in a house that protected me from the rain, kept me warm in the winter, was able to withstand large gusts of wind, and provided me with the comfortable place for living I had hoped for, then the builders needed to follow the plans. If the materials are used in any other way than what the architect intended, then it really doesn't matter how they are used—because you won't end up with a house. Having blueprints doesn't just make building the house easier; it makes it possible.

The house serves as an illustration for our lives in so many ways. As the verses from Psalms 139 mentioned earlier pointed out, God has drawn up the blueprint for all of mankind, as well as for our individual lives, way before any of us were born (see Ps. 139:13,16). From the moment man and woman walked on this earth, God knew what we needed and what would work best to fulfill us as humans. But even so, beginning in those early days of the Garden of Eden, mankind thought he knew a better way to do it. Really? Yep.

What would happen if the on-site plumber decided that the bathrooms really didn't need water pipes? I mean, sure the blueprints called for them, but the plumber decided that the architect didn't know what he was talking about. Besides, if he didn't have to put in the pipes, think of all the time that it would save him. But is saving time really what is needed? My wife, who is a special education administrator, often says, "Sometimes you have to go slow in order to go fast." In other words, you have to take care of the beginning steps, the foundational concepts, before you can go on to the next items. Similarly, taking the time to put in the pipes will make a huge difference in the functioning of the bathrooms. You can certainly leave out the pipes and save time now, but then you will be hauling buckets of water in from the well for the rest of your life. Not a wise plan.

While the plumber puts in pipes, the framers nails lumber. As the electrician runs wire, the roofer lays shingles. Each person performs his specific task with the bigger picture in mind. If the electrician attempts to wire the house before the framer has erected walls, there will be a confounding problem. Each laborer performs his task with an eye to the notion—"I am building a house." Until they catch that vision, that are just pounding nails. Similarly, it is essential that we catch that vision for life. As Myles Munroe states, "Until purpose is discovered, existence has no meaning."[8] He further comments, "Life without purpose is time without meaning."[9]

As we begin to examine the purpose of life, just like the building contractor, it is essential that we start with the "big picture"—the blueprint, the destination. I submit for your consideration (I sound like Rod Serling from *The Twilight Zone*, if you are old enough to remember that show) that we must begin with the ultimate "big picture"—and that is all of eternity. We are clearly told in numerous places throughout Scripture that we weren't created just for a few years on earth, but for all of time.

Eternity is a tough concept to grasp. So we poke at it humorously. Woody Allen was quoted as saying, "Eternity is a very long time, especially towards the end."[10] We tell jokes about questions that St. Peter asks at the pearly gates. We often talk about Heaven as if it were some mythical "make all my wishes come true" place in the sky. Yet, all of our jokes aside, Heaven and hell are both real places. Second Kings 2:1, Matthew 5:12, Matthew 7:21, Luke 10:20, Second Corinthians 5:1, Philippians 3:20, Hebrews 12:23, and First Peter 1:4 is a list of Bible verses that doesn't even make a dent in all of the scriptural references that talk about Heaven, how we can know that we can be there, and some glimpses of what to expect. We have to begin to fix our eyes on the "big picture."

I love to hike. However, I don't love heights. OK—I am downright petrified of heights, which makes it really crazy that I have hiked about a dozen of Colorado's "fourteeners." For those of you who live in states with no mountains, I am referring to mountains whose peaks are at 14,000 feet or higher. Some mountains I do fairly well on, and others, well—I have found myself hugging the mountain for dear life. I remember one such summer hike nearly 25 years ago with my boys. There were spots on this particular hike that had me near the edge of panic—really! I mean about ready to call the search and rescue choppers to come and get me. All I could do was stare at the ground and put one foot in front of the other, while my boys were thoroughly enjoying the scenery of the mountains, the canyons, and the full panorama of sights. I recall that as my oldest son, Jeremy, rounded a corner ahead of me, he remarked, "Ooh, Dad's not going to like this." My heart began to pound harder, and my hands became slippery with perspiration. Needless to say, this hike was not very enjoyable.

Many of us live life this way. We are focused solely on the next step on the ground. Our complete and total picture guiding us is where we stand at the moment. We haven't looked up to see the big picture on which God wants us to focus. If our view is small, if our vision is limited, is it any wonder that we wander around in endless tiny circles?

If we want to do more than walk in circles, then we have to be willing to trust the Creator of Heaven and earth, look up from staring at our feet, and focus on the "big picture"—the reasons that God put people here and what He has called us to do with the time allotted to us as we begin eternity. As author and speaker Bob Shank stated so well in his book *Total Life Management*, "If you are not aligned with God through personal submission, quite frankly, any direction is equally viable. It doesn't matter which way you're going. It's a short-term trip, anyhow. But for the person tracking with God's purpose, this life is a warm-up for the main event!"[11]

I don't know about you, but hiking the mountain while focused solely on not falling off is not much fun. When I do that, I miss what the hike is all about. It is much more enjoyable when I am able to look out and marvel at the view of where I am going. Similarly, when I look intently into God's purpose for my life, I begin to live— really live, now and with continuity into eternity.

~~~

I mentioned earlier that in talking with my students I sometimes note that not many people are "thinkers." No, I am not suggesting that you pose like a well-known sculpture, looking deep in thought. But I am encouraging you to think about your life, your direction, and your impact. You see, being busy really has nothing to do with whether or not we will have any impact on the world. Touré Roberts ratchets this up a notch when he says, "Purpose requires concentration. It mandates that we set goals and objectives daily, and stick to them. Purpose requires that we qualify every activity in our lives. No time or situation should be random, and everything should have meaning. Even if you decide to spend the day resting or doing nothing at all, it should be according to what the purpose of your life is."[12]

While some might think his perspective is a little extreme, it does cause one to think. For example, I wonder how many of us work hard at jobs we don't like in order to make money to take the next vacation? For some, life literally becomes about living from vacation to vacation. However, for others, while they enjoy vacationing, they are more likely to see their time off as an opportunity to connect with family, relax, and recharge so that they are better able to go back to work and function with a renewed level of excellence. They return more prepared to pursue their purpose. Please don't misunderstand. I am not saying there is a right and wrong perspective here. It is not that simple. But what I am saying is that the lens I choose to view life through will have a significant impact on how I feel and how I approach my day-to-day activities.

Examining Our Days

Psalms 90:12 states, *"Teach us to number our days aright, that we may gain a heart of wisdom."* I love the perspective offered by commentary author Albert Barnes: "The prayer is, that God would instruct us to estimate our days aright: their number; the rapidity with which they pass away; the liability to be cut down; the certainty that they must soon come to an end; their bearing on the future state of being."[13] He continues on to say, "The prayer is, that God would enable us to form such an estimate of life, that we shall be truly wise; that we may be able to act as if we see the whole of life, or as we should do if we saw its end."[14] In other words, the psalmist is saying, "Think." Examine life—its beginning, it brevity, its end; make sense out of it, and live it with a passion to fulfill what God has entrusted you with.

Carl Sagan is quoted as saying, "We are rare and precious because we are alive, because we can think."[15] Indeed, we can think. We can seek the wisdom of God. We can give thought to our days. And yet, we can also choose the exact opposite. I can spend all of my free time watching mindless sitcoms on television. I can spend hour after hour marinating my brain in YouTube videos. I can waste my weekends partying and staying inebriated. And I can do all of this under the guise of "rest and entertainment." In her book *What Is the Point?* Misty Edwards comments on this trend when she aptly states, "We do not understand that hours and hours of this plants seeds into the soil of our minds that are not immediately reaped, but over time the fruit of this kind of waste will be seen as our minds grow dull, causing our spirits to grow dull."[16] This kind of dullness ultimately leads us to meaninglessness and despair. But we don't have to live that way. It is truly a choice. I can choose to simply exist until life ends, or I can embrace life and all that God intended for it to be.

~~~

I spoke earlier in this chapter about the crossroad I had come to over 30 years ago and my driven search to find answers to the essential questions of life. Once I arrived at my two undeniable pillars of truth—1) that God is, and 2) that His Word provides us with His directions for this life—then the hunger of my soul turned to know those instructions. At that point, I read the Bible from cover to cover in 30 days. Now I don't write this as some point of pious pride. I tell you that for the sole reason that you might have some insight into the desperation and urgency of my need to know what my brief few years on this planet were all about. I voraciously consumed the Scriptures to find the answer to those questions of "what?" "where?" "when?" and "why?" with which I began this chapter. This book is the result of my quest to answer those questions—to understand God's purpose.

There are many books out there about "finding God's will." I find that the majority of people want God to be their "Magic 8-Ball" or "Cosmic Genie" that will give them answers to the specific questions of their day—questions such as "Where should I live?" "What job should I accept?" "Whom should I marry?" "How many kids should I have?" "What kind of car should I buy?" And the list goes on and on. Please know that you will find in here a chapter that addresses decision making in relation to God's will. However, the bulk of the material comes from a core belief that God's Word continually emphasizes that He is far more interested in who we are than what we do. As Rick Warren remarks, "We are human beings, not human doings."[17]

The masses walking about this earth want the answers to many of the day-to-day questions mentioned above. They will read books to learn the formula for finding God's will (sorry to break it to you, but there isn't one). They will take "StrengthsFinder" and various other assessments to sort through career possibilities (though many of those have some value). They will consult mediums and tarot card readers (which God clearly condemns). But rarely will they attempt to *know* the Creator of the universe, who alone understands it all. Rarely are they willing to do the relational work of digesting His Word so that they can better know Him. The truth of the matter is simply this—if I genuinely want to understand life and my reason for existing, it is absolutely understandable. But the answers to life's core questions are found only in the God of creation and His written instructions!

~~~

A couple of logistics here. This book is divided into three sections as we explore three distinct arenas for understanding the purpose of life and our purpose in it. I have made every effort, throughout this text, to put in **bold** any Scripture reference that is purposive in nature. I long for this book to be helpful to you regardless of your life experiences, your mistakes, your successes or failures, or your stage of life. While I have authored other books, I have hungered for decades to write this one. I believe that this is the most important manuscript I have written to date because it speaks to the core of our being. And yet, I understand the enormity of the task at hand. Therefore, it is truly with all humility that I ask you to journey with me through the pages that lie ahead. I will strive to do my best to honor God and honor you in this quest.

Section One

OVERARCHING PURPOSE #1

LOVE GOD WITH EVERYTHING IN YOU

"Love the Lord your God with all your heart and with all your soul and with all your mind." This is the first and greatest commandment (Matthew 22:37-38).

Chapter Two

He Longs For a Relationship— Relating with My Creator

"If God is not the captain of your ship, then you have just boarded the Titanic."
—UNKNOWN

I want to begin this chapter with an exciting story. Many years ago, there was a woman who was married and had a niece who resided with her. She lived on a farm and enjoyed cooking in her kitchen as well as canning fruits and vegetables. The woman was a respected pillar in the community, and all of her neighbors liked her. One day, there was an unusually terrible storm with extremely strong winds. She and her husband managed to avoid injury, but her niece suffered a pretty nasty bump on the head. However, the young girl recovered, and life in the town continued on steadily.

How did you like the story? Did it have you riveted to your seat? Were you hanging on each word, compelled to quickly read the next? No? OK. Well, how about if I were to tell you the story from the niece's viewpoint. What if I were to tell you that the storm was actually a tornado that ultimately led this young girl to the far away Land of Oz? Included in the narrative are witches (good and bad), munchkins, a lion, a scarecrow, and a tin man who required regular oiling. OK—now this is starting to sound a little more exciting. This story has promise. Who knows, it might even be made into a movie someday.

You see, in the first version I made the aunt (Auntie Em) the star of the story. Or perhaps I should say I tried to. It was not a very gripping tale because the adventure was not about her; it was about Dorothy, her niece. If the moviemakers had told the tale from Auntie Em's kitchen, my guess is that none of us would have heard of it, let alone watched it. Yet, we often live our lives as though we are Dorothy when we are really Auntie Em.

I know that you are probably thinking, "What in the world is he talking about?" I am describing the differences in the story depending on who is standing at center stage. One of our truths that we anchored down in the previous chapter was that God is and that He created this planet and all that is on it—including us. From a historical perspective, we see that God created man because He is relational; when mankind became too wicked to survive, God saved a remnant through a man called Noah; God chose a man named Abraham to become the beginning of a nation of people who would become known as God's chosen people; God rescued this nation from an oppressive tyranny, safely leading them out of Egypt; God would lead this people throughout generations; God knew that this nation of Israel would be unable to remain sinless and perfect, He knew that they could never be good enough, so He sent them a

Redeemer, a Savior, His Son; God made it so that man would never have to worry or guess as to whether or not he would make it to Heaven because He gave all those who would accept this Messiah the guarantee of eternal life with Him; and God has promised to come back for us and take us home.

The common thread that runs through all the pieces of the above narrative is God. God is, God cared, God did—God is at center stage of the narrative. When we remember holidays and festivals that range from Christmas to Yom Kippur, from Passover to Easter, they are not about what people did; they are about what God did because He is the star of the story. If what we celebrate in these holidays is what presents we want, our repentance, people hurriedly getting out of Egypt, or where we are going this year for Easter brunch, we have missed it BIG TIME. Those celebrations are truly about (respectively) the fact that God sent His Son, God forgives sins, God rescues, and God redeems. We are onstage in what might be considered to be "bit" parts or supporting roles because here is the deal—God is the star, and we are not. When we lay all of this out rationally, we understand it. But even still, we tend to live our lives as though the story is about us. And when we do that, the confusion and disillusionment begin. You see, when we think that we are in the lead and then things don't go our way, we find ourselves frustrated and upset. We become like the prima donna actor or actress who storms offstage because the scene didn't go as we wanted.

But how different life looks when we take ourselves out of that lead role. When we recognize that God is the star as the director of human history and salvation, the pressure is actually off of us and our efforts to make the show a hit. Because the reality is, we can never pull that off. But He can! I love the following statement from the book *Life with a Capital L*: "Embracing that I am part of the larger story of God's glory will change the way I live out humanity. It will change the way I eat, drink, do the dishes, and mow the lawn. It will change the way I pursue my vocation and enjoy my vacations. It will change the way I love, laugh, and cry."[1] Once I realize that this life is about what He has in store, then I no longer have to go "find" my purpose. Instead I awaken to His purpose.

Here is the great thing about this awakening—I don't have to consult some mystical spiritual crystal ball in order to know how to live. There is no confusion or ambiguity in what God calls us to. The truths of God's desire and direction for our lives are clearly declared in His written Word. Yet, as I recently heard someone state, "Complaining about a silent God while our Bible is closed is like complaining about not getting texts when my cell phone is turned off."

~~~

As we set out to be awakened, I remind you of my promise to put Scriptures in bold that are purposive in nature. Also, rather than list every Scripture, I have worked to cluster them in themes and then discuss them in more detail within those broader categories.

Relating through Faith

"The most important **[command]**,*" answered Jesus, "is this: Hear, O Israel, the Lord our God, the Lord is one. Love the Lord your God will all your heart and with all your soul and with all your mind and with all your strength"* **(Mark 12:29-30)**.[2]

This is the first and greatest commandment. This is God's first purpose for our lives—that we love and relate to Him with all of our heart and soul, with our very being. This is a choice that we actively make. It is not passive. God's first purpose for our lives is that we love Him. And in doing so, we allow Him to love us. At Mt. Sinai God gave Moses and the Israelites the Ten Commandments (see Exod. 20:1-11). In actuality, the first four of those commandments are summed up in this one statement of Jesus in Mark 12. **Because**

if I love God with all that I am, I will not have any other god, I will not have any idols, I will not misuse God's name, and I will rest one day a week as God did after creation.

Whether I read this command to totally love our Creator in Moses' words in Deuteronomy or in Jesus' words in the Book of Mark, to embrace this begins from a place of faith. The writer of the Book of Hebrews says it this way: *"And without faith it is impossible to please God, because anyone who comes to Him must believe that He exists and that He rewards those who earnestly seek Him"* **(Heb. 11:6).** Let this thought settle on you for a minute.

~~~

I can only imagine the overwhelming stress I would feel if I were in a Broadway production, I had three lines in the entire play, and I, for some odd reason, felt that the success or failure of the show rested on how I delivered those three lines—if I was convinced that whether the play ran for one night or for six months depended on me. But as soon as I were to accept that I was not the star and that all I was expected to do was contribute my lines in the short scene during the small act in the play, I would feel an enormous sense of relief and even freedom.

Similarly, once I allow my mind to grasp that God is at center stage, that the success of this thing called "life" rests on Him and not on me, I too can relax. Not only that, but knowing that my story is a piece of the greater story that began way before I existed and will continue long after I am gone is anchoring. The story is steady, even when I am not. I am called to show up during my scene (my lifetime) and deliver the lines on the page of the script that were handed to me. And it begins with this—love God with all that you are by being a person who has faith in who God is, what He has done, and what He has promised to do. When I am willing to do this, it changes everything. Now there are certainly still times when I may feel insecure, unimportant, or unloved. But how quickly those feelings turn around when I remember that I belong to God Almighty. I belong to Him and am loved by Him. It is because He first chose to love me that I am compelled in turn to love and commit my all to Him. In the words of T. C. Stallings, "God doesn't ask us to follow only principles in His Word; rather, He wants us to pursue Him first and foremost."[3] He wants a relationship with us.

Jeremiah 29:11 tells us that God knows the plans He has for us. He wants us to trust Him to work those plans in our lives. Faith is essential to that trust. **God wants us to believe in Him; to believe in the One, the Messiah He has sent; to believe in the prophecies; to believe that He hears and will answer our prayers; and to believe that He will return for us (see John 6:29; Matt. 21:22; 1 Thess. 5:20; Mark 11:24; Matt. 24:44; Mark 13:34,37; Luke 12:40; John 8:24).**

Faith Becomes Concrete

So, how do we relate to Him? Throughout human history, people have gone to all kinds of extreme behaviors to relate to God. We find recorded in Jeremiah 32:35 that people would offer their children as burnt offerings to the pagan idol Molech. Some even attempted to pursue this practice with God. Individuals belonging to certain monastic orders in the Philippines practice self-flogging with a cattail whip. This whip is flung over the shoulders repeatedly during private prayer.[4] Depriving oneself of certain pleasures has been deemed as important by many attempting to connect with and be accepted by God.

In Second Kings 5 we find the account of Naaman, who was a commander in the king of Aram's army. He was highly regarded by his master. So when he came down with leprosy, the king of Aram contacted the king of Israel on his behalf. Leprosy was a terminal illness, and Naaman's king had heard that there was a prophet in Israel. Naaman sent silver, gold, and clothes ahead of him so that the prophet Elisha would heal him. Elisha refused the gifts but sent the following message to Naaman: *"Go, wash yourself seven times in the Jordan, and your flesh will be restored and you will be cleansed"* (2 Kings 5:10).

Now here is where it gets interesting. Naaman went away angry and insulted. He had expected for Elisha to show up and wave his hand, perhaps say, "Abracadabra," and make the leprosy disappear. He didn't want to go wash in the dirty Jordon River. Fortunately, his servants convinced him to give it a try. Verse 13 records this interaction when it states, *"Naaman's servants went to him and said, 'My father, if the prophet had told you to do some great thing, would you not have done it? How much more, then, when he tells you, 'Wash and be cleansed'"* (2 Kings 5:13). These were wise words. Naaman listened, washed himself in the river, and was made well.

There is an extremely valuable lesson to be gained from reading this account. God doesn't necessarily ask us to do some monumental thing. Now, we would hopefully never contemplate something as atrocious as burning our children or as hurtful as flogging ourselves. But we might feel that we need to sell our homes and move to the slums of a Third World country in order to earn God's favor. Or perhaps we feel that a huge donation to a charity will be pleasing to God. We may even feel as though we have to deprive ourselves of enjoying anything in life in order to relate to God. But those things are just not true. I know that many sincerely feel that these kinds of sacrifices are required. However, as I frequently say, "Just because I feel a certain way doesn't make it true in reality."

Here is the truth, and honestly, it is a simple one—**obey God.** We need to have faith in our Creator, and we fully express that faith when we obey Him. We are clearly told in the Scriptures: **those who love God keep His commands (see Deut. 5:10, John 14:15); be careful to obey all His commands (see Josh. 1:7; 22:5); those who obey God will be the ones who enter Heaven (see Matt. 7:21); the Lord asks us to walk in obedience (see Deut. 10:12); God wants** us to obey because He is teaching us what is best for us (see Isa. 48:17); submit to God and the devil will flee (see James 4:7); hear and do what God instructs (see James 1:22); and obeying God is way more important than following human traditions (see Mark 7:8). We are promised God's blessings and compassion when we obey (see Exod. 15:26; Ps. 103:13). God wants us to understand that He doesn't desire elaborate sacrifices to offset our sins—it is His desire that we simply obey Him in the first place (see 1 Sam. 15:22; Prov. 21:3; Hosea 6:6; Matt. 9:13)—and that He wants us to enjoy the benefits of being obedient (see Prov. 3:1).

~~~

As you can see from just a sampling (there are many more) of the Scriptures—obeying God is the manner in which our faith becomes real. It is one thing to say that you believe in God or that you love God, but it takes on an entirely different reality when we demonstrate the truth of those statements by offering our lives in obedience to His instructions. As we love God with all of who we are, we find that we don't obey out of compulsion or some legalistic, life-draining attempt to earn His favor. But because we love Him, we know that He desires the best for us, and we trust Him with that. As Charles Swindoll states, "Disobedience always brings a cycle of complications."[5] God wants us to enjoy a life without the complications.

I love the comparison that Matt Heard makes when he appropriately states, "Instead of living like an orphan, it's me living like the accepted child of God that I am, responding to His love, and following His path."[6]

Faith and Obedience Are Expressed

And when they climbed into the boat, the wind died down. Then those who were in the boat worshiped Him, saying, "Truly You are the Son of God" (Matthew 14:32-33).

So, here is what happened. Jesus had been teaching in a remote area when it started to get pretty late in the day. The disciples wanted to send the people away so that they could go get food. However, Jesus took the only food that anyone had—five loaves of bread and two fish—and fed 5,000 men plus their wives and children. Wow! As you can imagine, after that kind of a miracle, the people didn't want to leave. But Jesus sent them on their way so that He could go up into the hills to pray.

He sent the disciples by boat to the other side of the lake. On the way, sometime between 3:00 and 6:00 A.M., they encountered some harsh windy weather that began to rock them around pretty good. As they rode out the storm, Jesus came walking on the water across the lake. That had to be quite a sight, one that was very unexpected, and they were terrified. But Jesus told them that it was Him and that they didn't need to be afraid. Boldly, Peter, one of the disciples, said, *"Lord, if it's You...tell me to come to You on the water"* (Matt. 14:28). Jesus said, *"Come,"* and Peter did (Matt. 14:29). All was well as Peter walked to Jesus until he allowed himself to become distracted, taking his attention off of Jesus and focusing it on the wind and the waves. Jesus reached out and saved Peter, then they both got into the boat.

I picture this scene like this: sitting in the boat are 11 frightened men, along with Peter, who is wet and also rattled. I see them with their jaws dropped and eyes wide open, and they are probably trembling (I know I would be). Their response—really, all that one could say: *"Truly You are the Son of God"* (Matt. 14:33). They knew who He was. They had put their faith in Him and had been following Him. But there comes a moment when the intellectual discourse runs dry and we are left with "Wow!" All we can do is confess—speak what is. In their case, they acknowledged who He was.

~~~

We first respond to our faith with obedience (or our attempts to be obedient). But that is quickly followed with an awareness that we can never perfectly keep every aspect of the law. We have blown it time and time again. Nevertheless, we bear down and try harder and still mess things up. In the Old Testament, sacrifices of animals were offered to atone for sins. Blood was shed to cover the ongoing disobedience. We read a few paragraphs ago that even though animal life was given up to pay for sins, God's desire was never for blood to be spilled. His desire was that we obey instead. As this understanding begins to percolate in my brain, I realize that I am absolutely dependent on God, and I am compelled to acknowledge that with my words.

But there is great news in the midst of all of this! While the Scriptures state **that unless we repent, we will perish (see Luke 13:5), the writer of Proverbs encourages us with the fact that whoever confesses his sins finds mercy from God (see Prov. 28:13). God's desires, instructions, and purpose for us in the midst of this realization is that we confess and repent of our sins. Acts 2:38 clearly commands us to repent and be baptized so that our sins may be forgiven. The apostle Paul, an educated Jewish man who had zealously persecuted Christians before he met Jesus on the road to Damascus, wrote that if we confess with our mouth that Jesus is Lord, we will be saved (see Rom. 10:9). We are also encouraged with the words of John that if we confess our sins, God is faithful and just and will forgive us (see 1 John 1:9).** What encouragement and assurance! As I get my head around what an amazing and all-consuming love God has for me, I find myself compelled to confess and repent of my sins. And in doing so, I am able to run into the arms of a loving God, where my future, where my eternity, is secure!

I Am Compelled by Love

I love my wife! You may be thinking, "OK, that's nice, but why are you telling me that?" Because I want you to know that I love my wife. Reading those words, you probably accept my statement at face value. But what if over coffee I began to declare the following: "Oh man, I can't believe it is almost Valentine's Day again. I guess I had better buy some flowers somewhere or else she will be mad. Can you believe it—she expects me to come home every night after work and give her a kiss? She wants me to even sit down and talk with her. I guess I had better act interested or I will be in trouble. Oh, I can't remember—did I tell you that I love my wife?"

What do you believe? You will probably observe my other words and actions and conclude that my relationship with her is really about checking off the boxes. It is motivated from a place of obligation—not love. As absurd as this may sound, it is far too common for us to approach God in this manner.

The Creator of the universe has chosen to love me, sacrifice His Son for me, and save me from my own wretchedness. And yet I find myself relegating Him to some recessed place in a corner of my life. I pull Him out of the corner during a crisis—a serious illness, a death, a job loss, and so on. But relating to Him—really pursuing an intimate relationship with Him? "Well, I don't want to be some kind of religious fanatic." We complain, "It's been a long week. Is it really necessary that I participate in a worship service? You mean He wants me to talk with Him regularly? I thought Christmas and Easter were regularly. OK, I will try to do better so that I'm not in hot water with Him." This doesn't sound like much of a relationship, does it?

God hasn't called us to "go to church" any more than my wife married me so that I would "play house." He has invited us to be in relationship with Him. Listen to what the Scriptures have to say in regard to our purposes in worship: **Give thanks to the Lord (see 1 Chron. 16:34; Ps. 136:1; Eph. 5:20). Serve Him with gladness and sing joyfully to Him (see Ps. 33:1; 100:2; James 5:13). Praise the Lord and rejoice in Him (see Ps. 147:1; 148:1; 149:1; 150:1; Phil. 3:1; 4:4). Continually offer a sacrifice of praise (see Heb. 13:15). Encourage each other with psalms, hymns, and spiritual songs (see Eph. 5:19). No matter how difficult or rotten your circumstances**

may be, always give thanks and be joyful in God (see Hab. 3:17-18; 1 Thess. 5:18). Notice that while there certainly may not be any apparent joy in my circumstances, my joy is in the fact that I am anchored in and loved by the God of all mankind. **Ascribe to the Lord glory and strength (see 1 Chron. 16:28).** As Rick Warren conveys, "But we are commanded to recognize His glory, honor His glory, declare His glory, praise His glory, reflect His glory, and live for His glory. Why? Because God deserves it."[7]

But how am I supposed to do this? Am I supposed to stand around and just sing all the time? Well, I certainly hope not. While I adore my wife, I don't want to spend every waking moment announcing, "You are the smartest, most beautiful woman on the planet." Don't get me wrong—she loves hearing that, and I love saying that, but if I just repeated it all day long, I can see her rolling her eyes and eventually saying, "Yeah, yeah, yeah." My wife wants a real, interactive relationship with me. She wants me to enjoy her, and she wants to enjoy me. This is what worship is about—falling in love with God and His Son.

My God and my Savior are not interested in me simply reciting some memorized liturgy or, worse yet, singing or repeating words I don't even understand just because someone has said that is what I should do to be religious. My wife enjoys receiving cards from me that express my love and affection. And I must admit, Hallmark and other card companies have managed to put into words my feelings better than I can sometimes. However, if my daily conversations with my wife were exclusively me reading cards to her that someone else wrote, I hardly believe she would feel that I was genuinely relating to her. She would much prefer my bumbling attempts at authentic expression over having me constantly recite another author's words.

~~~

Worship is singing songs to God, but not just that. Worship is praying honest, vulnerable prayers (talking) to God, but not just that.

Worship is honoring God by how I treat others, but not just that. Worship is using my money to help the poor, but not just that. You see, worship is not about one corner of my life that I designate as being for religious stuff. Worship is all of my life. I so very much appreciate the definition I heard, taught by Matt Heard when he was the senior pastor at Woodmen Valley Chapel: "Worship is my active, all-of-life response to the worth of who God is and what He does."

Yes, my worship is evident in a Sunday morning service. But it should also be evident in my Monday morning dialogue with a colleague or my Tuesday evening conversation with my spouse.

Everything that I do in life—from my parenting to my financial management—should demonstrate my "all-of-life response" to a God who is worth more than the most priceless jewel and who has done more for my existence than my mind can even begin to comprehend.

I worship the Lord when I enjoy Him. I worship Him when I praise Him. My worship is not something to be seen by others; it is totally and completely directed toward and for the benefit of my Father, who has given His all for me. My worship is truly for an audience of One.

~~~

It is so easy for us to pigeon-hole worship. I wholeheartedly believe that God is saddened when He hears us disparage the worship of others, whether that refers to a preference in style of music or time and location of services. It is not about the clothes you wear to church. It is about how you live your life.

Rick Warren provides the following examples, taken from Gary Thomas's book *Sacred Pathways*, of some of the various possible looks of worship:

> *Naturalists* are most inspired to love God out-of-doors, in natural settings. *Sensates* love God with their senses

and appreciate beautiful worship services that involve their sight, taste, smell, and touch, not just their ears. *Traditionalists* draw closer to God through rituals, liturgies, symbols, and unchanging structure. *Ascetics* prefer to love God in solitude and simplicity. *Activists* love God through confronting evil, battling injustice, and working to make the world a better place. *Caregivers* love God by loving others and meeting their needs. *Enthusiasts* love God through celebration. *Contemplatives* love God through adoration. *Intellectuals* love God by studying with their minds.[8]

Again—my worship is *every aspect* of how I live my life in relationship to God Almighty. Just as my love for my wife compels me to actively love her and honor her with the exclusivity of our relationship running through every fiber of my being, my love and commitment to the God who saves me compels me to do nothing less.

Purpose Recapped

1. Two Foundational Truths—

    #1—God is, and He knows what His creation needs.

    #2—The Scriptures are God's written instructions for how to live.

2. Overarching Purpose #1—To love God with all my heart, soul, mind, and strength.

    Sub-purpose #1—To relate to my Creator by:
    a. Having faith in Him.
    b. Putting that faith into action through obedience to His instructions.
    c. Confessing and repenting of my wrongdoings; acknowledging who God is and His

authorship and reign in my life.

d. Worshiping Him from the core of who I am in response to the depths of who He is.

Chapter Three

You're Not The Boss of Me— Relinquishing Control

*"We must be willing to let go of the life we planned
so as to have the life that is waiting for us."*
—JOSEPH CAMPBELL[1]

Walking down a side street in New Orleans, my wife and I came across a sign outside of a restaurant that was a tad unusual. While most would advertise their "great food in a fine dining experience," this one was different. This sign stated that the food was disappointing, the drinks were not all that cold, and the service was less than stellar. Now, I realize that this was a novel ploy designed to get one's attention—which it did. However, it also highlighted for me the fact that regardless of how much we want to be better than everyone else, we are flawed and imperfect human beings. We don't have it all together.

We live in an age where people have a very difficult time acknowledging this simple but dreaded fact. Characters on television shows like NCIS make statements such as "Don't ever apologize. It's a sign of weakness." Products on store shelves are always "New and Improved." Bumper stickers highlight how much smarter my honors student is than yours. My house is bigger, my football team is better, my vacation is cooler, and my car is faster. But why? Why do we strive to give the appearance that we are unflawed individuals? Because if I can somehow prove that I "have it all together," then I don't need anyone—including God.

Yet, this obsession is not new. Recorded in the Book of Luke is the account of the fool who in essence said in his heart, "I have crops coming in like crazy; I will tear down my barns and build bigger ones; I have all that I need; I am self-sufficient and don't need anyone; so tonight I will party like a rock star" (see Luke 12:16-29). But look at God's response to this "Eat, drink, and be merry attitude": *"This very night your life will be demanded from you"* (Luke 12:20).

Mankind has exhibited a history of wanting to be in control. Whether it was Adam and Eve eating the forbidden fruit, wanting to "be like God," or the people whose enlarged egos propelled them to attempt to build the Tower of Babel that would extend up to Heaven, men have wanted to rule. We have tried to reject God, ignore Him, relegate Him to the corner, lecture Him, demand fairness of Him—anything but accept Him. And yet, God is, and He is in control.

I am reminded of the excruciating trials that were experienced by Job in the Old Testament. And while his circumstances were horrific, they were only intensified when his friends came to visit. Now, one might think this would be a good thing, but his "friends" accused him of wrongdoing. I mean, why else would these trials be taking place? At least that was their reasoning. After Job defended himself time and time again, he finally responded in frustration, *"Oh, that I had someone to hear me! I sign now my defense—let the Almighty answer me; let my Accuser put His indictment in writing"* (Job 31:35). He had in essence demanded, "God, You are not being fair, and You owe me an answer."

Doesn't that sound just like us? Intellectually we know that we are not God. But if we are honest with ourselves, we somehow slide into a place where we begin to think about God as we would another person. We imagine that He is really just an older and more experienced version of ourselves. And if we think of Him as a being like us, well, then He does have to be fair and answer to us. But to assume such a position of ignorance can be costly. For two chapters God turns the tables on Job and begins to ask the questions that truly demonstrate man's level of ignorance. Listen to a portion of God's response: *"Who is this that darkens My counsel with words without knowledge? Brace yourself like a man; I will question you, and you shall answer Me. Where were you when I laid the earth's foundation? Tell Me, if you understand. Who marked off its dimensions? Surely you know..."* (Job 38:2-5). He goes on to question Job about light and darkness, rain and snow, the stars and constellations, animals giving birth, the flight of birds, and much more. Chapter 40, verses 1 and 2, read, *"The Lord said to Job: 'Will the one who contends with the Almighty correct Him? Let him who accuses God answer Him!'"* (Job 40:1-2).

Very quickly Job realized that he was out of his league. He had no answers for God. And neither do we—because we are not God. Like Job, we so easily display our ignorance about matters that only God comprehends.

Admitting Our Humanness

We are called into a relationship with our Creator. That is the first purpose of our existence—to love God with all of our heart, soul, mind, and strength. Engaging in relationship with the God of the universe requires us to understand the nature of that relationship. In other words, we are not relating to our equal but to our Maker. Grasping this principle completely changes the dynamics of the relationship. It allows us the privilege of relying and depending, not on a frail and flawed person, but on a being who is able to strengthen us and sustain us at every turn and in any circumstance. However, we come back to our need to admit that He is able to do that—and we are not.

It is for this reason that the Scriptures discuss the purpose of **humility**. In his first letter to Timothy, Paul writes, **"If you are rich, do not be arrogant and put your hope in your wealth, but put your hope in God, who gives you all you need" (see 1 Tim. 6:17). We are to humble ourselves and God will lift us up (see James 4:10; 1 Peter 5:6). Becoming humble like a little child, Jesus says, is essential if we want to enter Heaven (see Matt. 18:3-4; Luke 18:17). Humility is a posture for us to adopt not only in our relationship with God, but with each other. We are told not to think that we are "all that" (to use a contemporary idiom) and superior to everyone else (see Rom. 12:3). Instead, we are to consider others better than ourselves and ponder how we might put their interests ahead of our own ambitions (see Phil. 2:3). Jesus instructs us not to sit in judgment on each other but instead turn a critical eye to our own behaviors, to the things we need to correct in our own lives (see Matt. 7:1; Luke 6:37). Then we are in a better place to assist others with their struggles. We are even warned by Paul to be very careful during those times when we think we have "arrived" and that we have it all figured out, that we are undefeatable. Because it is in those times of arrogance that we are likely to fall (see 1 Cor. 10:12).**

In order for us to have a healthy relationship with our Creator, it is critical that we grasp our frailty and our absolute dependence on Him for our very existence and our future. Humility opens the door that allows God to pour Himself into us and bless us as He longs to do. **The writer of Hebrews encourages us to approach God's throne of grace with confidence. When we come before His throne in humility, we are promised mercy and grace (see Heb. 4:16). And it is His great compassion that enables us to have this confidence. God is more than ready to respond to us if we will choose to call on Him (see Jer. 33:3). James gets more specific with this in declaring that if we lack wisdom, we need only to ask God for it, and if we believe in His power to provide it, He will (see James 1:5-6).**

~~~

When my boys were young, we used to go camping frequently at a spot up in the Sierra Nevada mountains called Dinkey Creek. We built great memories there around fishing, swimming, hiking, making s'mores, telling stories, and so on. In this one particular swimming hole was a naturally created waterslide in the rocks. It was great fun to navigate the curves and splash into the pool below. That is, of course, unless you are three or four years old. I can still recall when my youngest son would tell me that he wanted to go down the slide. Setting him at the top, I would go to the bottom in order to catch him. While I knew that he was safe and that I would catch him, he would sit at the top and begin to cry, refusing to let go. I would go back to the top and tell him that it was OK and he could go down next time. He would adamantly say that he wanted to go down now. So, back to the bottom I would go, assuring him of my protection. You probably already know what is coming next. Yep, the tears began again as he clutched the rocks, refusing to let go. And yet, you and I both know that all he had to do was release his hold and the ride down would have been a blast. Now, a three-year-old certainly has no concept of humility. He just knows that he wants to perform this feat by himself. If only he would have accepted how broad my catch was, there would have been far fewer tears. How often we live as three-year-olds.

~~~

Sir John Templeton and Rebekah A. Dunlap articulate this thought well when they ask, "How can we cultivate a spirit of humility? A starting point would be allowing ourselves to be open to the possibility that our existence within a divine reality dwarfs our personal reality."[2] In other words, God is way bigger than I am—my thoughts, my feelings; all of me. And if I have embraced Him as my Redeemer and grasped His breadth and depth, I will realize how absolutely secure I am. Rabbi David Aaron describes the benefit of humility before God when he writes, "If we choose to make our persona the source of our identity and self-worth, then certainly we are right to fear that we will die, since all this will certainly pass away. But we need not be afraid at all. If we identify with God, and affirm that only God is the source of our self-worth, we will experience the immortality of our soul."[3]

As I am writing, I can't shake the lyrics to the Steven Curtis Chapman song "God Is God":

And the pain falls like a curtain
On the things I once called certain
And I have to say the words I fear the most
I just don't know

And the questions without answers
Come and paralyze the dancer
So I stand here on the stage afraid to move
Afraid to fall, oh, but fall I must
On this truth that my life has been formed from the dust

God is God and I am not
I can only see a part of the picture He's painting
God is God and I am man
So I'll never understand it all
For only God is God

And the sky begins to thunder

And I'm filled with awe and wonder
'Til the only burning question that remains
Is who am I

Can I form a single mountain
Take the stars in hand and count them
Can I even take a breath without God giving it to me
He is first and last before all that has been
Beyond all that will pass

Oh, how great are the riches of His wisdom and knowledge
How unsearchable for to Him and through
Him and from Him are all things

So let us worship before the throne
Of the One who is worthy of worship alone
Admitting we are not in control—nor do we want to be[4]

Steel Magnolias is a well-known 1989 film loaded with numerous stars. In this film set in the South, Sally Field plays the character of M'Lynn Eatenton. While she is a wife and a mother, in many ways she could have been an FAA air traffic controller. In the early scenes, we see M'Lynn's daughter, Shelby, played by Julia Roberts, getting ready for her wedding. M'Lynn's husband is shooting his gun in the air to scare the birds away from the wedding site, while the cranky neighbor storms across the yard with her dog to let him know what a menace he is. M'Lynn is determined to make this day perfect. She hides her husband's gun, works to keep her sons from inappropriately decorating the wedding car, takes her daughter to get her hair done, and attempts to pacify the neighbor.

While at the beauty salon, Shelby, who has diabetes, experiences a hypoglycemic episode, and M'Lynn goes into "super mom" mode, taking charge of the situation and bringing everything back into order. This is just a sample of what lies ahead.

Shelby's doctor had advised her against ever getting pregnant as it would push her body beyond what it could handle. However, she does become pregnant and M'Lynn is beside herself, angry that her daughter had gone against her expressed wishes as well as the advice of her doctor. Without getting into all of the details of the movie, let me just say that I get exhausted watching M'Lynn's efforts to control all of life around her. She seems to believe that she knows what is best for everyone and strives to get everyone to follow her lead.[5]

Aren't we all like that a little bit? It doesn't always take the form of some selfish agenda that we are trying to impose on the world around us. Sometimes it can come from a place of wanting to make people's lives better and may even result in our enabling people. But more often than not, I sincerely believe our driveness to control comes from a place of fear.

Think about it. How often do we find ourselves at work hesitating to empower those working for us out of fear that they won't do the job right—or at least not to our level of expectation? If you have had a teenage driver living in your home, recall the first time they were leaving to drive the car on their own. The potential problems and fears surrounding that are too numerous to mention. It is not uncommon in the midst of teaching someone to perform a given task that we state in exasperation, "I'll just do it myself." We fight against relinquishing control out of fear that the other person won't do the job as well as we will. And as baffling as it may seem, we sometimes have that same fight with God.

~~~

We began this chapter discussing humility because humility is the first step in trust. Recognizing God's ability to do what we are not capable of doing is necessary if we are to relinquish the reigns of control.

Many Scriptures reflect on the necessity of trust. **We are encouraged not to be weighed down with anxiety but with thanksgiving** to bring our requests to God (see Luke 21:34; Phil. 4:6). **Peter states that it is because of God's great care for us that He wants us to give all of our anxiety to Him (see 1 Peter 5:7). Matthew reminds us that God has the very hairs on our head numbered and that we do not need to worry about life (see Matt. 10:30; 6:25-34).** While we may not fret specifically about our next meal or that we don't have any clothes, we do worry about generating enough income to meet the other needs of life. **We are taught to look outside at the birds or the flowers and to think of how, without their worrying, God takes care of them. And then the Scriptures ask, "Are you not much more valuable than they?" (Matt. 6:26) Therefore, if we will simply make it our priority to first and foremost pursue God's Kingdom and His righteousness, He will take care of our needs.**

I am grateful for those passages that indicate God's promises to me that are attached to trust. **The psalmist tells us that if we will trust in the Lord, do good, and find our satisfaction in Him, He will give us the desires of our heart (see Ps. 37:3-4). If we are willing to cast all our worries onto Him, He will sustain us (see Ps. 55:22; Lam. 3:25).** And one of my favorite reassurances from God comes from Solomon's writings in **Proverbs 3:5-6:** *"Trust in the Lord with all your heart and lean not on your own understanding; in all your ways acknowledge Him, and He will make your paths straight."*

What a simple but powerful passage that is. And yet, people walk into my counseling office day after day ignoring this foundational principle. Refusing to place the full weight of their trust on the living God, ignoring His instructions that offer us peace, comfort, security, and satisfaction, they come in stunned when their "paths" are anything but "straight." I am usually surprised at their surprise. It would be much like my mechanic telling me not to put grape soda in my gas tank. But rather than heeding his advice, I go ahead with the grape soda idea only to watch my car being towed to the Firestone shop. Expressing my bewilderment to him would no doubt lead to his buddies talking about me in the back office, questioning the wisdom of even allowing me to own a car. Yet this is too often how we lead our short and precious time on this planet.

~~~

There is an account recorded in the Old Testament in the Book of Daniel regarding a dream had by King Nebuchadnezzar. In the dream was a large beautiful tree that was cut down. While the dream was much more involved than my one-sentence description, the importance of this account is Daniel's explanation to the king. The backstory to this situation is that the king thought he was extremely important and was not accountable to anyone, including God. He didn't need God and he would call his own shots. Daniel explains to Nebuchadnezzar that because he has chosen not to acknowledge that God is sovereign and in charge of this world, he would be driven away from the people, live among the animals, and eat grass like the cattle. This would be the case until the king recognized who was truly in control. Daniel urged the king to repent of his wrongdoing to avoid this. Unfortunately, the king continued on in his arrogant ways until all that he had dreamed took place.

However, it is Daniel 4:34 that gives you and me hope: *"At the end of that time, I, Nebuchadnezzar, raised my eyes toward heaven, and my sanity was restored. Then I praised the Most High; I honored and glorified Him who lives forever..."* No matter how far we may have removed God from the throne of our hearts, we can, in this very moment, turn and acknowledge that He is indeed in control of all that is—including our lives.

God is aware and knows the struggles that we face (see Prov. 5:21). He deeply cares for us and longs for us to entrust Him with our lives. The Messiah invites us to come to Him, *"all you who are weary and burdened, and I will give you rest"* (Matt. 11:28). But until we are mature enough to understand that God is working to build character in our lives, we will find it far too easy to harbor resentment toward God, our parents, a spouse, or anyone else who we believe has caused us pain. If we are honest, we will admit that we often find ourselves angry when things do not proceed in the way we would have done them if we were God.

~~~

The prophet Isaiah proclaims to God that *"we are the clay, You are the potter; we are all the work of Your hand"* (Isa. 64:8). I envision myself on a potter's wheel with God trying to shape me into something magnificent. However, because I can't see what He is making and I don't enjoy the shaping process, I am like clay that somehow manages to climb off the wheel. In doing that, I become just a blob of clay on the table. And yet, I then complain about the fact that I am a blob. And of course, I blame God.

We are encouraged to **consider it joy when we face trials because they actually test our faith, which produces perseverance, which in turn produces character, which leads to hope (see James 1:2; Rom. 5:4).** In the middle of difficulties it is very easy to forget that one of God's purposes for us is to shape our character. And yet, we fight God for control.

I love the following quote by Nicole Kidman to Tom Cruise in the movie *Days of Thunder*: "Control is an illusion, you infantile egomaniac! Nobody knows what's going to happen next…. Nobody controls anything. Now you've gotten a glimpse of that and you're scared."[6] Her quote is so profoundly true. And yet, I make my plans, I schedule my vacations, I fill slots in my appointment schedule, I speak about the future as though I were in control because…I have to confess, it is because I like the illusion. But if I am truly going to trust the One who made me to direct and bless my life, I have got to stay on that potter's wheel. **God's instructions promise that if I will cling to Him and His Word, I will "produce much fruit." But apart from Him, the results of my efforts are likely to be meager (see John 15:5).**

C. S. Lewis writes, "It would seem that our Lord finds our desires not too strong, but too weak. We are halfhearted creatures, fooling about with drink and sex and ambition when infinite joy is offered us, like an ignorant child who wants to go on making mud pies in a slum because he cannot imagine what is meant by the offer of a holiday at the sea. We are far too easily pleased."[7] He goes on to say in another work, "The more we get what we now call 'ourselves' out of the way and let Him take us over, the more truly ourselves we become."[8]

~~~

I fully realize that we have all experienced situations that just don't make sense—logically, humanly. We may have had friends or family betray us, finances fall apart, cars break down, you fill in the blank. Stuff happens that overwhelms us. We just don't get it. But God does.

Sometimes those difficult circumstances will make sense tomorrow, or next month, or next year, or perhaps not until we cross over to the other side of eternity. God is not limited to our time-framed existence. He is able to see all of the chronological scenes of our lives as...now. And He knows what is going on and why. It is my choice whether I want to connect and anchor myself to the God who made me or whether I want to crawl off the potter's wheel and take my chances on my own. But I must admit—as a lump of clay on the table, I don't do very well.

So what could life look like if I turned over the steering wheel of my life and let God drive? Giving up control to Him doesn't mean that I am released from responsibility, that I have no interests in the day-to-day activities of life. It actually leads to the exact opposite. If I began to live—to think, feel, and act as though God is in control of my life—how different might it look? I like the words of Charles Swindoll: "If you and I genuinely believed the promises of God, we would not have worried this past week as we have worried. We would not have tried to shoulder that enormous load that is beyond our ability to carry. We would not have rationalized wrong or made up excuses to cover our tracks."[9] He proceeds to ask: "Do you realize what a peaceful life you can live if you decide to live like this? Do you realize how relaxed you can be, how free of stress? Honestly. It is so helpful for me to remind myself: He is the One who is unfathomable. He is unsearchable. I'm neither."[10]

If I am willing to walk with God with unwavering trust, I will be able to live my purpose out under any circumstances. In his book *The God-Powered Life*, Rabbi Aaron sheds light on this way of thinking:

> There is nothing to look forward to in the future that this moment cannot offer you. You can serve the great [God] now and in any situation. When you are breaking up with your boyfriend or girlfriend, you can serve God by expressing understanding, compassion, and truth. When you are losing your job, you can serve God by showing love and accepting justice. When you are giving birth, you can serve God by knowing that you are bringing life into the world. If you are single or you are married, you can serve God right now. Do you think that you can serve God better when you're married than when you are single? If right now you are single, this is how you are supposed to serve God. Happiness is a choice available to us all because in whatever situation we find ourselves, we can choose to be of service and channel the presence of God into the here and now. Every day of our life can be purposeful and meaningful, passionately doing good and spreading love.[11]

While our circumstances are not always pleasant (sometimes they are beyond miserable), we have a choice whether we allow them to bury us or not. Yes, we can let them fall on us and crush us or, author Kenneth Wood suggests, we can climb up on top of the pile.

It will give us a better vantage point on our life.[12] The choice of perspective is ours.

The apostle Paul encourages us to **do everything without grumbling and complaining and make a decision to work at whatever it is we are doing, not as though we are doing it to please some person, but as though we are working for the Lord (see Phil. 2:14; Col. 3:23).**

Giving up control and trusting our present as well as our future with a God we can't presently see is easier said than done. But it is essential if we are to move from where we are to where we hope to be. It is not a simple flip of the switch though. It is a day-by-day decision—and, without a doubt, some days are easier than others.

~~~

It was Christmas Eve in the mid-1970s and I was a college student in Dallas, Texas. I had to work that day, but once I got off, I was going to drive to my cousin's home in Slidell, Louisiana, where I would meet my parents for Christmas. It is about a 500-mile drive, and I expected to arrive there around midnight. However, I remember getting into Louisiana and discovering fog thicker than I had ever seen. There were times when I could not see more than a few feet in front of me. What to do? I had some choices. I could pull off and discontinue the drive—but then I wouldn't get there for Christmas. I could turn around and try to head back to Dallas—but then I wouldn't get to my cousin's at all. Since visibility was poor, I could simply stop—but then I would likely get run over by a semi-trailer truck. Or I could continue on, slowly and carefully, moving 10 or 20 feet at a time. If what I could see was 20 feet, then I would go 20 feet. Once I went that distance, I could see another 20 feet, so I would move that far. I didn't have to be able to see from where I was clear to Slidell all at once. I trusted, from having read my map (this was way before the days of GPS), that the road I was on most assuredly went to Slidell. I knew that. So, if the fog allowed me to see 20 feet at a time, then I would confidently drive those 20 feet. Sometimes I was granted 100 yards so I took it. One mile after another I drove, arriving at my destination at about 3:00 in the morning. Did I want to get there quicker? Certainly! But by continuing to trust the road and faithfully drive with the distance I could see, I made it there in time to celebrate Christmas.

I trust God. I know that He is here. My confidence need not be in what I can't see. My confidence is in He who holds my road in His hand. As He reveals to me tomorrow, perhaps next month, or even the next year, I will faithfully live His purposes knowing that whether it is midnight or 3:00 in the morning, He will take me where He wants me to go.

Hmm—I think I will stay on the potter's wheel.

Purpose Recapped

1. Two Foundational Truths—

    #1—God is, and He knows what His creation needs.

    #2—The Scriptures are God's written instructions for how to live.

2. Overarching Purpose #1—To love God with all my heart, soul, mind, and strength.

    Sub-purpose #1—To relate to my Creator through: faith, obedience, repentance, and worship.

    Sub-purpose #2—To relate to my Creator by:
    a. Walking humbly with Him.
    b. Giving up my feeble attempts at control and trusting God with my journey.

Chapter Four

Hurry Up and Slow Down—Developing an Authentic Connection

"Actually, you had a pretty great life, but you were looking down at your phone and missed it!"
—UNKNOWN

In this first section of this book, we have been exploring how to relate to God. We have examined issues ranging from faith and worship to humility and trust. But really…how badly do we want to relate? The Scripture that is the undergirding for this section says, "Love God with all your heart, soul, mind, and strength" (see Matt. 22:37). Hmm. That sounds like more than some half-hearted lip service in a Sunday morning service. It sounds like a full-on investment of myself. But what exactly does that look like?

"A young man came to Socrates to say, 'I want knowledge.' 'How badly do you want?' 'I must.' And Socrates took him to the beach and waded out up to their necks and pushed the other under the water in a ferocious struggle. When he surfaced, he asked, 'What did you want the most?' 'Air, I wanted air!' When you want knowledge like you wanted air, under water, then you will get it."[1] I would contend that when we want to love, relate, and know God with the same intensity that this young man wanted air, we will get it.

Unfortunately, it is very easy for us to become like sheep who get lost simply by nibbling at the grass in the field and never looking up. They eat away, wandering to wherever the grass is, without paying attention to their location. We fail to see life in the larger picture because we get so focused on and caught up in the present moment.

Stop

"Stop, look, and listen," was the phrase that many of us learned as young children. I can still remember, as we would approach to cross the street, holding the hands of other children. We were to "stop" before walking into the street, "look" both directions for oncoming traffic, and "listen." This could be listening for anything that was coming that we hadn't seen or perhaps listening for instructions if there was an adult present.

Imagine, if you will, that you are planning a road trip. You need to make sure that you have a map (or perhaps a GPS), hotels reserved for lodging, packed bags, and money for gas and food. As you stand there in the driveway with all your stuff, you appear ready to go. But something is missing...hmm...oh yeah—a car. We need a vehicle to put our things in so that we can drive to our destination.

Now, if you are like I am, you probably figured that if we were discussing a road trip, the car was assumed. I certainly understand that. I am simply making a point that we can have all the stuff we want, along with plenty of money, but without the car, it is going to be a challenging trip.

Similarly, we have been discussing necessary components and actions in our relationship with God. In this chapter, I want us to pause for a moment to look at the "car"—the vehicle that is necessary for growing us in our relationship with God. Beginning with the first step—to "stop."

~~~

Remember the Sabbath day by keeping it holy. Six days you shall labor and do all your work, but the seventh day is a Sabbath to the Lord your God. On it you shall not do any work, neither you, nor your son or daughter, nor your manservant or maidservant, nor your animals, nor the alien within your gates. For in six days the Lord made the heavens and the earth, the sea, and all that is in them, but He rested on the seventh day. Therefore the Lord blessed the Sabbath day and made it holy (Exodus 20:8-11).

The word *Sabbath* is not a word that is used much in our culture outside of a religious context. That Hebrew word, *sabbat*, means "to cease or desist."[2] It is one of the Ten Commandments. But what does it really mean in a practical day-to-day sense?

For the Jewish people, it is indeed a very sacred command. While God had created all that existed, He had enlisted man to maintain and take care of that creation (see Gen. 2:15). Mankind was given jobs and responsibilities. And just as God finished creation and rested on the seventh day, people are to do their jobs and then cease, resting on the seventh day from their work. They are also to allow their servants and animals to rest on that day.

Historically, with the development of the synagogue, the seventh day of the week became a day of worship and of studying the

Scriptures.[3] The Sabbath was meant to be a blessing to man, but unfortunately, as time went on, it also became a day burdened with heavy restrictions and rules. We see this played out whenever Jesus reached out to do good on the Sabbath—whether He was healing the sick or picking food to eat. The religious leaders were more concerned about their well-refined legalistic practices than they were about the welfare of people. In response to this, Jesus clearly states God's intent when He says, *"The Sabbath was made for man, not man for the Sabbath"* (Mark 2:27). But what did He mean by that?

He meant that we need to "Sabbath." We need to cease from our work and rest. Our Creator knows every detail about our existence. He knows how He designed us and what we need to function best. He knows that we need rest. Without it, we don't function efficiently. This is not only true for us, but as the command in Exodus indicates, it is a principle that is true for our children, our workers, our animals, and even the land. In Leviticus 25:1-13, we see that the land was to be allowed to rest every seventh year and after seven seven-year periods there was what was called a Year of Jubilee. This was a year of rest, celebration, and even restoration.

~~~

Rest sounds as though it would be easy. But the Israelites found it difficult. While wandering in the desert, God gave them a substance called manna that they gathered six mornings a week to make their food. God said that on the sixth day they could gather twice as much and then they could rest on the seventh day—no gathering necessary. Here they were, given the day off, and still, many went out on the seventh day looking for manna.

Unfortunately, I identify with that mentality way too much. I have always wanted to "do." I don't like being idle. My wife will sometimes say that she thinks I could be busy doing stuff 24/7. While I disagree that it is that bad, I do admit the tendency. I remember back to certain times of my life when I worked far too much, thinking that I would get a lot more accomplished. But the problem was that I never operated at peak efficiency. I was tired, scattered, and unfocused. I was operating at maybe 75 percent but couldn't even see it. I didn't need to do more; I needed to stop and rest. As I heard my friend Jimmy Dodd say in a message one time, "We do not rest because our work is done. We rest because God commands it."[4] And God doesn't command it because He is a killjoy; He does so because He loves us. He knows our design, and He knows what we need. We need to stop.

There will always be work to be done. There will always be another tomorrow to plan for. If I am not careful (and I have been guilty of this), I will rush past the fun and family time of the present in order to get to tomorrow. And once I get to tomorrow, I won't really be there because I will be hurrying to the next tomorrow.

Cease—desist—stop. When we do, Isaiah the prophet tells us, God will lead us to joy (see Isa. 58:14). Honoring the Sabbath was one of the ways in which the Israelites were identified as belonging to God. Similarly, resting one day a week—really resting—is honoring our God by honoring His creation. It is a necessary step if we desire to become all that He made us to be.

Get Quiet

"A greater poverty than that caused by lack of money is the poverty of unawareness. Men and women go about the world unaware of the beauty, the goodness, the glories in it. Their souls are poor. It is better to have a poor pocketbook than to suffer from a poor soul."[5] So many of us suffer from being unaware—unaware of what is all around us and unaware of what God desires to give to us. But why?

We are bombarded! Our poor brains don't seem to have a chance, as we are fed a constant stream of relatively useless information. If you watch much television, you have no doubt found yourself inundated with commercials. An overwhelming 36 percent of a typical hour of television is dedicated to commercials.[6] You cannot log on to the Internet without your attention being drawn to ads on the sidebar clamoring to motivate you to buy something. For far too many of us, the first thing we do in the morning at the sound of our alarm is grab our phone. We feel compelled to see who has e-mailed us, texted us, or Facebooked us. I know—I have been guilty of it too.

A couple of years ago I had a strange experience. My wife and I were out of the country for a week and my cell phone didn't have any service. Oh, I could have purchased some kind of international plan for a week, but it didn't seem necessary. And besides, I thought it would be nice to be detached from my cell phone for a few days. This first 24 hours were the most interesting. Every time I felt the slightest vibration, I reached for my pocket with the phone in it. I continually reached for my phone thinking I had better check e-mail or perhaps Facebook. But it was turned off.

Finally, I took the phone out of my pocket and locked it up in the hotel safe—I mean, after all, I had no service so there was no need to carry it. For the next 24 hours my pocket felt empty, and I would have brief moments of panic, thinking I had lost or misplaced my phone. I couldn't believe what a slave I had become to that electronic device.

By the time 72 hours had gone by, I no longer was driven to find and check the phone. I was *free*! Free to enjoy my vacation, free to focus on my wife, free to relax—completely relax. But first I had to turn off the noise—the noise of life demanding my attention. I had to get quiet.

~~~

We have learned not to do "quiet" well. As a matter of fact, many of us are downright uncomfortable with quiet. I have seen many high school students who can no longer study without some kind of visual or auditory stimulus—such as music or television—in the background. I have even had some therapists tell me they are convinced that this information overload—this sound and sight pollution—has created ADHD-like symptoms in the frontal lobe of the brains of many individuals.

While we may be able to adhere to the first admonition of "stop," of ceasing the activity, we have a far more difficult time with arriving at "quiet." It is all too easy to fill the void of activity with the saturation of noise.

We have come to expect God to show up with fireworks and miraculous signs. Sometimes He does. But if we come to expect that, there is a good chance we may miss His direction in our lives.

The prophet Elijah in the Old Testament experienced a similar struggle. In an account recorded in the Book of First Kings, Elijah is convinced that he is the last of the faithful prophets and that the political and religious leaders were all out to kill him. God directed him to go stand on the mountain. I love the vivid description of the following words:

> *Then a great and powerful wind tore the mountains apart and shattered the rocks before the Lord, but the Lord was not in the wind. After the wind there was an earthquake, but the Lord was not in the earthquake. After the earthquake came a fire, but the Lord was not in the fire. And after the fire came a gentle whisper. When Elijah heard it, he pulled his cloak over his face* (1 Kings 19:11-13).

This imagery seems so appropriate for the 21st century. I am wowed by the high-tech explosions generated in a movie like *Star Wars*. The extravagance of a Disneyland fireworks spectacle takes my breath away. And while I may expect for God to speak in these sensory overload extravaganzas, He is more likely to be found, when the smoke-filled air is cleared and the explosions have gone silent, in the quiet of "a gentle whisper."

The challenge for me, if I am to be able to hear God's whisper, is that I have to learn to get quiet, stay quiet, and live quiet.

~~~

Lysa TerKeurst, author of *The Best Yes*, shared the following in a 2015 radio interview:

> When I have an overwhelming schedule, I stop paying attention to that still small voice that the Lord has when He directs me during the day. And so, when I'm rushing here and rushing there, I'm not able to focus on maybe the Lord directing me, "Go hug that child right now and tell them three reasons why you think they're amazing, because that child needs your support as their mom right now." Or I'm not able to walk across the restaurant at lunch and say a kind word to somebody. Because for me, the Lord is always wanting to instruct me and to encourage me to be a light in this dark world.
>
> And then all of a sudden, I wake up and I recognize I've turned into a checklist Christian. Like I will get up in the morning. I'll read my Bible. I'll pray. Instead of saying ugly words, I'll try to say nice words that morning. And then, you know, check all those things off my list and rush into my day and leave the Lord behind. I forget that when I pray and when I read my Bible, I've invited the divine presence of God to do life with me that day.[7]

The Lord of the universe desires to give me His best, but I have to position myself to hear Him. As we were instructed when we studied for our written driver's license test, we have to "Come to a full and complete stop." We then have to clear the noisy clutter from our brains and get quiet. Or as the psalmist says, *"Be still, and know that I am God..."* **(Ps. 46:10)**. And then, maybe as Elijah did when he pulled his cloak up over his face, we will recognize—*This is it. This is the encounter I have been wanting. This is the Lord is speaking to me.*

Think

I can get so busy in life that I just rush through things and don't think. I have a tendency to get up in the morning and just rush through my task without stopping to think about what I'm really doing, I don't think about "should I be doing what I am doing" or "do I want to be doing what I am doing?" Sometimes I need to just get away out of my own little world and just stop and think for a moment. Think about it right now—you and I are standing on a ball that is spinning at 1,000 miles per hour. We're flying around this ball of fire, it's like one million times our size, traveling at 67,000 miles an hour, and we think it's just another day. This place is amazing. It's gorgeous. Don't miss it. The whole message of the Bible is about the Creator who loves us and wants to give to us. If you missed out on that, you're going to miss the whole point of your life.[8]

I don't want to miss the whole point of life. But, as I mentioned in the first chapter, if I am to truly grasp "Why am I here?" it is going to require some critical thinking, thinking that doesn't allow me just to make it up as I go.

~~~

I remember when I was a kid hearing about people who didn't believe in airplane flight. No doubt this was probably in the early part of the 20th century. I was told that some individuals would get on a plane but would somehow believe that it was a really fast train and that what they saw out the window were manufactured projected images. Similarly, ever since the Apollo moon landings, there have been those who do not believe that man ever stepped foot on the moon. They hold to a belief that the images shown on television were actually staged somewhere in a desert setting or even in a Hollywood-type studio. In other words, they just made up reality as they went. While their fictitious version does not change reality, it is certainly one way to avoid thinking through the events with their rational mind.

Now the truth of the matter is that what I believe about something doesn't change reality. For example, if I choose not to believe in gravity and then jump off the Sears Tower (renamed the Willis Tower in 2009) in Chicago, I will hit the ground and die. Reality will not be altered because I choose to ignore the laws of gravity. If I decide not to believe in airplane travel or the moon landing or God's authorship of life, reality is not changed. While I may decide that the purpose of life is winning the Nathan's Famous Hot Dog Eating Contest in New York City, my belief doesn't make it so. Now, I can hear some responding, "Well, it does for me." Which is true— if we are God. But, we are not. That is reality. Apollo 17 astronaut Harrison Schmitt phrased it this way: "If people decide they're going to deny the facts of history and the facts of science and technology, there's not much you can do with them. For most of them, I just feel sorry that we failed in their education."[9]

~~~

So, I have stopped the daily grind for a moment; I have shut off the noise of the world. And now, I embrace the opportunity to think. If my thoughts are consumed with *what kind of candy do I want to buy today?*, *when does the Star Wars sequel come out?*, *when is the next sale at Macy's?*, or *where can we go drinking this weekend?*, the shallowness of my connection to God may be revealed.

It is said that George Schultz, Secretary of Labor during the Nixon Administration, constantly faced intrusions, people wanting his time. Therefore, people were stunned when they discovered that he would close his door for an hour each day to think.[10]

Steve Ross, who was the architect of the well-known Time Warner merger in 1990, tells of the advice that his father gave him when he was on his deathbed. His father told him that there are three kinds of people: 1) those who work all day, 2) those who only dream all day, and 3) those who spend an hour dreaming before they work the rest of the day seeking to fulfill their dreams. His father told him, "Go into the third category because there's virtually no competition."[11]

As we begin our journey into critical thinking, the words of Paul to the Philippians are a good beginning point: *"Finally, brothers, whatever is true, whatever is noble, whatever is right, whatever is pure, whatever is lovely, whatever is admirable—if anything is excellent or praiseworthy—think about such things"* (Phil. 4:8).

Pray

It has been a busy day at work, but you finally arrive home. Getting out of the car, you walk past your children who are playing in the front yard. You continue on through the living room, where your wife is sitting, without saying a word. Once in the bedroom, you turn on the sports network and watch television for the next three hours before falling asleep. Aside from seeming incredibly rude and insensitive, the behavior may not appear too bizarre, as it goes on in many households every day. But here is the crazy part—the next day you proceed to talk to your coworker about how important your family is to you and how you love them more than anything. He or she might believe you, as long as they weren't a witness to the previous evening. Because had they been there, your behavior would make absolutely no sense.

While the story may seem a bit ridiculous, it is one that is lived out daily. We may casually comment that we love God but then never stop long enough to have a conversation with Him. If the dad in the story above wants to relate to his wife or children, he would have to first stop and quiet his thoughts and then engage his brain to think about them. Once he has done that, he would be prepared to talk with them. This same process is played out when we engage with our Creator.

Throughout the Scriptures, we find examples of men who prayed: the prophet Samuel (1 Sam. 12:18), King Solomon (1 Kings 8:30), Job (Job 42:10), King David (Ps. 5:2), and of course, Jesus (Matt. 14:23; Luke 5:16). Now, someone might question, "Well, why would the Son of God need to pray?" Actually, a better question might be, "Why wouldn't He?" Why wouldn't He talk with His Father?

~~~

I think we get confused by the word *pray*. You might think that it is something you are not good at, or that you don't know how to do it. But I want to dismantle that notion. Prayer is not some religious ordeal. There is no prescribed formula. Very simply—prayer is talking to God. Talking—we know how to do that. My wife wants me to talk with her. My kids like to have conversations. And our God wants us to talk with Him. We don't need flowery words or religious-sounding lingo. He simply wants us to come as we are and talk with Him.

We are encouraged to have private conversations with God and to have regular and continual talks with Him (see Matt. 6:6; Rom. 12:12; 1 Thess. 5:17). We are to pray for our leaders (see 1 Tim. 2:1). God wants us to talk with Him about our troubles (see James 5:13). We are to lift up our hands in worship and converse with Him (see 1 Tim. 2:8). We are even told that when we are severely ill, we should have the church leaders come and pray for us (see James 5:14).

In one account, Jesus told His disciples a story about a widow who went to a judge (an uncaring, crooked judge, I might add) seeking justice. The judge ignored her and put her off. However, she was persistent to the point that he finally gave in. Jesus uses this example to encourage us **not to give up in our requests to God (see Luke 18:1-5).** If an unjust judge will eventually hear a widow's request, how much more will a just God listen to those He loves?

Now, I am certainly aware that we all have had requests that we are convinced God either doesn't hear or doesn't care about. My intent is not to tackle those frustrations here. I am not God, and much like Job learned, God's ways are beyond my comprehension. But what I do know is this—just as my wife may not fulfill my every request, she still wants me to talk with her about the things that are important to me. Similarly, God wants to me to relate with Him.

How would you feel if the only time your spouse spoke to you was when she was dashing through the room and, even then, only told you what she wanted you to do? If you are like I am, you probably would feel used and unvalued. Yet this is often exactly how we treat the Maker of the universe.

"But I am busy. I just don't have time to talk with God." When I find myself thinking these thoughts, I realize that I have forgotten how desperately I need and depend on God. Martin Luther is famous for remarking, "I have so much to do today that I'm going to need to spend three hours in prayer in order to be able to get it all done."[12] I must learn to see my conversations with God as the most powerful and efficient use of my time.

Meditate

Now before you begin to think that you are going to have to sit cross-legged on the floor in a monastery chanting, let me put your mind at ease. Lots of words could be used in place of "meditate." Words like *ponder, ruminate, cogitate, study*, or *contemplate* are just a few. However, because I like the summary nature of the word *meditate*, I am going to stick with it here. But what does it mean? I like the thoughts of well-known author Rick Warren: "Prayer lets you speak to God; mediation lets God speak to you. Both are essential to becoming a friend of God."[13]

Think about that for a moment. I am friends with my wife—first and foremost. And that early process of becoming friends was able to happen because I spoke to her and she spoke to me. If it had been nothing more than my talking, the friendship would have been short-lived. But because it was two way, our relationship developed.

"OK," you say. "That makes sense with your wife. But how does that work with God? How do I do it? How do I meditate?" Again, I appreciate Rick Warren's explanation of this idea: "If you know how to worry, you already know how to mediate. Worry is focused thinking on something negative. Meditation is doing the same thing, only focusing on God's Word instead of your problem."[14]

God speaks to us through His Word. So is it any wonder that if I spend three hours watching television and three minutes listening to God, I might live in a state of confusion about direction in my life? Meditation allows me to connect with the God of creation, and when I connect with Him, I am led by Him—both by His written instructions as well as the promptings of His Spirit. When I fail to allow Him to lead in my life, I have a blundering tendency to hold back when He is indicating to move forward, or worse yet, to rush in when He is saying to wait.

When we cultivate a praying/meditating or a talking/listening relationship with God, we develop the opportunity for greater clarity and satisfaction in our lives. Gallup surveys indicate that the closer people feel to God, the better they feel about themselves.[15] Of course King David declared this truth roughly 3,000 years earlier when he said that the person who is truly happy and fulfilled is the one who consistently meditates on God's Word. When we are willing to do that, we become like evergreen trees that are constantly being replenished by fresh streams of water—whatever we do prospers (see Ps. 1:2-3). It doesn't get much better than that.

~~~

Loving God with all of our heart, soul, mind, and strength is about relating to the Redeemer of our souls and aligning ourselves with His purposes. I resonate with the following statement by Rabbi Aaron: "We study Torah[16] to know what God wants. We pray in order to want what God wants. We obey the commandments in order to live what God wants."[17]

Purpose Recapped

1.   Two Foundational Truths—

     #1—God is, and He knows what His creation needs.

     #2—The Scriptures are God's written instructions for how to live.

2.   Overarching Purpose #1—To love God with all my heart, soul, mind, and strength.

     Sub-purpose #1—To relate to my Creator through faith, obedience, repentance, and worship.

     Sub-purpose #2—To relate to my Creator by walking humbly and giving up control while trusting Him.

     Sub-purpose #3—To relate to my Creator by:
     a.   Stopping to rest.
     b.   Getting quiet at the core of who I am.
     c.   Thinking about the things that are important to God and in life.
     d.   Talking on a continual basis with God.
     e.   Listening for His responses—both through His Word and through godly people.

Section Two

OVERARCHING PURPOSE #2
LOVE YOUR NEIGHBOR

"Love the Lord your God with all your heart and with all your soul and with all your mind." This is the first and greatest commandment. And the second is like it: "Love your neighbor" **(Matthew 22:37-39).**

Chapter Five

My Neighbor Might Be Easier—Marriage

"Perhaps the greatest opportunity for fulfilling one's potential lies in creating a lifelong, synergistic partnership with another person."
—KENNETH WOOD[1]

As we begin this next section, I want to revisit with you the direction that we are headed and remind you of the intentionality with which we are moving.

First, you may have picked up this book dealing with purpose because you are genuinely searching to understand what this life that you are living is all about. Or, second, you may be trying to make an important decision in your life, potentially regarding a career choice or spouse selection, and you were hoping for a three-step formula that would clearly tell you what to do. While we will eventually get to some information that could be helpful in decision-making, you have probably realized that this book is much more about the former (the purpose of life) than it is about the latter (career choices, etc.). However, once we lay down the foundations of purpose, specific choices will become more manageable.

Section 1 examined the priority foundational purpose from our Creator—*loving God with every fiber of our being*. Now we turn our attention to part two of our overarching purpose, which is to love our neighbor.

—~—

"Which one of these three do you think was a neighbor to the man who fell into the hands of robbers?" The expert in the law replied, "The one who had mercy on him." Jesus told him, "Go and do likewise" (Luke 10:36-37).

Here was the scenario—a Jewish man was on a trip when he was mugged. He was robbed, beaten, his clothes were shredded, and he was left half dead. As he lay on the road in this condition, three individuals walked by. The first was a religious leader, who intentionally walked on the opposite side of the road to avoid the man. The next was a Levite, a man from the priestly tribe of Israel, who also made it a point to avoid the wounded man. Finally came a Samaritan. Now for those of us living today, that doesn't mean much. We simply think, "A person from Samaria—no big deal." But without getting into the explanation as to why, let me just say that the Jews and the Samaritans despised each other—a lot. And yet, even though that was the case, this Samaritan stopped, helped him, bandaged his wounds, took him to the local Holiday Inn, paid for the man's care, and came back to check on him. Wow—not bad for a man who had such animosity toward the other one's ethnicity. And yet Jesus held this example up of what loving our neighbor entails—loving the difficult, loving those who seem unlovable.

You may be thinking, "OK, but what does that story have to do with marriage?" Great question. Hang tight and we will come back to this.

~~~

Early after the beginning of creation, recorded in the second chapter of Genesis, is the account of God's relationship with Adam. God had charged Adam with certain responsibilities (we will talk more about this in Section 3) and had determined that Adam would be able to fulfill these better if he had a companion.

> *So the Lord God caused the man to fall into a deep sleep; and while he was sleeping, He took one of the man's ribs and closed up the place with flesh. Then the Lord God made a woman from the rib He had taken out of the man, and He brought her to the man. The man said, "This is now bone of my bones and flesh of my flesh; she shall be called woman, for she was taken out of man." For this reason a man will leave his father and mother and be united to his wife, and they will become one flesh (Genesis 2:21-24).*

This passage sets the foundation for the marriage relationship: the husband and wife are to leave their families and become one. The passage here talks specifically about becoming one physically, which we will discuss more in a minute. But I would submit that in joining with my spouse, I become one physically, emotionally, spiritually, financially, and a host of other ways. The Scriptures expand upon this in Matthew 19:6 when Jesus states that once we become one physically, we *"are no longer two, but one."* In other words, my purpose, or even the image of who I am, is modified.

Recently, one of my wife's students invited us to a "Painting with a Twist" party. A number of kids and staff members were all together in a room with an instructor, trying to paint the same picture. While we were all given the same assignment or purpose, the results looked quite different from one another. Each individual went about painting their understanding of the picture in their own manner. However, my wife and I decided to do one canvas together (maybe because she felt sorry for my pathetic painting skills). It was interesting that once that decision was made, our manner of engaging the project changed. In other words, our approach wasn't dictated by my ideas or pursued only along the lines of her thoughts. We communicated about how best to tackle the project. We shared chalk, paints, and paint brushes. And once we started painting together, the picture could no longer solely belong to one or the other of us. The painting was under joint authorship.

This is a picture (no pun intended) of God's design for marriage. He knows how He built us, and He knows that people were not designed to be alone. While I recognize that there are some people who prefer to be single and truly enjoy doing life solo, most prefer to journey with a spouse. We are, for the most part, naturally wired that way. God's desire is that with the support of our mate, we become even more capable of achieving our God-given purposes.

～～～

We are reminded almost daily of the fragility of marriage in the United States in the 21st century. Nuclear-family households now account for less than 20 percent of American homes.[2] Whether we are discussing the high and destructive divorce rate, the trends toward cohabitation, or people miserably hurling insults across the house at each other for years, we are talking about the things that miss the target of God's ideal for us. As we have already seen, God's instruction manual tells us that in marriage we become one; we become united. **The Scriptures go on to say that this is such a sacred bond before God that we are not to divorce (see Matt. 19:6; Mark 10:9; 1 Cor. 7:10-11).**

Now, I recognize that Scripture teaches some limited reasons for divorce such as unfaithfulness (see Matt. 19:9) and abandonment (see 1 Cor. 7:15), but these situations are never God's desire. As a matter of fact, if you read Jeremiah 3, you see that God understands the need for divorce sometimes. But He clearly expresses His hatred for the practice (see Mal. 2:16) because He knows that betrayal, hurt, and devastation that are caused by divorce.

C. S. Lewis likens divorce to the "cutting up a living body, as a kind of surgical operation."[3] He goes on to state that it is "more like having both your legs cut off than it is like dissolving a business partnership."

The word translated "united" in marriage (see Matt. 19:5) is really a word that means "glued together" or "bonded." The image is that of two pieces of wood that are glued and clamped together. Once they are bonded, they are meant to function as one piece. So, one might ask the question, "Can they be separated?" Well—sort of. I can get something wedged in between them to pry them apart, but what happens? Sometimes they come apart with splinters sticking out, while other times huge chunks of wood are broken off in the process. The lesson I learn from that is that I really should avoid gluing the boards together unless I am planning to leave them together. Similarly, uniting myself with another person is an undertaking that should be reserved for those who are committed for life (see Rom. 7:2-3; 1 Cor. 7:39). God doesn't tell us this in order to somehow limit our fun—He gives us these instructions to spare us pain and to bring us peace and satisfaction.

A 2016 article reports that "baby boomers are divorcing at an unprecedented rate. Divorce among people over 50 is so prevalent today it has its own moniker: 'gray divorce.'"[4] But why, if divorce overall is so damaging, do people run to it so quickly? I would contend that for many, if they have been wandering around for decades, going through the motions of life, not having a clear understanding of their purpose, they may find themselves unhappy and unfulfilled.

Without God at the center of the equation, it is easy to search for and jettison the things that they perceive as possible causes to their unhappiness. Spouses are often one of the first things to go.

~~~

As my wife and I were painting our picture together in the earlier account, our palette only had four or five different colors on it. And yet, we were able to paint in a greater variety of colors by mixing the paints together. Depending on how I mixed the blue, green, and white, I could create a variety of colors and shades in the initial scenes of water that we were painting. But here is what was interesting—as soon as I combined black and white, I could only paint gray. Black and white no longer existed, but the perfect gray did. I could not take my paint brush at that point and paint black if I wanted to. The two colors were no longer two but were now one new color.

So how are we to do that in a world that perceives marriage as so impermanent? We have to go back to our guidebook—God's Word. And there we discover something that is key to this concept of marriage for life—"covenant." We find reference to the marriage covenant in Malachi 2:14. The Bible talks about the permanence of marriage in Matthew 19 and Mark 10. Our marriage relationship is compared in Ephesians 5 to the relationship that God has with His people, which is continually referred to in Scripture as a covenant relationship (see Deut. 5:2). But what exactly does that mean?

In our culture today we typically use the terms *covenant* and *contract* interchangeably. Thinking that they denote the same thing, people conclude that the deal is simply—"you do your part, and I will do mine. But if you fail to do yours, then I am not obligated to follow through." But that is a far cry from what a covenant entails.

I like the following clarification that comes from an article by Chris Cree: "With a contract, if one agreeing party does something in violation of the contract then it is considered broken. The whole contract becomes null and void. Basically the signers of a contract agree to hold up their ends as long as the other signatories hold up theirs too. With a covenant, both parties agree to hold up their ends *regardless* of whether the other party keeps their part of the agreement. A violation of a covenant by one party doesn't matter as far as the other party's responsibility to continue to do what they agreed to do."[5]

We see this demonstrated throughout the Old Testament in God's dealings with Israel as He continually reaffirms His covenant (see Exod. 19:5; Jer. 7:23; and many other passages). When Israel would violate the covenant, as they did more times than one can count, God did not give up on His relationship with them. (See the Book of Hosea.) Oh sure, there were consequences to their choices; at times there was punishment and even exile from their land, but God remained present. And it is that ever-present mind-set that He calls upon us to adopt in our marriages. It is by grasping this principle that we create the possibility of security, fulfillment, and a lifelong supportive companionship. That is our purpose in marriage, and as mentioned earlier, our marital relationship is a piece of our individual purpose puzzle.

I want to suggest four steps toward developing and strengthening a covenant marriage—a relationship for a lifetime.

Step One in "How?"—Knowing God

"The Talmud[6] teaches that a man and a woman who do not have God in their marriage will not have a lasting relationship."[7] This is reinforced in Old Testament teachings such as Deuteronomy 7, when God tells the Israelites not to marry those from nations who were idol worshipers. To marry them would result in people's hearts and minds being compromised. They would begin to worship idols made by men instead of serving the Living God. We see historically that this very thing happened, which contributed to Israel's frequent wandering away from God.

This same principle is reflected in New Testament Scripture when the apostle Paul writes, *"Do not be yoked together with unbelievers. For what do righteousness and wickedness have in common? Or what fellowship can light have with darkness?"* **(2 Cor. 6: 14)** This is a recognition that whom I choose to journey with will impact my life.

~~~

I want you to imagine that you and I decide to take a road trip together. We have been talking at length about how much we enjoy Mickey Mouse, the Matterhorn, Splash Mountain, and so on. We conclude that basically, we just love Disney. So, we pack up the car with containers of trail mix and a cooler of drinks, and off we go.

Now, from my location in Colorado Springs, we head down I-25 through New Mexico. As we get into Albuquerque, I start to turn right onto I-40. Puzzled, you ask, "Hey, you made a wrong turn. Where are you going?" I reply with, "No, I didn't make a mistake. This is the way to Disney." You respond curtly by saying, "You have to turn around. It is the other direction."

By now you have probably realized that we had two different destinations in mind; I thought we were traveling to Disneyland, while you had your sights set on Disney World. At this point, we have to make a decision: either you talk me into turning the car around and heading to Florida, or I convince you that California is the better destination. Of course there is a third option, and that would be that one of us gets out of the car and rents a separate vehicle because we are set on going two different directions.

This is the issue being addressed in the Scriptures above. If I am a servant who belongs to God, how easy will it be to travel with someone not headed in the same direction? And we are not simply talking about theme parks but about our destination for eternity. Living God's purpose for us to its full potential requires us first to address this issue of being bonded together with a believer.

Touré Roberts takes this a step further when he says, "Everything in life has purpose, even who you decide to marry."[8] He encourages couples to consider their purpose in life when choosing a mate. Think about the wisdom of this for a moment. Wouldn't it make sense to have a partner who supports you in your purpose as well as for you to be invested in his or hers? In order for that to happen, our spouse selection needs to be much deeper than just whether or not we both like ice cream and old movies.

Step Two in "How?"—Sexual Intimacy

Now I am well aware that as some of you read this subtitle heading, the hair on the back of your neck is bristling and you are tempted to close the book and be done. But please don't. There certainly have been many who have used and abused Scripture for their own selfish agendas. And all I can say about that is they were dead wrong and were dishonoring both you and God in doing so.

At the same time, I don't want to ignore something that God has designed to physically and emotionally unite us. We are told in First Corinthians 7 that there is a great deal of sexual immorality going on and rather than have that continue, men and women should marry (see 1 Cor. 7:2). The writer goes on to emphasize the importance of this connection when he says that **we have a responsibility to meet each other's physical needs (see 1 Cor. 7:3-5). We are not to go for extended periods of time with a lack of sexual connection unless we have agreed for some reason to do so. And even then we are to make sure that we reconnect physically. Failing to do so creates a dangerous vulnerability in our marriage.**

Other passages remind us of the sacredness and exclusivity of our sexual connection. Malachi 2:15 notes the fact that through this joining, God has made us one in both flesh and spirit. The writer of the Book of Hebrews clearly tells us that *"marriage should be honored by all, and the marriage bed kept pure, for God will judge the adulterer and all the sexually immoral"* **(Heb. 13:4).** He is recognizing two important principles here. First, sex is designed for those who are married. It is not for us to engage in with anyone except for our spouse. Secondly, marriage is to be respected. That means I don't flirt with another man's wife, and I would expect that they would not attempt to test the parameters of my marriage either. I like the imagery used by King Solomon in Proverbs 5:15-17. He compares the sexual connection you have with your spouse to waters flowing from a well, saying, *"Drink water from your own cistern, running water from your own well.... Let them* **[the waters***]* *be yours alone, never to be shared with strangers"* **(Prov. 5:15,17).**

The intimacy that God has created for me to experience with my mate is for her and for her alone. I always want to be careful never to take what belongs only to her and give it to someone else. And this doesn't just apply to sexual intercourse. It includes any physical touching that my spouse would be uncomfortable with were she present. It also encompasses personal secrets, flirting, inside jokes, and intimate conversations with the opposite sex. I can't emphasize enough that connecting with another person in any of these ways is robbing from my wife the things to which **only** she is entitled.

Step Three in "How?"—Interdependence

"Independence!" It is a sacred value in this country. I remember the celebrations that were held when we reached the 200-year anniversary of America's Declaration of Independence from England. And now we are nearing the 250th birthday of that event.

Movies that proclaim "Freedom!" such as *Braveheart*, or that contain a refusal to submit to outside forces, like the science fiction thriller *Independence Day*, all hold to that same premise—that we are strong and will submit to no one.

Certainly, this core belief is important to embrace in various areas of life. However, when it comes to the marriage relationship, we have taken it to an extreme. I remember lyrics from the chorus of that 1970s song by Helen Reddy, "I Am Woman":

If I have to, I can do anything.

> *I am strong*
> *(Strong)*
> *I am invincible*
> *(Invincible)*
> *I am woman.*[9]

The song was no doubt a response to decades of women being undervalued and oftentimes being viewed as second-class citizens. It was a natural and understandable reaction.

But you see, it was never God's intent that either gender be taken for granted, that men or women would be deemed of more or less value than the other. While we all have a certain level of independence, God has called us to rely on each other. Read these words in First Corinthians 11:11-12: *"In the Lord, however, woman is not independent of man, nor is man independent of woman. For as woman came from man, so also man is born of woman. But everything comes from God."*

~~~

When describing the ideal relationship between husbands and wives, the Bible uses the word *submit*. *"Submit to one another out of reverence for Christ"* (Eph. 5:21). But for so many of us, that idea of "submitting" conjures up related words and phrases like *surrender, acquiesce, capitulate, kowtow, relent, eat crow, give in,* or *throw in the towel*. These synonyms bring feelings of weakness and powerlessness, and most of us want nothing to do with them. But what if we considered similar words, but ones with a more positive connotation—such as *agree, defer,* or *yield*—in the context of an interdependent relationship?

Men and women were never meant to be walked on or viewed as inferior to each other. We clearly see at the beginning of time that God created man and woman equal but different. They were designed with unique gifts, strengths, and talents, all of which were needed for a full and complete relationship. It is into this "equal but different" context that we see so many of the Bible's instructions for marriage offered. **Women are encouraged to defer to the husband's leadership in the marriage because husbands are instructed to lead (see Eph. 5:22-33; Col. 3:18-19; 1 Peter 3:1). However, it is important to understand how the men are called to lead.** It is not an "I am in charge so you have to do what I say" kind of leadership. **Husbands are called to lead with love—a sacrificial love, a love that demonstrates a willingness to lay down my life and my agenda for the welfare of my wife. When I read the Ephesians passage, I discover that it is my responsibility to present my wife back to God better than I found her—a pretty tall order. I even find that the effectiveness of my prayers can be directly connected with how I treat my wife.**

~~~

A lack of understanding of these principles has led clients in my office to tell me why discovering their God-given purposes means that they should leave their marriage. One individual said to me, "I didn't consider God's direction or will when I married my husband. But now that I am seeking His purpose for my life, I realize that I married the wrong man." The person making this statement has failed to understand what a covenant marriage is. As life coach Bob Shank writes, "Sorry, but no way. If you're involved in relationships with people by covenant (as in marriage), or by contract (as in a business situation), then you stick to your guns in that relationship for the term of the agreement (for marriage, that's for life!)."[10]

In my interdependent relationship with my spouse, I have built a unique set of connections. Every decision I make impacts her and therefore must be considered in light of her needs. Each decision she makes related to time, money, energy, location (and a host of other factors) affects my life as well. Whether the decision is related to the car, the house, the kids—they all affect both of us. Therefore, we do life together and make decisions together as we strive to be each other's biggest fans.

A side note here—it is critical that we invest in each other interdependently, especially during the season of life when the kids are at home. Otherwise, when you get to the "empty nest" stage, you will be looking at each other wondering who this stranger is living in the house with you. Reconstructing your marriage once the children are gone is far more energy draining than investing in each other all along. Tragically, far too many divorces take place at this stage.

God has given us purposes in His Word that align us as well as purposes (that we continue to discover) that complement us and our oneness. As a result, we champion each other's purposes, continually cheering each other on. Because truly, as a husband, a part of my calling is to support my wife's purposes just as she supports mine. I am better able to fulfill God's directions in my life because I am married to my wife. Without her, I am convinced, the going would be slower. That is "interdependence."

Step Four in "How?"—Love

Love as distinct from "being in love" is not merely a feeling. It is a deep unity, maintained by the will and deliberately strengthened by habit; reinforced by (in Christian marriages) the grace which both partners ask, and receive, from God. They can have this love for each other even at those moments when they do not like each other; as you love yourself even when you do not like yourself. They can retain this love even when each would easily, if they allowed themselves, be "in love" with someone else. "Being in love" first moved them to promise fidelity: this quieter love enables them to keep the promise. It is on this love that the engine of marriage is run: being in love was the explosion that started it.[11]

A familiar Scripture passage frequently recited in weddings says it this way: *"Love is patient, love is kind. It does not envy, it does not boast, it is not proud. It is not rude, it is not self-seeking, it is not easily angered, it keeps no record of wrongs. Love does not delight in evil but rejoices with the truth. It always protects, always trusts, always hopes, always perseveres. Love never fails"* (1 Cor. 13:4-8a).

What both of these authors are conveying is this—love is a choice. My marriage is a choice. How I treat and relate to my spouse is a choice. It is my choice whom I marry, to be physically and emotionally united in a covenant marriage for life, to be interdependent, and to treat my mate with the kindness, love, and respect that she deserves. Whether or not I treasure my wife is completely up to me. And if I am choosing to embrace God's overarching purpose in my life of "loving my neighbor," it is first demonstrated in how I love my spouse.

~~~

Thinking back to the passage I discussed earlier in this chapter regarding the Jewish man who was beaten and robbed, we saw that the man from Samaria reached out and loved the man whom his people would have considered unlovable. Notice that there is no discussion regarding whether or not the Samaritan had fond feelings for the robbery victim. We are simply told that he loved the man— he acted with loving choices that were for the benefit of the stranger.

Many reading this might find it easier to love a stranger than to love their mate right now. You may be one who has been deeply wounded by harsh criticisms, disrespectful behaviors, and even betrayal by your husband or wife. And honestly—they seem unlovable to you. Yet even in these most difficult of circumstances, God has purposed that we would treat our partner with the loving behaviors described in First Corinthians 13.

Perhaps this part is easy for you because you are intimately connected with your partner. If so—super! But if not, I want to encourage you to decide to begin loving the difficult "neighbor" in your spouse today. It is a critical part of your purpose.

Purpose Recapped

1. Two Foundational Truths—

    #1—God is, and He knows what His creation needs.

    #2—The Scriptures are God's written instructions for how to live.

2. Overarching Purpose #1—To love God with all my heart, soul, mind, and strength.

    Sub-purpose #1—To relate to my Creator by: having faith, being obedient, confessing and repenting of my sins, and worshiping God with everything in my life.

    Sub-purpose #2—To walk humbly with God by giving up control and trusting Him.

    Sub-purpose #3—To connect with God through a lifestyle of quiet—praying and listening.

3. Overarching Purpose #2—To love my neighbor.

    Sub-purpose #1—If I am married:
    a. Committing myself to traveling together with my mate down the road God has us on.
    b. Being united and intimate—physically, emotionally, and spiritually.
    c. Developing an interdependent relationship with my husband or wife.
    d. Making the choice to love my spouse in my words and actions in all circumstances.

Chapter Six

My Neighbor Might Be Way Easier—Parenting

*"The way we talk to our children
becomes their inner voice."*
—PEGGY O'MARA[1]

I ran into a stranger as he passed by,
"Oh excuse me please" was my reply.
He said, "Please excuse me too;
I wasn't watching for you."
We were very polite, this stranger and I.
We went on our way and we said goodbye.
But at home a different story is told,
How we treat our loved ones, young and old.

Later that day, cooking the evening meal,
My son stood beside me very still.
When I turned, I nearly knocked him down.
"Move out of the way," I said with a frown.
He walked away, his little heart broken.
I didn't realize how harshly I'd spoken.
While I lay awake in bed,
God's still small voice came to me and said,
"While dealing with a stranger, common courtesy you use,
but the family you love, you seem to abuse.
Go and look on the kitchen floor,
You'll find some flowers there by the door.
Those are the flowers he brought for you.
He picked them himself: pink, yellow, and blue.
He stood very quietly not to spoil the surprise,
You never saw the tears that filled his little eyes."
By this time, I felt very small,
And now my tears began to fall.
I quietly went and knelt by his bed
"Wake up, little one, wake up," I said.
"Are these the flowers you picked for me?"
He smiled, "I found 'em, out by the tree.
I picked 'em because they're pretty like you.
I knew you'd like 'em, especially the blue."
I said, "Son, I'm very sorry for the way I acted today;
I shouldn't have yelled at you that way."
He said, "Oh, Mom, that's OK.
I love you anyway."
I said, "Son, I love you too,
And I do like the flowers, especially the blue."
—Author unknown

I love that poem—well, maybe a better way of saying it is that I am convicted by that poem. It is very easy for us to get so caught up in the busyness of our day-to-day activities that we take our family members for granted, give them the crumbs of our energy (not our best stuff), and even abuse them with the curtness of our responses. And yet, this is not what we were called to do.

We begin to examine our next topic of significance under our overarching purpose of "loving our neighbor"—parenting. **From the beginning of creation, God told Adam and Eve,** *"Be fruitful and increase in number"* **(Gen. 1:28). In other words, "Have kids and populate the planet."** Now, if you don't have children, it is in no way necessary for you to feel as though you have dropped the ball. That is certainly not the case. It is easy to see that early on this admonition was of high priority as there were not yet other people on the planet. However, as I sit writing in 2017, the world's population is nearing 7.5 billion people.[2] I think that we have done a pretty good job at "increasing in number."

So, while this chapter on parenting will look not so much at the need to make babies, it will examine the importance of what we do with them should we decide to make them.

The Goals of Parenting

So, we have to ask ourselves, "What is the goal of having kids and of parenting?" In talking with parents, I have become convinced that the vast majority of them have no more clarity about parenting than they do about their purpose in life. Young parents have been heard to say, "I am having a baby so that there will be someone who will always love me." While I understand the sentiment, I am afraid this misses the mark. Similarly, others have stated, "I had kids because that is what we thought we were supposed to do."

I recall during my days of working in an inner-city high school in central California when a student of mine wanted me to meet his dad. I walked up to the dad and introduced myself, relating what a great son he had—a diligent worker, kind hearted, and of strong character. The dad's first words to me were, "Well, as soon as he turns 18, he has to be out on his own." I can only imagine how his son felt hearing those words. My guess is that this dad had less than a clear purpose for parenting. And yet, according to a Pew Research Center report published in *The Washington Post*, 18-year-olds aren't moving out at the rate they once were. For children ages 18–34, a greater number of them are living with their parents over all other living arrangements.[3]

During the late 1800s and early 1900s, it was not uncommon for couples to have large families of 10, 11, or even 12 kids. My grandmother came from a family of this size. As there was a larger agricultural population then, couples had numerous children partly to have more hands to help with the farming.

I want to suggest four reasons that I believe God has given us children.

1. Psalms 127:3 tells us that children are a "reward" from God. Whether it was the early historical need for help at home or the 21st-century need of having children to assist us as we get older, I think most parents would agree that they have been rewarded by having children.

2. King Solomon says that our children can bring us joy (see Prov. 23:24). When we are privileged enough to see our children become caring, independent, responsible adults, I think that most would agree—we are filled with joy.

I think of my oldest son as an example. There were certainly difficult seasons in his life and, as a result, in our relationship. But as I watch him today as a young father, I am impressed by the dad and husband he has become. I am proud of him, and my heart is filled with joy.

1. Our relationship with our children is representative of the relationship that God has with us. Luke 11:11-13

states, *"Which of you fathers, if your son asks for a fish, will give him a snake instead? Or if he asks for an egg, will give him a scorpion? If you then, though you are evil, know how to give good gifts to your children, how much more will your Father in heaven give the Holy Spirit to those who ask Him!"* As parents we experience a wide range of thoughts and emotions as we navigate parenthood. In doing so, we have the opportunity to gain great insight into God's love and care for us.

2.   It is God's desire that we raise children who will live in a manner that honors Him—with lives demonstrating His love. In other words, we fill this world with children who obey their Creator by doing the very things we have been talking about—loving God and loving people. This is the ideal that God has desired from us since the beginning of time.

~~~

Parenting expert Dr. James Dobson writes, "Raising children who have been loaned to us for a brief moment outranks every other responsibility."[4] Having grown children as well as a grandchild, I can attest to just how brief these moments are. Of all the responsibilities that I have had in my life, without a doubt, being a parent has been one of the most significant ones with which I have been entrusted.

Raising a child from newborn to adulthood might be compared to planting a garden. Once I have prepared the soil in the spring, I have to begin to plant seeds. The kinds of vegetables that I want to eat will determine whether I plant green beans, carrots, squash, or cucumbers. If I am to enjoy my zucchini in the summer, then I am going to have to carefully plant and nurture those seeds. In her book *Give Them Wings,* Carol Kuykendall describes the nurturing that is required of us as parents. If we want to raise godly, independent, responsible adults, then it will require us to nurture the following seeds in our children's lives: seeds of faith, confidence, character, perseverance, kindness and compassion, sexuality, and practical coping skills.[5] Because the reality is, if we don't nurture those components in our kids' lives, someone else will. And when that is a person not of our choosing or society at large, we will watch our influence evaporate.

Some have expressed that parenting is the most natural thing in the world. While I suppose that giving birth is natural (easy for me to say as a guy), parenting is more like building an airplane in flight. (I am thinking that would be a more than challenging task.)

I remember the excitement and anticipation of the birth of my first child. We had read all the books about having a baby and faithfully went to Lamaze classes. We practiced all that we were taught, and I knew I had this "breathing" thing down pat. But then this baby was born. As I held my new son for the very first time, a wave of incredible responsibility washed over me. I suddenly realized that this wasn't about having a kid because all our friends were doing it and we were supposed to as well. This had nothing to do with fitting into an American norm. This newborn was a real live person—a person for whom I was responsible. I suddenly woke up to the fact that my life was no longer about me. I was being entrusted with my son, and for the next two decades I needed to make the most of it.

Did I know what I was doing? Not a clue. Oh sure I had read some books about babies, but I knew very little about parenting. This was definitely going to be "on-the-job training." Fortunately, we are not left on our own to figure this parenting thing out. First, we have our own parents as resources. Now, if your parents did a pretty good job, it may be easy to want to pick up some of their skills. However, if you were raised in a severely dysfunctional household, you may be trying to get as far away from those strategies as possible. Second, you probably know other parents who have successfully progressed down the parenting road further than you and can offer you some valuable wisdom. And third, you have God's example as a parent as well as His instructions.

Discipline = Discipleship

Now you may see the subheading "Discipleship" and be a little confused, thinking, "What does this have to do with parenting?" A lot! You see, the words *discipline* and *discipleship* come from the same root word, which I believe gives us profound insight for parenting. "Discipline" denotes the idea of "training to act in accordance" with a set of rules. It involves activity that is designed to improve one's skills.[6] Similarly, "disciple" also embodies this idea of "teaching or training."[7]

Now I wonder, as you read those definitions, if they throw you a bit. For many parents, when you mention the word *discipline*, what they actually think of is *punishment.* They use the terms interchangeably. You know—"That behavior can't be tolerated. He is going to have to be *disciplined.* I am thinking we should take his cell phone away for a week"; "I can't believe she came in after curfew again, and she was so blatant about it. We will have to *discipline* her this time for her disregard of our rules. What do you think her punishment ought to be?"

I would submit the idea that "punishment" may not accomplish what we originally thought that it would. Typical consequences when punishing include yelling, making threats, giving putdowns, taking things away (not always inappropriate), and hitting. Punishment teaches our kids to behave in a certain way only for the purpose of getting something (be that a reward or a privilege) or simply to avoid trouble—not to cooperate. It may teach our kids to fear and resent us. It can definitely damage the relationships we want to have with them. Punishment can even stimulate revenge.

Discipline, on the other hand, begins to teach our children how to take charge of their own lives by making some of their own decisions. This is made possible because it teaches them to learn from the consequences of their choices. Discipline shows respect for both you and your child. The consequences fit the misbehavior, are about the behavior, are firm but friendly, allow choice, and most importantly, are about the future—not the past.

~~~

As parents, **we are charged with the responsibility of raising our children to become godly individuals, and this won't happen without discipline. Knowing this, King Solomon wisely tells us,** *"Do not withhold discipline from a child..."* **(Prov. 23:13). He also encourages us to** *"discipline your son, for in that there is hope..."* **(Prov. 19:18).**

Too often, parents react to children. A child may have broken a rule, or blatantly disregarded a parent's instructions. Mom or Dad become livid and then punish in anger. I have been there. I remember what it is like. Teens know exactly which buttons to push to send us over the edge—and they do it. A rational mind wonders why teenagers would intentionally do something that will lead to their parents blowing a gasket. Here is the secret—teens want some control. If you don't raise them with mutual respect, giving them options and choices when age appropriate, they will find very inappropriate ways to get control. They know that when they do or say a certain thing, fireworks will shoot out of your ears. While it may not be pretty, for that moment, they are in control. Then what happens? It often becomes an emotional slugfest. Insults are hurled at each other, profanity fills the room, and ultimately some over-the-top punishment is meted out while the child stomps out of the room. Parents and children alike are breathing fire, and no one wants to be anywhere near the other one. The relationship is damaged—sometimes severely.

When children misbehave, I have seen parents huddle together to devise what new punishment will "show them who is boss." Finding ourselves in this position, we can be pretty certain that we have missed the boat on discipline. I appreciate the words of Old Testament commentators C. F. Keil and Franz Delitzsch: "The teacher should not seek correction as the object, but only as the means."[8]

Our goal is not the punishment; our goal is changed behavior, and that needs to be our focus. As Solomon said in Proverbs 19:18, if we are working for corrected behavior, we are working with hope for a changed future.

~~~

Effective discipline begins early. **Proverbs 13:24 reads,** *"He who spares the rod hates his son, but he who loves him is careful to discipline him."* The imagery of the rod here is in the context of a shepherd with his sheep. A shepherd's rod was used at times for gentle guiding, while on other occasions it was used with a firmer strike. But I want to focus for a moment on the word *careful* in this verse. A better translation here might be "intentional." As parents, we are intentional in disciplining our children. We don't wait until they are 12 years old to begin disciplining them. Again taking advantage of the insights of Keil and Delitzsch: "A father who truly wishes well to his son keeps him betimes under strict discipline, to give him while he is yet capable of being influenced in the right direction, and to allow no errors to root themselves in him."[9]

We love our children so much that we begin teaching and training (disciplining) when they are young and pliable. Whether we are teaching them not to run out into traffic, how to practice good study habits, or how to discern friends of good character, the younger we begin, the more likely it is to stick. **As parents, we are instructed that our discipline should be intentional.**

~~~

One final passage with purpose for us as parents that I want to explore is an often-quoted one: *"Train a child in the way he should go, and when he is old he will not turn from it"* **(Prov. 22:6).** Many parents have looked to this Scripture for hope when their child has wandered off to the pigpen in that faraway land (see the story of the prodigal son in Luke 15). For the parents whose child is caught up in a drug addiction, is involved in destructive relationship, or has rejected the values of their parents, they cling to this passage hoping for some kind of guarantee. While I don't believe there is any kind of promise here, I do believe there is sound advice. Two impactful principles are at work that I want us to explore.

First, there is what I would call a "stacking the deck" strategy. By that I mean, if I build a relationship with my children, if I begin teaching them early with an intentionality that focuses on the future, there is certainly a greater chance that they will not wander from it, or at least not as far as they might have otherwise. And even if they do seem to reject the values that I hold dear, there is a greater chance that they will return to them as they mature and begin their own families. Certainly, as a parent, there is hope in this principle.

Second, Solomon is teaching us that effective parenting takes a developmental approach. When he states, *"Train a child in the way he should go…,"* it carries the idea of a limb on a young and developing tree (Prov. 22:6). Some have read this passage as "Train a child in the way he is bent," referring to a young, tender branch. In other words, our teaching, training, and discipline should fit with where our children are developmentally.

Would we tell a four-month-old child who carelessly knocked a lamp off the table to go sit and think about their careless behavior? Of course not. OK, then how about we have a conversation with them rationally explaining why they need to be more considerate of other people's possessions? That is ridiculous because it is not developmentally appropriate.

Solomon is telling us in this proverb that our discipline does not look the same for a five-year-old as it does for a seventeen-year-old. While we may think we have this parenting thing figured out when they are one, we are in for a rude awakening because they are going to turn two. But here is the challenging part—as they progress through different stages of development, we have to learn to adapt our methods of discipline. If we will, there will be a greater chance of success. If we don't, there is more likely to be rebellion. You see, we want our children to work at growing and acting more mature. We want *them* to work at it. However, we often find ourselves resistant to investing the same energy.

In working with a parent recently, I tried to address this very issue. As they described the behavior of their high school student, I could clearly hear in their voice a weariness that comes with doing battle in a developmentally inappropriate way. I offered some strategies that I knew if they would work to implement consistently over time, there would be improvement. During the next conversation, the parent was venting about the same issues and the same conflicts. Inquiring as to whether they had begun to alter their way of relating to a more developmentally appropriate method, as I had suggested, they responded with, "I tried it once, and it didn't work." Defaulting back to their old patterns that hadn't worked before, they continued to use methods that did not work in the present either. If we hope to experience greater success in our parenting, "the method ought to be arranged according to the degree of development which the mental and bodily life of the youth has arrived at."[10]

One other thought I would suggest here is that we need to consider how each child is "wired." I have seen parents who have a passion for a particular career field. It may be engineering, or it could be medicine. Rather than consider that their child might be more artistically inclined or have a heart for the social sciences, they coerce their child to pursue what is important to them as parents without taking into account how the child "is bent." We do our children a grave disservice when we push our agenda onto them.

Advancing the Relationship "as" Children

"Honor your father and your mother, so that you may live long in the land the Lord your God is giving you" **(Exod. 20:12)**. *"Children,*

obey your parents in the Lord, for this is right. 'Honor your father and mother'—which is the first commandment with a promise—'that it may go well with you and that you may enjoy long life on the earth'" **(Eph. 6:1-3). Colossians 3:20 adds that to honor your parents** *"pleases the Lord."*

As parents, it is relatively easy to expect our kids to respect, honor, and obey us. I mean, this is the fifth of the Ten Commandments. So it must be important. Because we work hard to provide for our families and raise and train our children, we may feel we have earned and deserve this respect. But what about when we are the children—grown children?

"Well, I'm an adult now. I am my own independent person. I don't have to do this anymore." No, we don't obey our parents as we did when we were young children living at home, but I would suggest that "honoring" our parents is a lifelong command. For some, this comes easily. I recognize that for others, this may be difficult, especially if your parent was abusive, unloving, or perhaps even absent. And yet, we are called to "honor our parents." So, how do the majority of us do that?

I want to suggest a few practical approaches that can help you in this area. First, you can avoid speaking negatively about your parents (and if you're married, this includes your in-laws). It is so easy to grumble and complain about things that our parents do. And if you are the spouse of the one who is complaining, it can be easy to jump on the bandwagon, helping to heap more negative perspective onto the pile. It is our job to work toward gratefully seeing our parents through the most positive lens possible. That includes helping our spouse to do the same with regard to his or her parents. Sure it is easy to take pot-shots at controlling, divisive behaviors that our parents may exhibit. But resist the urge to do so. Strive to accentuate the positive rather than amplify the negative.

Gary Chapman adds, "You honor them in such practical actions as visiting, telephoning, and writing, whereby you communicate to them that you still love them and want to share life with them. 'Leaving' must never be interpreted as 'deserting.'"[11]

Recalling how our parents took care of our physical needs when we were young, we will probably be called upon to assist with their physical needs as they age. Seeing this as a privilege and an opportunity, rather than a burden, is a component of "honoring."

Now I should probably include here that if you are a younger person living at home and you are reading this, then yes, you have to clean up your room (and probably other things you don't want to do). Obeying your parents is definitely a reflection of how you honor them.

Empower Your Children

I sat with a father in my office yesterday listening to his frustrations. He and his 15-year-old son seem to be locked in mortal combat on a daily basis. As is typical, the father wants to bark orders and have his son respond promptly and without question or argument. The 15-year-old wants to talk about it and wants fairness and justice. The more the son asks questions, the angrier his dad becomes, displaying greater frustration and unreasonableness. In return, the 15-year-old explodes with his own anger, and a relational meltdown ensues.

Wisely, the apostle Paul writes, *"Fathers"*—and this is equally true for mothers—*"do not exasperate your children; instead, bring them up in the training and instruction of the Lord"* **(Eph. 6:4). He adds to this in Colossians 3:21 by saying,** *"Fathers, do not embitter your children, or they will become discouraged."*

Thinking back to one of our earlier goals of parenting—if my desire is to raise children who love God and others, I may need to ask myself, "Is my style of parenting encouraging and empowering my children, or do they want to pull their hair out and get away from me as fast as they can? Am I measuring my words so that I am assisting my children in their development, or am I letting my words flow unfiltered so that I can get what I want in the moment? Am I teaching my kids in a manner that will lead them to embrace God and His desires for them, or will they run from God as fast as possible because of the harsh, critical, and demeaning approach that I take with them?"

More individuals than not seem to have been raised in some level of dysfunction. The challenge for us becomes taking the time and making the effort to learn new and different parenting skills. I will suggest some resources at the end of this chapter to help you in your quest to become more effective as loving parents.

~~~

In his book *The Seasons of God,* Richard Blackaby makes an intriguing observation. He writes, "The best parents…have been those who grew up with their children."[12] He is acknowledging the reality that few, if any of us, begin parenting with a full box of parenting tools. We typically have a couple—maybe diaper changing and burping skills. But as our children grow and we need additional tools, it is critical that we grow with them, that we gain new skills to enable us to parent effectively at all stages of their development.

Of course, this means that we have to be present. We are hindered in our ability to parent if we are absent. Parents can go AWOL for a variety of reasons. There may have been a divorce resulting in reduced parenting time. Occasionally a mom or dad has literally abandoned their family. Other times, the parents are around, but they are not truly present. While some may be away from home frequently for business-related travel or military deployment, others are physically present but mentally or emotionally absorbed in everything from hobbies to ESPN. Parents may be absent by necessity, design, or default. Please understand, I know that everyone's circumstances are different. So there is no judgement intended here, simply observation.

I absolutely know how it feels to come home from a long and tiring day of work. At those moments it may be that all I can think about is propping my feet up and "vegging out" in front of the television. And certainly we all need some time to rest and recharge. Yet, effective parenting requires that I show up—physically, emotionally, intellectually, and spiritually. There is no question that it is far easier to bark orders than it is to have a reasonable discussion (be that with my kids or my spouse). But relationships that are designed to last require my full participation. They are work, as are most investments with rewards, and they are worth it.

~~~

"Finally, all of you, live in harmony with one another; be sympathetic, love as brothers, be compassionate and humble" **(1 Peter 3:8).** While Peter is employing words that ideally describe all our relationships, our interactions with our children are certainly included in this command. We are reminded that our three-year-old will not remain static—they will develop, grow, change, and at some point, eat most of the groceries. One day they will leave, whether that be for college or a new job. They will move out, and our connection with them will transition. Yes, we are still their parents, but it takes on a different flavor. My grown children are still my children, but they are adults, and we have become friends. I still want to be in their world, and I want them in mine. Therefore, I encourage you, whether your kids are still at home or are out in the world, to grow with them; invest the energy required to have relationship so that you can "live in harmony" with them with compassion and humility.

Resources

As a therapist and a professor, I can assure you that there is no shortage of parenting resources out there. Sorting through them can be a daunting task—so overwhelming in fact that many parents throw up their hands and decide to just "wing it." While I understand the frustration, I also know that getting new or additional tools requires (like everything else we are learning to "purpose") intentionality.

With that in mind, I want to offer just a handful of parenting resource suggestions here. These are just a sampling, but they have been tried, tested, and found to be supportive and effective for many parents.

- *Parenting with Love and Logic* (2006) by Foster Cline and Jim Fay
- *Parenting Your Out-of-Control Teenager* (2001) by Scott P. Sells
- *The New Dare to Discipline* (2014) by James Dobson
- *Raising Self-Reliant Children in a Self-Indulgent World* (2000) by H. Stephen Glenn and Jane Nelson
- *Bound by Honor* (2000) by Gary and Greg Smalley
- *Relief for Hurting Parents* (1998) by Buddy Scott
- *Spare the Rod* (1988) by Phil E. Quinn

Purpose Recapped

1. Two Foundational Truths—

   #1—God is, and He knows what His creation needs.

   #2—The Scriptures are God's written instructions for how to live.

2. Overarching Purpose #1—To love God with all my heart, soul, mind, and strength.

Sub-purpose #1—To relate to my Creator by: having faith, being obedient, confessing and repenting of my sins, and worshiping God with everything in my life.

Sub-purpose #2—To walk humbly with God by giving up control and trusting Him.

Sub-purpose #3—To connect with God through a lifestyle of quiet—praying and listening.

3.   Overarching Purpose #2—To love my neighbor.

Sub-purpose #1—If I am married: traveling with my mate through life, being united, relating interdependently, and loving in all circumstances.

Sub-purpose #2—If I have children:
a.   Viewing my children as a blessing and an opportunity to raise individuals who love both God and people.
b.   Loving my children by effectively disciplining and shaping them.
c.   Honoring my own parents.
d.   Empowering my children.

Chapter Seven

Finally...My Neighbor—Relating with Others

"You can't change how people treat you or what they say about you. All you can do is change how you react to it."
—UNKNOWN

Under our umbrella purpose of "loving our neighbor," we have, up to this point, looked primarily at family—spouses and children. In this chapter, we will broaden our scope to include everybody else. As you may recall, in Chapter 5 we examined Jesus' explanation of just who qualifies as our "neighbor." The conclusion from that narrative was that pretty much everyone falls into the "neighbor" category.

In this chapter, we will explore four progressively deepening levels of relationships with others: 1) actions we take that are primarily external in nature, 2) internal processes that impact our external relationships, 3) more intentional relations as a community of God-loving people, and finally, 4) relationships of accountability—with ourselves and with others.

Relating Externally

Promoting justice, prohibiting gossip, and providing for the poor are three distinct areas that require us to make some intentional choices. They are probably the most emotionally safe ways of interacting with people. In other words, there is not much risk involved. We don't really have to get too involved personally—we can more or less operate at a distance. And yet, they are biblical principles that are essential to the well-being of people.

Promoting Justice

"Truth, justice, and the American way." These are words from the beginning of the 1950s television show *Superman*. The idea of justice is often equated with fairness, evenhandedness, impartiality, or neutrality. When thinking of the legal system, we often picture the scales of justice, which speak to the expectation of a fair and impartial hearing from a judge. But I wonder how we view justice at a more personal level? Does it have application beyond the court system? One news network claims that they try to make sure their approach to the news is "fair and balanced." They strive to be "just" in how they report events. But what does justice look like at a personal level, and how do we administer it?

I believe that Rabbi Aaron is correct when he asserts that "the highest Torah value is justice."[1] It is a value that is reflected repeatedly throughout the Scriptures. **The Bible tells us not to steal, lie, or deceive each other (see Lev. 19:11). We are not to pervert justice, show partiality to the poor or favoritism to the great, but are to judge fairly (see Lev. 19:15; James 2:9).** King David elaborates further on this when he asks the question, "Who will dwell in the Lord's sanctuary?" (see Ps. 15:1). Listen to his description in Psalm 15 of the person who exemplifies a lifestyle of justice: *"He whose walk is blameless and who does what is righteous, who speaks the truth from his heart and has no slander on his tongue, who does his neighbor no wrong and casts no slur on his fellow man, who despises a vile man but honors those who fear the Lord, who keeps his oath even when it hurts, who lends his money without usury* **[interest]** *and does not accept a bribe against the innocent. He who does this things will never be shaken"* **(Ps. 15:2-5)**.

Old Testament prophets encouraged individuals **to** *"...seek justice, encourage the oppressed. Defend the cause of the fatherless, plead the case of the widow"* **(Isa. 1:17)**. *"...Administer true justice; show mercy and compassion to one another"* **(Zech. 7:9)**.

When we find ourselves asking how we should live and what are we supposed to do, we can't get a much clearer response from God than what we find recorded in **Micah 6:8**: *"...what does the Lord require of you? To act justly and to love mercy and to walk humbly with your God."* If we would regularly remind ourselves of this purpose statement, our focus would take on immediate significance.

Jesus reaffirms this thought when He warns against getting caught up in all the religious rules and regulations. Fitting into a framework of rules is fairly easy to do and doesn't require a lot of thought. But He says that so often when you do that, *"you have neglected the more important matters of the law—justice, mercy, and faithfulness..."* **(Matt. 23:23)**. **And those are the matters that God is most concerned about.**

Prohibiting Gossip

Gossip is insidious and destructive. But how often do we find ourselves listening to someone talk about the poor choices and bad behaviors of some person whom we know? No doubt, most of us would give a politically correct answer if asked whether we think gossip is harmful. Well of course we do—yet we continue. I have even seen gossip flourish in Christian circles. However, we are much more couched about it. We might be less likely to say to someone, "Hey, did you hear about Tom having an affair?" because that is too crass. Instead we will say, "We need to pray for Tom because I heard he is cheating on his wife." Perfect—gossip camouflaged in Christianese.

Biblical instructions speak openly about the damage caused by our careless conversations. The writer of the Book of Proverbs writes, *"A perverse man stirs up dissension, and a gossip separates close friends"* **and** *"A gossip betrays a confidence; so avoid a man who talks too much"* **(Prov. 16:28; 20:19).** Both the Old and New Testament entreat us **not to go around slandering people (see Lev. 19:16; James 3:11).**

As we will see later, it is not God's intention that we use our conversation to belittle and tear down our fellow man. But when we gossip, that is exactly what we are doing. When discussing unfaithful spouses, many have heard it said, "If he or she will cheat with you, they will cheat on you." The same understanding is equally true here. People who will gossip to you will gossip about you. Yikes! When we are in the middle of listening to a juicy story, we are not usually thinking this—but we should be.

God does not want us destroying someone with our wagging tongue. This is exactly what gossip is and can do. So, here is my advice—if you have a tendency to talk negatively about others, stop it! As a matter of fact, ratchet it up to a level even beyond that. The next time someone begins to gossip to you, ask them to stop. Tell them you don't need to know this information. You might even ask them if they have talked to the other person about what they are preparing to tell you. Odds are that they haven't, but they should be.

I had a roommate in college who used to say, "Don't believe a thing that you hear and believe only about half of what you see." This was great advice, as things aren't necessarily all that they seem.

And when it comes to what we hear, that is more often than not a mangled mess.

Similar to a decision to operate from a mode of fairness and justice, gossip is a choice we make. Yet with both of these concepts, there is not much personal risk. We can simply begin to make different choices about what we communicate, determining to speak only things that are helpful instead of harmful.

Providing for the Poor

King Solomon made some astute observations when it came to those who are less fortunate than ourselves. **He said those who are blessed or happy are those who are kind to the needy (see Prov. 14:21). In his great wisdom, he noticed that when we are kind to the poor, we are rewarded, we will lack nothing, and we honor God (see Prov. 19:17; 28:27). However, if we oppress the poor, we show contempt for our Creator and we will not be answered when we are in need (see Prov. 14:31; 21:13).**

Jeremiah the prophet asks the question, "What does it mean to know the Lord?" He then answers the question in chapter 22, verse 16, by writing that **if a person is truly connected to God, it will be reflected in how he or she defends the cause of the poor and needy (see Jer. 22:16).**

New Testament passages cause us to examine our priorities as God followers. **We are told that amassing money and material objects is not nearly as important as having less and taking care of the poor. And when we take care of the poor, we are storing up treasure in Heaven (see Matt. 19:21).**

Jesus even makes it more personal when He says that when we take care of those who are hungry, thirsty, in need of clothing, sick, or in prison, it is as though we were doing those things directly to Him (see Matt. 25:34-46; Heb. 13:2). That is a clear indication of just how big of a deal this is, as well as how much He cherishes us.

I am grateful for the words that James writes about religion. Unfortunately, when we usually hear it remarked that someone is very religious, we often think that they must follow lots of rules and traditions and go to church and pray zealously. But listen to these words: *"If anyone considers himself religious and yet does not keep a tight rein on his tongue, he deceives himself and his religions is worthless. Religion that God our Father accepts as pure and faultless is this: to look after orphans and widows in their distress and to keep oneself from being polluted by the world"* **(James 1:26-27).**

I want to suggest that taking care of the poor is a very intentional act. While it may look different for all of us, it much more significant than handing a couple of dollars out of our car window to the guy on the corner by Walmart with his dog and his cardboard sign. As a matter of fact, I have visited with some of those individuals, and they have indicated that upwards of 70-80 percent of panhandlers are collecting money to support their drug habit. I believe that if we are to honor God by taking care of the truly needy, it may require us to do some homework. This could result in a variety of responses. You might sponsor children through an organization such as World Vision or Compassion International, become involved in a prison ministry, support an orphanage, or participate in providing foster care for children in need. Your active involvement can look very different than mine and God will be pleased with us. But the point here is this—**relating to the people of the world in God-honoring ways requires our intentional, thoughtful actions. We are to purpose ourselves to live in ways that provide justice to all, build people up with our words rather than tearing down, and demonstrate God's love in taking care of those in need.**

Relating Internally

While the external acts described above are critical aspects of how God wants us to relate to each other, they are choices that still keep us somewhat at a distance from our emotional selves. We don't risk much at our core when we choose not to gossip or to administer justice. However, it is God's desire to take us deeper in our relationships. Let's take a look at three components of relating at this level: guarding our mouth, forgiving, and peacemaking.

Guarding Our Mouth

While I have labeled this "guarding," which comes from David's prayer in Psalms 141:3 to *"set a guard over my mouth, O Lord,"* a better word might be "managing." Now, it is easy to think, "OK, well I can manage what I say and learn to bite my tongue at times. That doesn't seem like too much of a risk." But honestly, the risk doesn't come so much in not saying certain things—it comes in listening.

The Proverbs writer instructs us to **listen before we give an answer; to do otherwise would be foolish (see Prov. 18:13). James says it this way:** *"…Everyone should be quick to listen, slow to speak and slow to become angry"* **(James 1:19).**

Invariably, when I see people engaged in what seems like mortal verbal battle, most often they are much more focused on "getting their point across," "defending themselves," or "making sure that they make themselves clear." When individuals are more concerned about being understood than they are about understanding the other person, this is what happens.

Why is it so difficult to stop talking and listen to the other person? We all have struggled with that at one time or another. Are you ready for the answer? Fear. Fear that the other person will confront us about our own behavior—which none of us get too excited about. Fear that they will point out something we have done that has caused hurt or damage in the relationship. Yet, if our desire is to have an intimate, healthy relationship with people, being vulnerable and listening, even if it is at times uncomfortable, is essential.

Proverbs 12:18 states that *"Reckless words pierce like a sword…"* And **Matthew reminds us that on the Day of Judgment, we will** give an account for our careless words (see Matt. 12:36). Other passages remind us that we should be people of our word (see Matt. 5:33-37). If we state something, people should know that they can count on us to follow through with what we said. Our word should be solid. We are not to lace our conversations with obscenity (see Eph. 5:4). As a matter of fact, as people who serve a loving God, there should not be any "unwholesome" talk coming from us (see Eph. 4:29). Instead, our conversations and relationships with people should be full of grace (see Col. 4:6).

In the Book of James, we see that the power of the tongue to control a person's life is compared to the bit in a horse's mouth, the rudder of a ship, or even a small spark in a forest (see James 3:1-6). He says that an entire forest can be set ablaze simply because of that spark. Our inability to (actually our decision not to) control our tongue *"corrupts the whole person"* (James 3:6). As such, it is imperative to *"...keep a tight rein on* **[your]** *tongue..."* (**James 1:26**).

We find it so easy to let our tongue wag, leaving relational destruction in our wake wherever we go. I appreciate the reminder by Charles Swindoll that "the lowest level of conversation is people. The next level is events. The highest level is truth and ideas."[2] Our conversations need to be words that will advance truth and build up people.

Offering Forgiveness

"To be a Christian means to forgive the inexcusable, because God has forgiven the inexcusable in you."[3] Forgiveness is one of the most difficult issues over which people stumble. We all have been wronged. Occasionally it is hurt caused by someone's unkind words. Other times it may be a more serious offense that has deeply wounded us. For others still, it may be a level of abuse that one deems absolutely unforgiveable. Forgiveness can be tough.

One author describes forgiveness as "the process of giving up your rights to be angry, vengeful, judgmental, or resentful and allowing God to be the righteous judge in your situation."[4] Honestly, if enough pain has been inflicted upon us, we can experience serious struggles with forgiveness. And yet, the level of seriousness that Scripture takes on the subject indicates that it is not something we can simply dismiss, even when we find it excruciatingly difficult.

In this area of forgiveness, Scripture is clear. **We are called pure and simply to forgive. Luke writes,** *"...If your brother sins, rebuke him, and if repents, forgive him. If he sins against you seven times in a day, and seven time comes back to you and says, 'I repent,' forgive him"* **(Luke 17:3-4)** You may be thinking, "Seven times—are you kidding me?" Hmm, well let's take it up a notch. As Jesus was teaching on the subject of forgiveness, Peter asked Him how many times he should forgive another person? He asked Jesus if he should forgive up to seven times. Listen to Jesus' response: *"I tell you, not seven times, but seventy-seven times"* **(Matt. 18:22). In other words, it is not tied to a number. You continue to keep on keeping on when it comes to forgiving people.**

While I know that many people have been hurt in immeasurable ways, I wonder if we have experienced lies, rejection, and betrayal any worse than what we have heaped upon God? We have sinned against the very Creator of our souls. And yet, when we ask Him for forgiveness, we find that through the sacrifice of His Son, we can receive it. **We are instructed to forgive others as God has forgiven us (see Col. 3:13; Eph. 4:32).**

Jesus told the story of a man who owed a particular king millions of dollars. Now, this man couldn't even begin to make a dent in his debt. So the king was going to sell the man, his wife, his children, and all that he had to pay toward the debt. Matthew records that *"the servant fell on his knees before him* [the king]. *'Be patient with me,' he begged"* (Matt. 18:26). The king took pity on him and canceled the debt. Notice that the king didn't reduce the debt or give him extra time to pay it. He wiped the slate clean. Wow! That is incredible.

But watch what happens as the story continues. It seems that this servant then went out—a free man—and found someone who owed him a few dollars. He grabbed this man and began to choke him and demand payment. When the man begged for mercy and patience for paying the debt back, you would think that the servant would grant a reprieve, much like what had been done for him. But the exact opposite happened—he had this one who owed him such a small amount thrown into prison.

As you might imagine, when word of this got back to the forgiving king, this self-centered servant was called in to account for his behavior and was thrown into prison and tortured—all because he was so unforgiving. **You see, it is crucial that we understand that if we want the forgiveness of God, we must be willing to forgive others. Scripture even goes so far as to say that if we don't forgive others, we cannot expect that God will forgive us (see Matt. 6:14-15).** As you may have gathered by now, this forgiveness stuff is serious business.

Not only are we to forgive when someone asks for it, we are even to actively seek out the person who has wronged us. **In Mark 11:25, we are told that if we remember that we are holding something against another person, at that moment we need to forgive them. In Matthew 5:23-24, we are even instructed that if we remember that someone holds something against us, we should seek them out in order to make things right.**

I want to address one important distinction about forgiveness, and that is that forgiveness and trust are not the same thing. When someone has wronged me and asks for forgiveness—I give it. When that someone has wronged me, doing the same thing repeatedly, and asks for forgiveness—yes, I am to offer it, but it might be a wise idea not to put myself in the position again of being hurt until trust has been rebuilt. Forgiveness addresses the past, while trust addresses the future.

Forgiveness means that I let go and no longer hang on to my hurt, anger, and resentment. However, it doesn't mean that I should jump back into a normal relationship with the offender. I may need to give the relationship some space and wait to see if the person who wronged me becomes trustworthy again. If they do not, I may choose not to be in relationship with them—but that doesn't necessarily mean that I haven't forgiven them. God has not called us to live as abused doormats. It is appropriate to set good boundaries, which actually can be the foundation of healthy relationships. Our Father does not expect us to continue in dysfunctional relationships when a change is clearly indicated. He desires that we would embrace the change that is needed for that relationship to flourish.

Being Peacemakers

"Blessed are the peacemakers, for they will be called sons of God" **(Matt. 5:9). The Bible repeatedly states that we are to make every effort to live in peace and harmony with each other (see Mark 9:5; 1 Thess. 5:13; Heb. 12:14; Rom. 12:16; Col. 3:15).**

Certainly I think that most of us would nod our head in agreement with this statement. And yet, we have best friends bickering, siblings who haven't spoken in years, marriages that have deteriorated into a cold war, political parties that refuse to find common ground for cooperation, and countries that have been at war for so long that the people can't remember a time without conflict. All one has to do is pick up the morning paper to be reminded that we are not at peace.

And yet, Paul, the ex-persecutor of Christians in the early church, says, **we who are disobedient sinners (that would be all of us) have been reconciled to God when we allow God's Son to be the Messiah who paid our debt to God for us. Jesus reconciled us** to the Father, and in turn, Paul says, God *"gave us the ministry of reconciliation"* (2 Cor. 5:18). In other words, we have not been called to quarrel, bicker, demean, argue, or live in conflict with the people around us. Instead, we are empowered to mend relationships wherever possible and to live in peace and harmony with each other. It is not our job simply to accept peace if we encounter it. We are to pursue peace.

Relating as a Community

As a young boy, I recall living in neighborhoods in Oklahoma in which we knew everybody: the family across the street, the two elderly sisters who lived a couple of doors down from us, or the couple next door with the pristine lawn. We were a community. Fast forward to the 21st century, where it is not uncommon to live in a home for years and never even meet your next-door neighbor. So, we now have new developments that include a "community center." This may be where the swimming pool is located, or it may include a building that you can rent for parties. For many, the closest they come to "community" is Facebook. But it is certainly a very different definition of community.

There was a time in our country when "community" was centered around the church or the synagogue. The majority of citizens were connected to some degree with one of these institutions. People shared a common set of characteristics or interests, and there were qualities that distinguished them from the society at large. Unfortunately, we have lost much of this common connection as a culture—which is part of the reason why the government has stepped in to take care of certain needs that used to be met by the members of the religious community.

While I recognize that many have had negative experiences with individuals and organizations, this does not negate our need for community. It may simply indicate that we need to reexamine how we do it. I have high regard for the German pastor Dietrich Bonhoeffer, who was martyred by the Nazis. In the course of his writings, "he suggests that disillusionment with our local church is a good thing because it destroys our false expectations of perfection. The sooner we give up the illusion that a church must be perfect in order to love it, the sooner we quit pretending and start admitting we're *all* imperfect and need grace. This is the beginning of real community."[5]

I love the example of community that is pictured in the following passage: *"Two are better than one, because they have a good return for their work: If one falls down, his friend can help him up. But pity the man who falls and has no one to help him up! Also, if two lie down together, they will keep warm. But how can one keep warm alone? Though one may be overpowered, two can defend themselves. A cord of three strands is not quickly broken"* (Eccles. 4:9-12).

~~~

In our deepening exploration of "loving our neighbor," relating with this picture of community involves a little more emotional risk. Living in community means that we have "more skin in the game," to borrow a financial phrase. We begin to experience a vulnerability that comes with greater intimacy. Yes, we run a greater risk of being wounded by others, but we also open ourselves up to the possibilities for rich, vibrant relationships.

As a group of people who are committed to obeying and following the Creator of the universe, we are indeed different from the culture at large. We are united by our common love for God and His Son and our pursuit of His purposes for our lives. Unfortunately, we sometimes think this means that we always have to be compatible with one another. That couldn't be further from the truth. Our unity is rooted in our pursuit of God, not in our ability to always enjoy each other. But this commonality in faith encourages us to make efforts to stay in healthy relationships rather than to be quick to discard them when things get difficult.

The Bible teaches us that as believers, our family consists of those who pursue the will of God (see Matt. 12:48). As family members we serve each other (see Mark 10:43-45), we practice hospitality (see Rom. 12:13), we laugh and cry with each other as we experience the ups and downs of life together (see Rom. 12:15), and we do our best to have the same love and to be united in our spirit and our purpose (see Phil. 2:2). We humbly take ourselves off our selfish pedestals and view others as important (see Phil. 2:3). Being intricately connected as family means that we strive to solve differences within our community rather than dragging each other into court (see 1 Cor. 6:4).

God designed us from the beginning of time to be wired for relationships. While we like to think of ourselves (especially in this country) as strong, independent, and needing no one, God knows just how dangerous that is. The reality is that we are weak and fragile but thrive when in genuine, caring relationships. Like coals in a fire, functioning within an *authentic* community of believers helps to keep us centered in God's love and His design for our lives. Likewise, when a coal is removed from the fire and set aside, it grows cold.

Let me emphasize the importance of authenticity. I have been involved with groups of believers who were pretentious at best and deceptive at worst. Trying to connect with that level of dysfunction is worse than being isolated. God does not want to condemn us to lifelessness. His desire is that we would relate as "real" people in genuine, life-giving relationships. As Pastor Rick Warren clearly expresses, "Pretentiousness repels but authenticity attracts, and vulnerability is the pathway to intimacy."[6] He goes on to say, "At some point in your life you must decide whether you want to impress people or influence people."[7]

Relating with the Risk of Accountability

Engaging as a community of believers requires that we become vulnerable, learning to lean on each other for our needs. But there is an even deeper level of relating for us to explore. Accountability is about the standard to which we hold ourselves, the criteria to which we hold others in the community, and the expectation that we will have permission to speak truth reciprocally into one another's lives.

Self-Accountability

Have you ever been on a diet but walked into a pastry shop just to see what kind of donuts they were making on that particular day? Probably not. Because if donuts are your weakness and you walked into the store anyway, you would probably leave with a donut—or 12—in your hands. Perhaps "bear claws" aren't your weakness, but ice cream, cookies, alcohol, tobacco, or gambling are. If you want to resist those temptations successfully, it becomes critical that you stay away from them. Some are unlikely to overindulge, while for others—set a carton of ice cream in front of them, and all bets are off. That is one of my personal weaknesses.

Similarly, the Bible speaks of sin as something that we must resist and even run from. **We are instructed to be on our guard, that when people entice us to do what we know is displeasing to God, we are not to give in (see Prov. 1:10; 2 Peter 3:17). God says that we are to eliminate such things as** *"sexual immorality, impurity, lust, evil desires and greed"* **in ourselves (Col. 3:5). Anything that causes us to sin must go on the chopping block as part of an effort to purify ourselves (see Matt. 18:8-9; Mark 9:43-47; 2 Cor. 7:1).**

"If you know a particular situation, person, or thing will cause temptation to invade your life, avoid those situations, people, and things. Don't tell yourself you're strong enough to fight temptation on your own when it comes your way."[8] These are helpful words of advice. Otherwise, we create our own problems. Now I don't know about you, but I encounter enough problems in life that I don't need to be out creating my own. As a matter of fact, I don't know of a greater guilt than the guilt that comes from mistakes of my own choosing.

Accountability to the Authorities

As I turn on the network news, images of rebellion fill the screen on an almost daily basis. Civil disobedience has become popular, with attitudes like "No one is going to tell me what to do" seeming to be the norm rather than the exception. Yet, this is not God's design.

We are told clearly that God has established the authorities for mankind's benefit; whether it be the government or any other institutional authority, He has allowed it to be in place. **His purpose for our lives is that we would submit to the authorities (see Titus 3:1; Heb. 13:17; 1 Peter 2:13). As the apostle Paul writes in the Romans 13:1, if we rebel against the governing authorities, we are rebelling against God.**

Granted, there are situations where a leader might give orders that are contrary to God's Word (see Acts 4:19). In which case, we are to obey God. But for most of us, this is not a conflict that we face. Our struggle tends to be more around a lack of humility and an unwillingness to put ourselves under the authority of our leaders. These leaders include those ranging from governors and policemen to bosses and school officials. We are called to willingly place ourselves under their leadership.

Accountability for Who and What Influences You

If you have been a parent, especially of teenagers, you probably recall those moments when you knew that your kid was hanging out with friends who weren't good for them. Of course, trying to get them to change friends was like pulling teeth. As a loving parent, you only wanted your child to pick friends who would influence them positively. You knew that their having the wrong friends could bring disastrous consequences.

Our Heavenly Father cares about us in the same way, which is why He tells us to avoid the following: mockers (see Prov. 9:8); foolish men (see Prov. 14:7; 23:9); hot-tempered people (see Prov. 22:24); those who drink too much alcohol (see Prov. 23:20); those who claim to be followers of God but are sexually immoral, greedy, slanderers, drunks, or swindlers (see 1 Cor. 5:11); and those who are lazy and refuse to work (see 2 Thess. 3:6). As the letter to the Corinthian church points out, "...*Bad company corrupts good character*" (1 Cor. 15:33).

Similarly, we are instructed to avoid "godless chatter" (see 2 Tim. 2:16); "hollow and deceptive" philosophies (see Col. 2:8); and "every kind of evil" (see 1 Thess. 5:22).

Now some may read these passages above and be convinced that God is a cosmic killjoy. However, that could not be further from the truth. Just as we know how easily influenced our children are, God knows how very true that is of us all, even as adults. Very simply— He gives us these wise instructions to protect us. The importance of hanging out with those who believe the precepts of God cannot be overemphasized. King Solomon accurately expresses that we take on the characteristics of those with whom we spend time: "*He who walks with the wise grows wise, but a companion of fools suffers harm*" (Prov. 13:20).

Not only are we influenced by people, but we are influenced by the media as well. Author Bruce Waltke refers to the "Medusa syndrome" in his discussion of how television and media can harden our hearts. "We watch it, and we become like it."[9]

If I long to escape the limiting entanglements of a dark and dying world, if I desire to soar with the God of the universe, then I need to surround myself with those life-giving influences—regardless of what others think.

I love the story of Francis of Assisi. He was the son of a rich man and was given all the benefits of such. When he was younger, he was caught up with the partying "in-crowd." But then he heard the words of Jesus telling him to sell all and follow Him. Those words were powerful, and he chose to believe and follow them. But that decision came with a cost. His father rejected him, and his friends abandoned him. Even so, he walked away from the life of riches to obediently follow Jesus.[10] His life modeled the priority of love and service and influenced men and women for generations. Clearly, he chose who and what would influence him.

Accountability for Who You Influence

Allowing others to speak truth into our lives can be edifying yet uncomfortable. But now it gets even harder, because we are called to hold others accountable. I recognize that this is not a popular concept in the 21st century. It is much easier to adopt a philosophy of "live and let live." "I need to mind my own business and just let others mind their own." Yet, this is the exact opposite of what God calls us to do. *"As iron sharpens iron, so one man sharpens another"* (Prov. 27:17). If we are to stay sharp and on track, we need to hold each other accountable to the truths of God.

We have to remind ourselves repeatedly that God knew what He was doing when He made us. He knows our propensity for wandering as well as what is needed to keep us clearly directed. However, if we are going to be able to hear His words, we must be willing to humble ourselves, put down our own "Well, this is what I think" agenda, and be attentive to His instruction.

I find two accountability principles in the Scriptures. The first involves the relationships we have with other believers. These are people who, like us, claim to believe God's Word for their lives. **Jesus provides clear instructions in Matthew 18:15-17 for how we can go about lovingly confronting those who have wronged us or those who have been caught in sin, always in an effort to restore a**

relationship (see Gal. 6:1). We are also to warn those in our community who are divisive pot stirrers (see Titus 3:10). They are a detriment to harmony and cooperation. Too frequently, Christ followers want to look the other way and hope that the problem will just go away. But it doesn't. "You shouldn't act as if everything is just fine when one of your Christian companions is promiscuous or crooked, is flip with God or rude to friends, gets drunk or becomes greedy and predatory. You can't just go along with this, treating it as acceptable behavior."[11] While I am not responsible for how those outside of the family of believers behave, I certainly owe my God-following companions the faithfulness of accountability.

Proverbs 27:6 reminds us that *"faithful are the wounds of a friend…"* (NASB). Or stated another way, if I care enough about you, then I will lovingly confront you regarding your sinful behaviors. I can think back to times in my own life when the faithful confrontations of a friend saved me from serious mistakes that could have hurt numerous people.

The second principle of accountability concerns our duty to warn. If you or I saw a young child about to step into the deep end of a swimming pool, we would frantically attempt to prevent it. Can you imagine if your child stepped into the pool and suffered harm while another adult watched? I doubt that their protestations of "I didn't think it was any of my concern" would appease us. **In the writings of the prophet Ezekiel, God says that when we see people perpetrating evil or when we see evil or destruction about to overtake or harm someone, we have a duty to warn them. If we do, they might be spared. If they refuse to listen to us, then their destruction is their responsibility (see Ezek. 3:18-19). However, if we fail to warn them and they are destroyed, we are told that we will be held accountable for their deaths (see Ezek. 33:6).**

Accountability for Being There

Many people like superheroes such as Superman, Batman, and others. It seems to me that one of the reasons for this is that we like the idea of being able to have all the power we require and not need to rely on the support of anyone else. Now, your kid may have a Batman costume, but they definitely still need you—and we need each other. Knowing that need, the Scriptures make a foundational connection in their instruction. **It is essential that we encourage each other with wisdom and build each other up (see 1 Thess. 5:11; Col. 3:16). Paul goes on to say that we should** *"...encourage the timid, help the weak, be patient with everyone"* **(1 Thess. 5:14). Supportive "in the trenches" relationships are also evident when you** *"...confess your sins to each other and pray for each other..."* **(James 5:16). And we are able to do all of this because we regularly get together (see Heb. 10:25). In order to "be there," we have to be committed to doing life together—through the fun times as well as the gut-wrenching challenges, through the parenting years and the empty nest season, through marriages, divorces, births, and deaths. Authentic community requires commitment.**

Accountability with a View Toward Eternity

"Hold on to instruction, do not let it go: guard it well, for it is your life" **(Prov. 4:13). In relating to and loving others, it is critical that we guard against false teaching, cherish God's instruction, and teach God's Word to a lost and spiraling world (see Matt. 16:11; 28:19). Eternity is at stake, and we are making a clear and intentional choice to live this life guided by the Spirit of God (see Gal. 5:16-26). Truly loving others necessitates that I live for eternity.**

Purpose Recapped

1. Two Foundational Truths—

    #1—God is, and He knows what His creation needs.

#2—The Scriptures are God's written instructions for how to live.

2. Overarching Purpose #1—To love God with all my heart, soul, mind, and strength.

   Sub-purpose #1—To relate to my Creator by: having faith, being obedient, confessing and repenting of my sins, and worshiping God with everything in my life.

   Sub-purpose #2—To walk humbly with God by giving up control and trusting Him.

   Sub-purpose #3—To connect with God through a lifestyle of quiet—praying and listening.

3. Overarching Purpose #2—To love my neighbor.

   Sub-purpose #1—If I am married: traveling with my mate through life, being united, relating interdependently, and loving in all circumstances.

   Sub-purpose #2—If I have children: loving my children as a blessing from God by shaping them, by honoring my own parents, and by empowering my children.

   Sub-purpose #3—Relating to others by:
   a. Relating externally: promoting justice, prohibiting gossip, and providing for the poor.
   b. Relating internally: guarding my mouth, offering forgiveness, and being peacemakers.
   c. Relating as a community.
   d. Relating with the risk of accountability: accountability to yourself, to the authorities, for who and what influences me, for my influence on others, in being there, and with a view toward eternity.

Chapter Eight

Don't Touch My Stuff—Wealth

"You weren't born to pay bills and die."
—ANONYMOUS

The year was 1888. Alfred Nobel, a Swedish chemist, had made his living inventing and producing dynamite. While he had grown extremely wealthy from this, he sat distraught on this particular day. His brother had just died in France. While that was grief enough, it was amplified by an unintended realization.

As he picked up the French newspaper to read his brother's obituary, he instead found his own. It seems that the editor had confused the brothers and had written the following headline: "The Merchant of Death Is Dead." His obituary told of a man (Alfred) who had become rich by helping people kill each other.

At that moment, shaken by what he read, Alfred resolved to use his wealth in a manner that would leave a different legacy. Eight years later, when he died, he had left more than nine million dollars to fund awards for people whose efforts worked to help mankind. We know the awards as the Nobel Prize.[1]

This man had the ability to do whatever he wanted with his wealth, and he determined to use it to leave a lasting legacy and to make a difference.

~~~

Money! It, or the lack of it, can consume us. For many, it seems as though we never have enough. We take our paycheck, pay the bills, and do our best to figure out how to make what we have left last until the next paycheck. Others may have more money than they know what to do with. My son-in-law sells cars for a Mercedes dealership in Colorado. A couple of years ago, he sold a car that cost $280,000. No, I didn't put too many zeros in that figure. Someone actually paid that. Now of course my first thought was, "That is someone who has more money than sense."

However, my suspicion is that there is someone somewhere that could say that about any one of us. We may not spend $280,000 on a car, but how about that 60-inch-screen television in your living room? For a homeless person, our purchase of a big-screen television may lead them to say, "That is someone who has more money than sense." For others it may be the latest video game console or the newest Gucci purse.

If we have plenty of money, we perceive those who don't as poor. If the nickels and dimes don't stretch far enough, we view others as rich. We have a tendency to put people in one of these two categories: rich or poor. But I would submit that regardless of how we view ourselves, we all have wealth.

Now I know that when most think of wealth, they see visions of piles of gold coins, the gated homes of the rich and the famous, NFL stars earning millions per game, and women (or even men) flashing expensive, extravagant jewelry. And while wealth can certainly indicate opulence and fortune, it can also refer to "anything that has utility and is capable of being appropriated or exchanged."[2] In other words, regardless of how much or how little we have—we all have wealth.

For many years, Dan, my financial planner, owned his own company. I loved the tagline on his business publications—"A Wealth Management Organization." It certainly wasn't that Dan helped only the "rich" (pretty obvious, as he was providing services for someone with as little money as I had). It was more related to his approach. His desire was to assist individuals and families in managing whatever they had, whether that be a large stock portfolio, a simple savings account, family heirlooms, or a shoestring income. We all have "wealth" of some sort to manage.

~~~

Through the years, many stories have been printed regarding how individuals have approached their "stuff." Some are "rags to riches" stories, while others have been more of a "riches to rags" journey.

~~~

Joy, the 2015 movie based on the life and struggles of Joy Mangano, details her rise to fame in the 1990s. A divorced mother of three, she invented the Miracle Mop, becoming an overnight success on QVC. But without giving away the movie plot, know that her success came only after being mortgaged to the hilt and facing bankruptcy and other professional obstacles. It was her persistence in pursuing what she believed in and managing what she had that contributed to her long-term success.[3]

~~~

At 42 years of age, Gerald Muswagon, of Winnipeg, Manitoba, in Canada, won ten million dollars in the lottery after buying a two-dollar ticket. It seemed as though his money problems were over and he would never have to worry about finances again. "He bought a new house that he promptly turned into a self-proclaimed 'party pad' and it was also alleged that he bought eight brand new big screen television for friends in a 24-hour shopping stint."[4] While certainly, at one point, Gerald had plenty of money, without appropriately managing it, he soon found it gone. His "party pad" led to a lifestyle involving high levels of alcohol and drug abuse. Following a poorly run and failed business and eventual run-ins with the law, he found himself broke and working a minimum wage job doing heavy lifting just to get by. In 2005, he hanged himself.

~~~

Born Gonxha Agnes Bojaxhiu in 1910, Mother Teresa of Calcutta won the Nobel Peace Prize in 1979.[5] Even though she died in 1997, she remains a vivid example of "managing what she had been given." Believing she was called to the slums of Calcutta, Mother Teresa washed the sores of children, cared for the old and the sick, and nursed people dying of hunger and tuberculosis. It was her soul's desire to serve God by serving "the unwanted, the unloved, and the uncared for." As might be expected, when she was awarded the Nobel Peace Prize, she asked that the $192,000 in prize money be given to the poor.

~~~

I recall watching Mel Gray, the NFL wide receiver for the St. Louis Cardinals, play in the 1980s. I am not a Cardinals fan, but I clearly remember watching him play against my beloved Cowboys. As the two teams were division rivals at the time, I saw him in numerous games. Mel was selected to play in four straight Pro Bowls (1974-1977), and he caught passes in 121 consecutive games between

1973 and 1982.[6] With his amazing speed, abilities, Pro Bowl selections, and notoriety, one would think that upon his retirement, he would be pretty well set financially. However, that was not the case.

While I remember his playing days, even more clearly I recall my conversations with him. Mel was originally born in Fresno, California, and he had come back there to live after his retirement. While working as a counselor with inner-city students at Roosevelt High School in Fresno in the early 90s, I got to know Mel. He had taken a job at the school as a campus security officer. He was still fast and could chase down students if he needed to—successfully. Yet, the Pro Bowl player could not afford to buy some of the necessities of life. It was not uncommon for teachers and staff members to donate clothes and other items to Mel. Managing what he had was not a strength of his.

~~~

Warren Buffett became a billionaire in the 1990s and has been considered by many to be one of the most (if not the most) successful investors in the world. In 2015, he was the third wealthiest person in the world.[7] Now one would assume that a person with a fortune of his size would live in some lavish mansion. Not so for Mr. Buffett. He still lives in the house that he paid $31,500 for in 1958. Even when adjusted for inflation, this would still make the house purchase only equivalent to approximately $260,000.[8]

Now one might wonder, "Why would a person with as much money as he has still live in such a modest home?" I would suggest that Mr. Buffett knows how to manage wealth. His personal frugality and the financial principles that have led him to stay in the same home all of these years are the same principles that have made him one of the wealthiest people in the world.

~~~

Managing what has been entrusted to us is an important scriptural concept. We see this reflected in stories found in Matthew 25 and Luke 19. Jesus tells of a man who gave his servants various amounts of money with the expectation that they would properly and wisely manage it while he was away on a trip. When he returned, the man interacted with each servant differently based upon how conscientious they were as managers (see Matt. 25:14-30; Luke 19:11-27).

Another word that is not used much today to describe this practice is *stewardship*. It carries with it the idea of managing property or finances that belong to someone else. This idea is demonstrated by the manner in which an employee manages their employer's business or how a financial advisor manages their client's money.

Likewise, we are stewards or managers of what belongs to God—which is everything. He has entrusted us with all that is His—from this planet, to our material stuff, even to relationships. Psalms 50:10 states that God owns the cattle on a thousand hills. He made everything, and it all clearly is His. We are simply allowed to hold some of it in our hands and manage it for a season. Unfortunately, we often forget this and selfishly act as though we "own" stuff. With our hands closed tightly, we maintain a firm grasp on what we think belongs to us. And in doing so, we lose sight of our role as managers.

We are going to spend time in this chapter examining just what God's desires are for us in this realm. And if are able to get our head around this, our lives are likely to be changed in amazing ways.

Honor the Lord

The wisdom of King Solomon is expressed in the following: *"Honor the Lord with your wealth..."* **(Prov. 3:9).** What we are to do with our money and possessions, at a conceptual level, is really that simple—honor the Lord. Whether God has given you plenty, with a sizeable income and many possessions, or He has given you little, with a meager paycheck and a few material goods, you are to honor Him with your wealth.

Now, you may be thinking, "Well, that sounds simple enough, especially if one has plenty. But I can't be expected to do much when I have hardly any money. What kind of craziness is that?" But listen to the words of the apostle Paul: *"...I have learned to be content whatever the circumstances. I know what it is to be in need, and I know what it is to have plenty. I have learned the secret of being content in any and every situation, whether well fed or hungry, whether living in plenty or in want. I can do everything through Him who gives me strength"* (Phil. 4:11-13).

Paul indeed gets it. At times, he found himself feeling pretty blessed in his circumstances. Other times he was hungry and even in prison. Yet he learned the secret, which is relying fully upon the Lord and His sustaining care and love. When Paul says that he can do all things through Him (Christ) who gives him strength, he has not set off to tackle and conquer some great feat of faith (see Phil. 4:13). It would be like somebody boldly proclaiming that they were going to climb Mt. Everest and they are sure to be successful because "I can do all things through Him who gives me strength"—"never mind that I have no equipment, training, or experience." No, Paul is clearly laying out a life of faith and trust. He says that our reliance upon God is to be so unwavering that no matter our circumstances—whether we are rich or poor, whether we are living with abundance or barely getting by—whatever our situation—we decide that God gives us the strength to do all things. And that includes honoring God with our circumstances—with our wealth.

We honor God by serving Him, determining to make a difference with our energies, making an impact with our money, allowing God to prepare us for more, and determining where we will focus our hearts. Let's examine these five areas.

1. Serving God

Most of us have, at one time or another, had a "boss." They may have been called a "manager," a "supervisor," an "executive director," a "vice president," or one of a number of other titles. But the bottom line is that we were answerable to them. I don't know if you have worked for two bosses at the same time, but having two individuals with unique personalities and different agendas can be a tough road to walk—especially if they are not on the same page, or worse, are in competition with each other, each jockeying for position. If you have been unfortunate enough to be in that situation, you probably had experiences of wanting to please one but not so much the other.

Jesus acknowledges this dilemma in saying, *"No one can serve two masters. Either he will hate the one and love the other, or he will be devoted to the one and despise the other. You cannot serve both God and Money"* (Matt. 6:24). And yet so many try.

Conversations with teenagers about career plans can be quite intriguing. Sometimes a student will share with me their dreams to teach kids, design buildings, or play a sport. Others have been heard to reveal their plans (and their hearts) by saying, "I just want to do something where I will make lots of money." Of this pursuit we are warned: *"…Watch out! Be on your guard against all kinds of greed; a man's life does not consist in the abundance of his possessions"* (**Luke 12:15**). Or as someone once said, "The greatest things in life are not things."

You see, God knows how our hearts work. If we set them on accumulating money and stuff, that will be our focus. We will ultimately develop blinders to everything else (including our purpose). I picture the pirate whose only goal is to get the treasure chest with the gold coins and jewels. And then when he gets them, his life is spent taking inventory of his loot. However, **if we seek first the Kingdom of God and His righteousness, He will take care of our**

material needs (see Matt. 6:33). It is up to us to make a choice—are we going to serve God, or will we choose money?

2. Making a Difference with My Energies

As stated above, we have a choice as to the direction of our pursuits. We can focus our attention on learning God's purposes for us and serving Him, or we can enslave ourselves to the almighty dollar. But either way, we will direct our energies somewhere. **Proverbs 23:4-5 reads,** *"Do not wear yourself out to get rich; have the wisdom to show restraint. Cast but a glance at riches, and they are gone, for they will surely sprout wings and fly off to the sky like an eagle."*

And yet how many people do we know (or maybe we have been some of them) who are more concerned with amassing their retirement nest egg, saving for the bigger RV or boat, or stepping up to the plusher home in the more enviable neighborhood? In order to accomplish this, many put in 60, 70, or 80 hours of work a week, to the exclusion of their family. Many parents have put more energy into building a financial nest egg for their children to inherit than they have put into building an enduring relationship with them. As Solomon asserted, riches are gone in a flash (see Prov. 23:5). It would be foolish of us to wear ourselves out in an attempt to simply "get more." As author Kenneth Wood writes, "God wants our devotion to be toward Himself, our families and the people which He brings into our lives to befriend." He further suggests that "God wants us to think less about making a bigger castle and more about making a bigger difference."[9]

3. Making a Difference with My Money

I often hear people offer the following quote: "Money is the root of all evil." However, that is not quite a true statement. The Scripture to which this refers actually states, *"For the love of money is a root of all kinds of evil..."* (1 Tim. 6:10). Therein is the problem—the love of money. Money itself is quite useful. With it we purchase food and clothes, pay for our children's doctors' appointments, and give thoughtful gifts to loved ones. When money serves us (as opposed to our serving money), great benefits can be experienced. Therefore, it is important for us to understand that we can use our finances to make both God and people a priority over money.

~~~

While there is no question that God doesn't need our money (I mean, let's face it—He created everything; if He needed money, He could just create more), if we are to be sold out to Him, He does need to be the priority in our life. And, without a doubt, one of the most significant ways that I indicate what is important to me is how I spend my money. I have a pretty good idea that if I look at your checkbook (or nowadays maybe your online bank statement), I will know what captivates your attention. By examining how you spend your money, I can catch a glimpse of whether your passion for golf is more important than your spouse, or whether your kids rank higher than your penchant for new shoes. Our financial dealings can paint a pretty accurate picture of our heart condition, which we will talk a little more about later.

In the Old Testament, we read about the concept of tithing—giving a tenth of our income back to God. **Giving from the beginning of one's income as opposed to giving from the scraps that are left at the end of the month was an important concept, as discussed in Proverbs 3:9. Malachi 3:10 reinforces this with urgings not to "rob" from God, which the prophet said was transpiring when people failed to bring their tithes and offerings to God at the temple.**

While the specific idea of tithing is not necessarily carried over into the New Testament, we find the principle of giving expanded upon with these words: *"Remember this: Whoever sows sparingly will also reap sparingly, and whoever sows generously will also reap generously. Each man should man should give what he has decided in his heart to give, not reluctantly or under compulsion, for God loves a cheerful giver"* **(2 Cor. 9:6-7).**

Another way of communicating this idea might be, "Gratefully demonstrate your love for God by where He is in your checkbook or credit card. Make Him the priority in your life."

~~~

But not only are we charged with providing for the needs of the temple (or church), we also are taught to use our wealth to take care of each other. *"On the first day of every week, each one of you should set aside a sum of money in keeping with his income..."* **(1 Cor. 16:2).** In this passage, Paul is talking about the collection he is making to give to those fellow believers who are struggling financially. **He is instructing people to look at their income and figure out what they can give to help those who are in need.**

I remember when I was in college that "Faith Promise Rallies" were popular in the church. The idea was that you would trust God to provide for whatever amount of money you would pledge for a given cause. It didn't matter whether you even had a job. You would promise an amount and trust that somehow, money would arrive so that you could fulfill that promise. I was not a fan of that concept in the 70s and I am even less so today. In his book *Decision Making and the Will of God,* Garry Friesen says it this way: "But to hold God to a promise that He hasn't put on the record isn't faith—it is presumption. Genuine faith must be anchored to verifiable promises."[10] I believe that God expects us to use the rational brains that He gave us, examine our income, and decide in our own heart what we are led to gratefully give to help others.

While contributing 10 percent of one's income is appropriate for many, someone else's circumstances may dictate that all they can give is 5 percent. Yet for others, it may be significantly more. Friesen goes on to tell a story of a wealthy man who had become a believer and wanted his financial giving to reflect his new priorities. He began by contributing 10 percent of his income to the needs of people but very quickly ratcheted it up to 40 percent. Making his money count in a God- and people-honoring manner was leading him to more carefully monitor where his money went. As Friesen writes, "He was amazed at how much money he had formally wasted on things he did not really need."[11] Ultimately, when the man examined how God was continuing to bless him, he landed on giving away 60 percent of his income every month. "Abundant giving and careful spending were his new responses to God's prospering of his life."[12]

Unfortunately, many are driven by gimmicks rather than rational and thoughtful decisions. My wife and I were recently watching an old episode of the television show *King of Queens*. Carrie's elderly father, Arthur, lives with her and her husband, Doug. Arthur had decided to respond to a station's fundraising campaign by donating a minimum amount so that he could receive a tote bag they were giving away. While it made for humorous interactions, being motivated to give because of some reward one will get is a lousy reason to contribute.

I endeavor to be thoughtful and send money to worthy causes. However, a tactic that makes me a little crazy is when well-intentioned organizations that do meaningful work begin sending me pleas for additional funds nearly every week. An emergency or budget shortfall arises, and they need my immediate help. I don't respond well to those. But understand, the reason they send out so many pleas is because they are effective. They know that most people have not "decided in their heart," and they can appeal to their emotions (see 2 Cor. 9:7). The Scriptures teach us to use our discernment abilities to meet the needs of others out of our abundance. Of course, we need to prioritize. "Out of my abundance" doesn't mean only after I have bought the new car, boat, and vacation home. It means that with what I have been blessed with, I am able to help those who are truly less fortunate. It is my belief that God expects for us to take care of our families first, our family of believers second, and others third. But I encourage you to listen to your own convictions in how God leads you in this arena.

4. Preparing to Be Trusted

Whether we envision money as a necessary evil or something we can't get enough of, we typically view it as something physical and outside of ourselves. But I want to suggest that our approach to wealth is very much a reflection of and a contribution to our spiritual health. As Damien Wills notes, "While material desires are in themselves not damaging, some material desires can actually delay us in achieving our spiritual purpose."[13] How we engage with finances is directly connected to our spiritual life.

In the Book of Luke, Jesus tells a story of a shrewd and dishonest manager. It is also in the 16th chapter that we read the warning mentioned earlier regarding our inability to serve two different masters. In verses 10-12, Jesus says, *"Whoever can be trusted with very little can also be trusted with much, and whoever is dishonest with very little will be dishonest with much. So if you have not been trustworthy in handling worldly wealth, who will trust you with true riches? And if you have not been trustworthy with someone else's property, who will give your property of your own?"* (Luke 16:10-12).

As a reminder of discussions in earlier chapters—we are only living in the blip on the timeline. Our brief existence on earth is not all that our lives are about. We are here to grapple with the weightier issues of eternity. God uses our years here to determine what He can entrust us with in His heavenly Kingdom. He is saying that if we are good stewards or managers of His stuff here, then He knows that He can entrust us with "true riches" in eternity.

Jesus talked more about money than He did any other subject, but it wasn't because He was concerned about money. He was concerned about our heart condition. And as Rick Warren states, "The Bible is very clear: God uses money to test our faithfulness as a servant."[14]

A recent client shared with me how deeply violated they felt when their daughter stole their credit card to make unauthorized purchases. She also allowed her drug-addicted boyfriend to come into her parents' house and steal items of value to use toward purchasing more drugs. As much as it grieved the parents, they have had to change the locks and forbid their daughter from coming to their house. Without question, she has proved herself untrustworthy.

When God examines our lives, I wonder what He sees. Does He find faithful children who are thoughtfully, diligently, and responsibly managing what He has loaned us for our use? Or does He discover selfish and inconsiderate children that are squandering what He has given them with no thought for Him or His other children in need? I am thoroughly convinced that we have been granted this time on earth to handle wealth as a period of preparation. He is preparing us, if we are willing and teachable, to be trusted with much greater treasure in eternity.

5. Determining the Focus of My Heart

I remember years ago when I was on church staffs in California, it always intrigued me to watch how uncomfortable people got when the pastor would teach about giving, tithing, and just money issues in general. Some felt as though the church was just trying to get into their wallets and get more money out of them. Whether or not that was true is not my point. As they say, "I have no horse in this race." I have no agenda to get you to open your checkbook and donate to any particular cause. I am simply reporting what the Scriptures teach regarding money, priorities, and making a difference.

In my opinion, **Jesus sums up the issue when He says,** *"For where your treasure is, there your heart will be also"* **(Luke 12:34).** While this concept doesn't apply only to money, it is certainly appropriate. What we spend our money on will captivate our attention, our passions, and our heart.

I remember in 1985 purchasing a brand-new Pontiac Firebird. I had planned for this, saved, spent time at the showroom picking out features, haggling over the price, and ultimately buying it. This car was my pride and joy. I continually perused it for scratches. Every Saturday I hand-washed it and cleaned its interior. It is certainly safe to say that this was my treasure, and as a result, it had my heart as well.

Now, please don't misunderstand what I am saying. I am not saying that we can't have toys and nice things. I am inquiring as to what our priorities are. Is my heart chasing money and material possessions, or is my wealth following my heart?

I am convicted by the words of renowned author C. S. Lewis:

> Charity—giving to the poor—is an essential part of Christian morality...I do not believe one can settle how much we ought to give. I am afraid the only safe rule is to give more than we can spare. In other words, if our expenditure on comforts, luxuries, amusements, etc., is up to the standard common among those with the same income as our own, we are probably giving away too little. If our charities do not at all pinch or hamper us, I should say they are too small. There ought to be things we should like to do and cannot do because our charitable expenditure excludes them.[15]

Money—it is without question necessary to live. But God never intended for us to gather as much as we could for the sole purpose of lavishing it on ourselves. He also intends for the use of it to be a part of our purpose, a part of why we are here on this planet. It is His desire that our use and management of money reflect a humble and surrendered heart. The ways that we handle our money should demonstrate that God is our priority, that the dollar doesn't distract us from the things that really matter in life, that we can impact people and the world and make a genuine difference with the wealth He has given us, that we are using our opportunities here to prove ourselves trustworthy, and that our

heart is focused on the treasures that truly matter. In these ways, we will honor God with our wealth. That is our purpose here.

In 2006, investment mogul Warren Buffet made a pledge:

> More than 99% of my wealth will go to philanthropy during my lifetime or at death. Measured by dollars, this commitment is large. In a comparative sense, though, many individuals give more to others every day.
>
> Millions of people who regularly contribute to churches, schools, and other organizations thereby relinquish the use of funds that would otherwise benefit their own families. The dollars these people drop into a collection plate or give to United Way mean forgone movies, dinners out, or other personal pleasures. In contrast, my family and I will give up nothing we need or want by fulfilling this 99% pledge.[16]

Humbly, Mr. Buffett admits the degree of his wealth and how his 99 percent pledge will not impact him the way a 5 percent, 10 percent, or 20 percent commitment might impact you or me. But I believe his point for us is a simple one—use what you have to make a substantial difference in honoring both God and people.

Purpose Recapped

1. Two Foundational Truths—

    #1—God is, and He knows what His creation need

    #2—The Scriptures are God's written instructions for how to live.

2. Overarching Purpose #1—To love God with all my heart, soul, mind, and strength.

Sub-purpose #1—To relate to my Creator by: having faith, being obedient, confessing and repenting of my sins, and worshiping God with everything in my life.

Sub-purpose #2—To walk humbly with God by giving up control and trusting Him.

Sub-purpose #3—To connect with God through a lifestyle of quiet—praying and listening.

3. Overarching Purpose #2—To love my neighbor.

Sub-purpose #1—If I am married: traveling with my mate through life, being united, relating interdependently, and loving in all circumstances.

Sub-purpose #2—If I have children: loving my children as a blessing from God by shaping them, by honoring my own parents, and by empowering my children.

Sub-purpose #3—Relating to others: externally, internally, as a community, and with accountability.

Sub-purpose #4—To honor the Lord with my wealth by:
   a. Serving God.
   b. Making a difference with my energies.
   c. Making a difference with my money.
   d. Becoming trustworthy.
   e. Deciding my heart's focus.

Section Three

OVERARCHING PURPOSE #3

LOVE YOURSELF

"Love the Lord your God with all your heart and with all your soul and with all your mind." This is the first and greatest commandment. And the second is like it: "Love your neighbor as yourself" **(Matthew 22:37-39).**

Chapter Nine

Do You Talk To Yourself?—
Relating With Self—*Part 1*

*"Sometimes God doesn't change your situation
because He is trying to change your heart."*
—ANONYMOUS

In the first two sections of this book, we learned that the beginning of God's purposes for us are wrapped up and fulfilled in how we love and relate to Him as well as how we love and relate to each other. And yet, in examining the passage in Matthew 22, we frequently overlook an essential component. You will notice that the Scripture says that we are to love our neighbor as we love ourselves (see Matt. 22:39).

Because humans naturally tend to be pretty self-focused, many of us had parents who worked hard to teach us to put other people first and ourselves last. As a matter of fact, you may have even been encouraged to discount yourself. To cater to yourself may have implied that you were selfish, and that simply wasn't OK. If this idea was carried to an extreme, thinking about and caring for yourself at all was critically looked down upon.

Yet, the Scripture is clear that we are to love others as we love ourselves (see Matt. 22:39). Certainly, we are to put others first, but we are still to love and take care of the person who God has made us to be. The reality is that if I don't know how to love myself, discovering how to love someone else will be extremely difficult. Therefore, learning to put our love in perspective is a significant part of our purpose and development.

You Are Unique

I love peaches—freshly picked, in jars, in a cobbler; it pretty much doesn't matter. Buying peaches at roadside stands in Fresno, where I used to live, was always a treat. California is the largest producer of peaches, especially the San Joaquin Valley, where Fresno is located.[1]

But imagine with me for a moment—what if a peach somehow acquired decision-making abilities and decided that it really wanted to become an orange? Since the greatest production of orange juice occurs in Florida, the peach seed decides to hop a bus (remember—we are imagining here), and heads to the Sunshine State. Once it gets there, it plants itself and waits. This seed has big plans. It wants to become a delicious orange and eventually be transformed into orange juice that will complement family breakfasts across the country.

As the growing season progresses, the orange seeds turn into trees with blossoms that burst into developing fruit. Likewise, the peach seed feels itself growing, just like the orange seeds. It too blossoms and grows into hanging fruit. However, when it looks in the mirror, it doesn't see an orange—it sees a beautiful peach. You might think, "Well, what's wrong with that?" But the peach is in distress. It doesn't want to be a peach. Longing to be an orange, when at its very core it is a peach, simply creates confusion and frustration.

As silly as that peach was to want to be an orange, we often discover that we are not that much different. If you are fully grown and have reached a towering height of five feet tall, I am guessing that your prospects for an NBA career are slim and dwindling. Conversely, if you are seven feet tall, I wouldn't recommend trying out for the Olympic gymnastics team. While you can certainly choose to do so, it honestly makes about as much sense as the peach hopping a bus to Florida. It would be much wiser for the peach to embrace all the glory of its peachness and find satisfaction in what God intended for it.

~~~

God has made you to be you—not someone else. If He had wanted you to be taller, shorter, blonder, more muscular, southern, musical, mathematical, athletic, extroverted (and the list goes on and on), He would have made you that way. He made you exactly the way that He wants you. The prophet Jeremiah recorded God's words to him: *"Before I formed you in the womb I knew you, before you were born I set you apart..."* (Jer. 1:5). Why do we have such a difficult time accepting this principle?

I love the way in which C. S. Lewis so matter-of-factly expresses this idea: "He makes each soul unique. If He had no use for all these differences, I do not see why He should have created more souls than one. Be sure that the ins and outs of your individuality are no mystery to Him; and one day they will no longer be a mystery to you."[2]

You are unlike anybody else on this planet—and it is by design. Yet how very hard we work to become like everyone else. You want to buy the latest outfit because your favorite celebrity is wearing it.

You seek out the plastic surgeon because you think you need a different nose, forehead, or other body part. Why? Because in our mind, we have established some arbitrary ideal that we think we are supposed to fit into. I am convinced that if everyone in the whole world were brunettes and God made me or you blonde, rather than revel in our uniqueness, we would probably dye our hair brown in order to be like everyone else. But you are not everyone else. You are exactly who God designed you to be. He knows your strengths, gifts, and abilities, and He has a destiny carved out just for you. As Charles Swindoll phrases it, "That's why He sends one person to the mission field in China and another to the bank building in downtown Seattle."[3]

You are unique. The sooner that you fully embrace the life God has "set you apart" for, the closer you will be to living a fulfilled and "abundant" life, enjoying the days that lie ahead.

Guard Your Heart

From a materialistic perspective, many might think that "loving themselves" means that they should pamper themselves, take luxurious trips, and, as I used to picture when I was a kid, have someone feed you grapes while you are being fanned with giant palm fronds. Yet I want to suggest that God desires for us to love ourselves, beginning with taking care of ourselves—particularly by taking care of our heart.

King Solomon articulates it this way: *"Above all else, guard your heart, for it is the wellspring of life"* **(Prov. 4:23).** Notice that he doesn't say, "Once you have earned plenty of money, once you have acquired all that your eye desires, once you have taken all the vacations that you want—then maybe consider guarding your heart." No, he clearly states, *"Above all else..."* (Prov. 4:23). I don't know what that means to you, but to me, "Above all else" means "Above all else!" Protecting my heart is the first and most important thing that I can do to love myself. As the passage appropriately indicates, our heart is the source from which our existence springs.

So often we get caught up in circumstances that are swirling around us, and they become the target of our energies. Yet God is "much more concerned with the attitude of your heart than the environment or the conditions in which you live."[4] But the question we begin to ponder is, just what does guarding our heart mean? I am wholeheartedly convinced that the single most dominant factor that contributes to the shaping of our heart is our thought life.

The Scriptures say that we were made in the image of our Creator (see Gen. 1:26). What this means, in part, is that we are also creative beings. As Touré Roberts writes, "The process of creation is this: you think it, you meditate on it, you envision it, you speak about it, and then you take action toward it."[5] He continues: "This is why we have to be very selective with our thought life."[6] It is for this reason that Jesus takes the stand that He does when elaborating on the Old Testament teachings regarding adultery. He instructs us that not only are we not to commit adultery, but that *"...anyone who looks at a woman lustfully has already committed adultery with her in his heart"* **(Matt. 5:28).** He knows that if we can think it, we can do it. And that is a very dangerous place to go.

So we have to examine ourselves and ask, "What influences and shapes my heart?" It has been reported that the average person in this country watches between 30-35 hours of television every week.[7] This is a passive activity that tends to generate more passivity and lethargy. In the name of "rest" and "entertainment," individuals will spend hours upon hours watching YouTube videos, searching the Web, and saturating their brains in mindless movies and sitcoms. Consider the effect that this can have on you. How different might we be if we spent even some of those hours focused on God's purposes for our lives?

The authors of the book *Why We Are Created?* liken the pliability of our brains to the "butterfly that assumes the color of the foliage on which it settles."[8] They state that what we contemplate, the things on which we focus our thoughts, we become. "If our minds are preoccupied with nonproductive thoughts such as worry, concern, gossip, failure, or resentment, then our thoughts are colored with these hues. If our focus is on positive traits such as joy, unlimited love, service, divine purposes, enthusiasm, diligence, and usefulness, the mind's hue again responds."[9]

Getting caught up in how we look and how things appear can drive us to a place of inauthentic living. We are reminded in the Scriptures that God is not impressed by one's outward appearance. He, instead, examines a person's heart (see 1 Sam. 16:7). First Chronicles 29:17 goes so far as to say that God tests our hearts and is *"pleased with integrity."*

Be Careful How You Live

In his letter to the Ephesians, Paul offers these practical words of instruction: *"Be very careful, then, how you live—not as unwise but as wise"* **(Eph. 5:15).** "Being careful" sounds like pretty sound advice, but just how do we do that?

Unusual weather conditions during the past couple of years have resulted in an abundance of potholes in the roads in Colorado. The voters approved the expenditure of millions of dollars in the state to begin to repair, and in many cases completely repave, the backlog of damaged streets and highways. It seems as though everywhere I drive I see orange cones that warn me to slow down and drive carefully. Otherwise I am likely to run over workers and probably drive my car into a hole in the road. Because I would rather not damage my car or hurt the workers, I am appreciative of these orange warning cones. I want us to explore seven "orange cones" that will help us in our quest to "be careful how we live."

Cone #1—Be Careful Not to Live Foolishly

Those whom God considers foolish are seen in a variety of circumstances throughout the Bible. For example, have you ever been around someone who gets offended at the drop of a hat? If so, you know how frustrating that can be. Therefore, it should come as no surprise that Solomon would write, *"A fool shows his annoyance at once, but a prudent man overlooks an insult"* **(Prov. 12:16)**. It is easy to see how the foolish person gets caught up in ridiculous quarrels. This is why we read, *"...do not be foolish, but understand what the Lord's will is"* **(Eph. 5:17)**. Keeping our focus on how we have been wronged is foolish. God would much rather we understand that His desire is for us to love, forgive, and be understanding of others.

My wife and I enjoy watching people—whether at the mall, the airport, or pretty much any public gathering. If you ever want to witness foolishness on full display, just go to a popular bar on a Friday night and people-watch. As the clock creeps toward midnight and then on to 1:00 or 2:00 A.M., behaviors grow more bizarre, embarrassing, and well—foolish. This is why we are warned **that we are not to get drunk, which leads to foolish behaviors (see Eph. 5:18)**.

Another interesting group of people to watch are those who stand with signs on street corners. It seems that it has almost become a challenge for some who have no desire to get a job to see who can get out the earliest to the best corner and discover how much money they can collect on any given day (at least where we live). Therefore, it might be easy to read the words *"If a man will not work, he shall not eat"* and think they were written for the 21st century **(2 Thess. 3:10)**. But they weren't. They were written nearly 2,000 years ago. Please don't misunderstand my intentions here. I recognize that the economy is tough and that some hard-working people have truly found themselves down on their luck and are legitimately in need of assistance. However, I am convinced that the majority of people on the street corner do not fit into this category. Instead, they perhaps reflect the experiences that come when we are not "careful how we live."

Cone #2—Be Careful to Actively Avoid Evil

While we might see some nuances to this warning, it is pretty straightforward: *"Avoid every kind of evil"* **(1 Thess. 5:22; see also 2 Tim. 2:22). Peter is a little more specific when he says it this way:** *"Therefore, rid yourselves of all malice and all deceit, hypocrisy, envy, and slander of every kind"* **and** *"...abstain from sinful desires..."* **(1 Peter 2:1,11).** This particular warning is so blatant that it is actually probably more like the radar speed sign that shows your speed and flashes "slow down" than it is a cone. Avoiding evil is rudimentary.

Cone #3—Be Careful to Live Wisely

Just as we read earlier that a foolish person is easily offended, the exact opposite is true of a wise man. *"A man's wisdom gives him patience; it is to his glory to overlook an offense"* **(Prov. 19:11). People are also wise in how they take advantage of opportunities they are given to relate to outsiders by demonstrating love and grace (see Col. 4:5-6).**

If I am living as a wise person, it is obvious to others because I am self-controlled (see 1 Peter 1:13), clear-thinking (see 1 Peter 4:7), and I am striving to be separate from the world and called out to be who God intends (see 1 Peter 1:15).

Cone #4—Be Careful by Actively Embracing

Sometimes when I am driving through road construction, I find that it is not always about just "avoiding" something—avoiding the pothole or avoiding the concrete barricade. Once in a while, there is a person with a flag. They may be asking me to stop because they have to let one lane through at a time. Or they might be directing me to detour or turn a certain direction. Similarly, the Scriptures encourage us to be careful how we live by taking intentional active steps.

As God followers who truly grasp the power of His saving grace, we are introduced as *"the light of the world"* (Matt. 5:14). With that dynamic gift and message, Jesus says that **we are to impact the world. We are able to do this most effectively when we allow that light to shine as a beacon of hope to others (see Matt. 5:16; Eph. 5:8-9) and when the character of God's love in our lives alters people and society in positive ways (see Matt. 5:13). As a matter of fact, when we live by reflecting God's priorities in our daily interactions, even a pagan world will be able to see God at work (see 1 Peter 2:12).**

Taking active, intentional steps in how we live as believers does not mean that we are to be loud and obnoxious. It saddens me to see the name "Christian" become synonymous with "Bible-thumping, boisterous busybodies." When that is the case, God is dishonored.

Jimmy Dodd talks about how there are two parts to our lives: the front stage and the backstage.[9] Just like in a theater, the front stage is the part that everyone sees—the elaborate scenery, the flowing curtains, the perfect lighting, and all that looks beautiful. However, if we were to visit the backstage, we might find lose wires, empty boxes, sheets hung to provide temporary costume changing areas, and just general disarray.

Unfortunately, we too often focus on our "front stage" persona without giving proper attention the "backstage" areas of our lives that need some cleaning up. Yet it is the "backstage" to which God wants us to direct our attention. He knows that if we only concern ourselves with our image and how we look, we could easily be a fraud. But if we quietly go about taking care of the less attractive parts of our lives, God knows that what people see will take care of itself—and it will be genuine.

We bring honor to God when we are not just a bunch of "talk" but when **our actions, in loving and taking care of others, back up the faith that we proclaim to have (see James 1:14-26).**

We bring honor to God when **we make it our ambition to lead a quiet life and mind our own business (see 1 Thess. 4:11-12).**

We bring honor to God when **we give less attention to how we dress and fix our hair than we do our inner self. Peter refers to this as** *"the unfading beauty of a gentle and quiet spirit, which is of great worth in God's sight"* **(1 Peter 3:4).** Here is where we have to ask ourselves what may be a difficult question: What do I value more—the things that are of worth to a spiraling society, or the things that are of great worth to God?

We bring honor to God when **we endeavor to travel with a partner who shares our purposes (see 2 Cor. 6:14).**

Cone #5—Be Careful How You Live Sexually

Sexuality seems to be a topic of ongoing discussion over many generations. Even in my lifetime I have seen the sexual mores take some radical turns. Thinking back to the 50s and into the 60s, society had some expectations with regard to behavior and dress. While teens were sexually active to a certain degree, they weren't blatant about it, except in certain circles. If a girl became pregnant, it was not uncommon to find her suddenly missing from school one day, having gone to live with a grandmother or aunt until after the baby arrived. Girls who dressed suggestively, wearing tight clothes or low-cut tops, were frowned upon and quickly garnered a reputation.

But toward the end of the 60s and into the 70s, society began to push mightily against sexual restrictions. And now in the 21st century, we have lost the art of embarrassment. One example of this is "sagging." When I worked as a counselor with at-risk students in a local school district, I would frequently see young men who would "sag"—wearing their pants with the waist sometimes down nearly to their knees, with their underwear hanging out for the world to see. Embarrassed? No. They are proud and in-your-face with their dress.

Young (and sometimes older) women dress in ways that they leave little to the imagination. When men can't seem to help but stare at their bodies, rather than blush, the women are proud because they have been able to capture the attention of the opposite sex, even if it is for the wrong reasons.

In being careful how we live, how we manage our sexuality is a definite part of the equation. Biblical instructions repeatedly point out God's creation, design, and guidelines for our sexual behavior. Sexuality is God-ordained; it is meaningful and beautiful—when enjoyed as He intended. While cultural norms change, God's designs for our pleasure and fulfillment remain constant. From Genesis and continuing throughout the Scriptures, we see that God created sex to be a part of the most intimate and unifying experience a man and woman can share. It has the power to connect and bind, which is the reason it was made for marriage, or it has the ability to hurt and damage in significant ways when cheapened and made casual.

Therefore, keeping sexuality in its proper perspective is key to maintaining healthy relationships. For this reason, we discover that **we are to abstain from sexual immorality (see Acts 15:20), and be in control of our own body (see 1 Thess. 4:3). In First Corinthians 6:18 we are told to go beyond simply abstaining or avoiding sexual immorality and to actually flee from it.** The image I see when I read that is Joseph fleeing from Potiphar's wife when she was sexually pursuing him. I know many men who have been caught in the hooks of pornography because they were going to walk or saunter away from it when in fact they should have been in a dead sprint away from it. I should point out that the word frequently used for "sexual immorality" in the New Testament is the same word from which the English word *pornography* originates. **This passage in First Corinthians goes on to elaborate that other sins are outside our bodies, but when we sexually sin, we are sinning against our own body.**

Finally, we are told that if we are a part of God's people, there needs to be not even a hint of sexual immorality among us (see Eph. 5:3). We are not to toy with the idea, flirt with it, or have any connection to immorality. If we are not careful how we live in this arena, it is one of the quickest ways to destroy our reputation, our marriage, our family, and our witness of God's work in our lives.

Cone #6—Be Careful to Stand Firm in Your Faith

God knows that our faith will be attacked. If we are effective in loving others, satan will work to take us out at the knees. If God is honored by our lifestyle, compromise is lurking around the next corner. For this reason we read that we should **be on guard and stand firm in the faith (see 1 Cor. 16:13-14); hold tightly to the teachings of the Scriptures (see 2 Thess. 2:15); and hold firmly to the faith that we profess (see Heb. 4:14).**

And not only is it important to be a person of faith, it adds substance when you know why you have faith. *"...Always be prepared to give an answer to everyone who asks you to give the reason for the hope that you have..."* **(1 Peter 3:15).** Your example and your testimony to others is strengthened when you are able to share why you believe what you believe.

Cone #7—Be Careful to Work Out Your Salvation

"...continue to work out your salvation with fear and trembling" **(Phil. 2:12).** The writer is not suggesting here that our salvation is up to us to figure out. God is the author of our salvation. The grace that we receive through Jesus is not up for discussion. It simply is. What this Scripture is telling us is that we are to be careful how we live that grace out. We are not to be casual and flippant about it. God's grace and love are enormously big deals, and, therefore, how we choose to conduct our lives, whether in public or behind closed doors, should be done with great care. In order to accomplish this, we have to decide what is important.

Americans in this day and time, probably more than ever before, are starving. I am not necessarily talking here about food. Most of us rarely struggle with physical hunger. Sure we may get a little cranky if we miss our mid-morning snack, but it is unlikely that we really go without food. Yet we are hungry—for something. We may try to fill that void with a variety of efforts—a new job, an exotic vacation, or buying more stuff. Yet, we remain unsatisfied. The Bible clearly indicates that this is about deciding what is important, what genuinely matters.

Viktor Frankl, who wrote the book *Man's Search for Meaning*, details his experiences in a German concentration camp. The Jewish prisoners, if they were fortunate enough to be chosen to live, were sent to a room where they were to strip naked and pile all their belongings in the center of the room. Hurriedly, the prisoners would undress, afraid that if they weren't fast enough, they would be beaten or killed. Very quickly, they all found themselves with just their naked existence. Frankl's important writings were contained in manuscripts that were rolled-up papers in his pockets. He pleaded, "I must keep this manuscript at all costs: it contains my life's work."[10] However, they too went into the pile.

One can only imagine how the life energy drained from prisoners, with many contemplating and some committing suicide. Frankl was devastated that in an instant, all that he had worked so hard for was gone. Yet as he reflected on the experience, he was able to talk about the freedom and spiritual power that were ultimately made available to him. He noted that in the prison camps, those who were religious tended to last longer than those who were more athletic but lacked the inner strength in their soul.

All of the prisoners were given camp uniforms that had belonged to people who had recently died in the gas chambers. As Frankl put on a used and dirty uniform, he reached into the pocket and found a small piece of paper. As he looked at it, he realized it had written on it the text of the Shema. The Shema is a part of the Jewish daily prayer book and comes from Deuteronomy 6:4-9. It begins with "[Shema]"—which means, "Hear, O Israel"—*"The Lord our God, the Lord is one"* (Deut. 6:4). Another Jew had managed to keep this hidden in his pocket. Frankl realized that while he had been forced to give up his collection of manuscripts, what he had received in return was of far greater value.

So, we have to ask ourselves, "What is of greater value? What really matters?" As Rick Warren suggests, "I must desire friendship with God more than anything else."[11] Passages such as John 15:14 and Romans 5:10 tell us that God desires friendship with us as well. God celebrates our uniqueness because He wants an individual relationship with you and me. I in turn choose to guard my heart and be careful how I live because I want the most intimate relationship that I can have with my Creator. I am purposed to enjoy Him.

Purpose Recapped

1. Two Foundational Truths—

    #1—God is, and He knows what His creation needs.

    #2—The Scriptures are God's written instructions for how to live.

2. Overarching Purpose #1—To love God with all my heart, soul, mind, and strength.

    Sub-purpose #1—To relate to my Creator by: having faith, being obedient, confessing and repenting of my sins, and worshiping God with everything in my life.

    Sub-purpose #2—To walk humbly with God by giving up control and trusting Him.

    Sub-purpose #3—To connect with God through a lifestyle of quiet—praying and listening.

3. Overarching Purpose #2—To love my neighbor.

Sub-purpose #1—If I am married: traveling with my mate through life, being united, relating interdependently, and loving in all circumstances.

Sub-purpose #2—If I have children: loving my children as a blessing from God by shaping them, by honoring my own parents, and by empowering my children.

Sub-purpose #3—Relating to others: externally, internally, as a community, and with accountability.

Sub-purpose #4—To honor the Lord with my wealth by: serving God, making a difference with my energies and my money, becoming trustworthy, and focusing my heart.

4. **Overarching Purpose #3**—To love yourself.

   Sub-Purpose #1—To relate with yourself by:
   a. Recognizing your uniqueness.
   b. Guarding your heart.
   c. Being careful how you live.

Chapter Ten

Do You Talk to Yourself?—
Relating with Self—*Part 2*

*"You can work for what you want or
settle for what you have."*
—SIGN AT THE UNIVERSITY OF COLORADO, DENVER

It was December 2015, and my wife and I were traveling to New Orleans. As we were reading about things to do there, you would think that I would have been most intrigued by the historic sites, the plethora of live jazz, or even the beignets served at Café Du Monde. While those were certainly items in which I was interested, what had really caught my attention was that the day before we were arriving, Blue Bell ice cream was going back on the shelves in Louisiana. You see, since they had issues in 2015 with listeria, the plants had been shut down for some time. As I am writing this, they still haven't returned to Colorado. So, if you are a crazed Blue Bell fan such as myself and have been experiencing severe withdrawals, perhaps you can understand my excitement as we were planning our trip. Now of course (though I can't imagine this), if you are not the ice cream fan that I am, you may have trouble understanding what all of the hoopla is about (but there is always therapy available for you).

As this chapter continues the conversation around "relating with ourselves," we will be getting up close and personal as we examine issues of health, growth, and success, and our enjoyment of life. For me, ice cream definitely impacts a couple of these areas.

Be Intentional with Your Health

"Do you not know that your body is a temple of the Holy Spirit, who is in you, whom you have received from God? You are not your own; you were bought at a price. Therefore honor God with your body" (**1 Cor. 6:19-20**). In this passage, we are shown clearly that God has given us these bodies as our vehicles with which we navigate life. Therefore, we probably want to take appropriate care of them.

As a kid, I remember how my dad would prepare for family vacations. I think that his unspoken motto was, "Don't worry about the car until the day before a road trip and then get it ready." It seemed as though, at a frantic pace, Dad would try to take care of everything related to the car on that day—oil change, brake issues, tire concerns, and some rattle or squeak that it had been experiencing for months. Invariably, he would become frustrated, and it was not uncommon for the beginning of the trip to be delayed a day or two. How much better it would have been for Dad to maintain the cars on a regular basis. Had he been more proactive, the car would have always been ready to make a trip. And I am also convinced that he would have experienced fewer mechanical problems, which in turn would have helped his cars last longer.

For those who make their living with their vehicles, such as truck or taxis drivers, they would never adopt my dad's approach to automotive maintenance. They know that if they did, they would be either in financial chaos or out of business—or both. No, because they are in business for the long haul, they know that vigilant maintenance is essential to the purposes of their business. Our bodies are not that dissimilar.

As we consider our desire to live on purpose with intentionality, we will take a brief look at eating and nutrition, resting, and exercising.

You Are What You Eat

"Do not join those who drink too much wine or gorge themselves on meat, for drunkards and gluttons become poor, and drowsiness clothes them in rags" **(Prov. 23:20-21).** I guess it is comforting to know, in some weird sort of way, that gluttony was a problem long before the 64-ounce Big Gulp drinks and the supersized combo meals. For as often happens today, Solomon warns that those whose lives are caught up in how much they eat and drink will become lazy and lethargic.

Modern science tells us that our overeating habits can actually shorten our lives. A study out of London reports that overweight people may die one year earlier than expected, obese individuals up to three years prematurely, and the severely obese could lose as much as eight years of their life.[1]

Fifty years ago, it was easy to think that obesity was rare, and we may not have even known anyone who fit into that category. However, there has been an unprecedented increase in the number of individuals who qualify for that label. There are predictions that by the year 2025 (not that far off), one-fifth of adults will be obese.[2] This same study went on to note that not long ago, the primary global concern was weighing too little. However, as incomes rise, access to cheap processed foods has increased. As surprising as it might be, excess weight is now a bigger concern worldwide than weighing too little. And, as would be expected, carrying around extra weight also comes with an increased risk of diabetes, heart disease, and a host of other health complications. I can't help but wonder if Paul had obesity in mind when he wrote, *"...their god is their stomach..."* (Phil. 3:19)?

Paying attention to what we put in our bodies has been an area of focus from early in the Old Testament. At one time, people believed that food guidelines from the Mosaic Law were arbitrary and didn't make sense. However, with the advantages of modern medicine and current nutritional information, biblical food instructions began to take on new significance. We even see some of the young Jewish men from the royal family, as recorded in the Book of Daniel, refusing to eat the king's food because they knew they would not be as healthy. They were granted permission to eat only vegetables and drink water (see Dan. 1:12-15). As a result, they were better nourished than all of the other men.

I could spend time writing about food or drink that have negative effects, such as diet soda. Studies show that the majority of people drinking diet soda typically drink more of them, because they are diet, and as a result consume more calories than those who drink regular soda.[3] I could report on foods that will do the most to strengthen your mind and body; namely, fruits and vegetables.

I would also mention that *when you eat* affects your weight. For example, those who work nights tend to gain weight.[4] Our metabolism is designed to work most effectively during daylight hours. The author of *You Are When You Eat* writes, "That late-night bowl of ice cream may all go toward your waistline."[5] Ouch—that has been a struggle I have certainly had to address.

As a matter of fact, she goes on to say that our digestive system needs at least 12 hours without interruption from food. This is why breakfast, which really means to "break the fast" from the previous 12 hours, is the most important meal of the day.[6] Of course I know lots of people who are in a hurry or feel as though they are not awake enough and simply skip breakfast. But for the sake of our metabolism, our brains, and our body, we really need to reconsider the importance of this meal. Just as breakfast is the most important meal of the day, eating late into the evening, when our metabolism is slowing down, is the exact opposite of what our body calls for. We are best off when we eat the largest meal of the day earlier. Studies continue to show that ignoring these simple guidelines has been implicated as a factor in diabetes, heart disease, cancer, and learning and memory problems.

Eating the right kinds of calories in moderation plays a role in our overall weight and our energy level. While there certainly have been diets that have advocated eliminating or significantly reducing your intake of carbohydrates or protein, we actually need both of these, as well as certain amounts of good fat. Three helpful resources I would suggest are *40-30-30 Fat Burning Nutrition*,[7] *None of These Diseases*,[8] and *Foods That Harm, Foods That Heal*.[9]

Yes, I realize I may be messing with your habits and preferences, but I am interested in your body working at its best so that you are better able to live out your purposes, and feel better while doing it.

One other item that I feel compelled to mention is the significant role that necessary vitamins play in our health. While I realize there is at times an overload of information out there, try not to allow that to overwhelm you to the point of just not thinking about it. Granted, if you are eating the nutrient-rich foods that your body needs, you may not have much of a need for supplements. But the one vitamin that I continually read that we don't get enough of is vitamin D. Low levels of this vitamin have been determined to affect brain function, the growth of nerve cells, memory, and to contribute to Alzheimer's disease and even mortality.[10]

Don't Forget to Rest

While we spent significant time in an earlier chapter looking at the concept of Sabbath, allow me to address briefly a couple of thoughts here as well. **The Gospel writer Mark reminds us that the Sabbath was made for us to rest (see Mark 2:27). Jesus offers us the invitation to fully rest by committing our lives to Him when He says,** *"Come to me, all you who are weary and burdened, and I will give you rest"* **(Matt. 11:28).**

In discussing the Sabbath and our definitive need for rest, Erik Rees writes, "Jewish rabbis taught that it was a day to let our souls catch up with our bodies. The word *Sabbath* actually means 'to catch one's breath.'"[11]

If you are like I am, you live far too often in a state of chronic sleep deprivation. We squeeze more and more into our day; we are on our electronic devices—our phone, computer, or iPad—right up until we turn out the light at night; and then we lie awake, staring at the ceiling with our minds running a hundred miles per hour. And yet we seem surprised when we are exhausted the next morning. A silly bunch we humans are.

One recent study from the American Academy of Sleep Medicine linked adequate sleep with "improved attention, behavior, learning, mental and physical health. And insufficient sleep increases risks for obesity, diabetes, accidents, depression, and in teens, self-harm including suicide attempts."[12] While this study makes clear recommendations for children of all ages, the two categories that I want to point out here are children ages 9 to 12, who require 9-12 hours of sleep per night, and children ages 13 to 18, who need 8-10 hours per night. I make mention of these age ranges in particular because in working with parents and kids, rarely do I find children who are getting this much sleep. Then parents are puzzled as to why their kids are sleepy all the time. According to the National Sleep

Foundation, adults ages 26 to 64 function at their best when they are able to snooze 7-9 hours each night.[13]

Yes, again, I know I am messing with habits, patterns, and busy schedules. But I am fighting for your right to be rested. You deserve it, and your body and mind would agree with me. The better rested you are, the better able you are to fulfill God's purposes for your life.

While we have already discussed in an earlier section the importance of dedicating time to connecting with our Creator through "being still" and focusing on His Word, I want to mention one other benefit of spending time with Him. MRI scans have demonstrated that the time I spend in meditation can actually change the shape of the part of my brain that is in charge of memory and learning.[14] And these physical changes can alter our mood, reducing fear, anxiety, and stress.

Get up off the Couch

Now I know many are really going to dislike me as we get into this last area regarding our health, and that is the dreaded word— *exercise*. **While Paul, in his letter to Timothy, emphasizes the fact that godliness is of greater value than exercise, he does still recognize that there is benefit to physical training (see 1 Tim. 4:8).**

I remember when I would be on the treadmill and my dad would call. He would ask me what I was doing, and I would tell him that I was working out. Without fail, tongue in cheek, he would tell me how he was going to outlive me because he never exercised. His logic went like this—he would say that all people are allotted a certain number of heartbeats and when they are gone, their life is over. Because I was exercising, my heart was beating faster and I was using up my allotted beats much more quickly than he was. Now, while he was being humorous, many live their lives with an exercise (or lack thereof) philosophy that is not too far from my dad's.

We all know that we need some form of exercise other than working the remote for the television. So I am not going to spend much time trying to drive that point home. Rather, I would like to offer just a few insights as to the best ways to pursue physical fitness.

First let me say that at the dawn of time, there probably wasn't much need for treadmills and weight rooms, as tending the Garden of Eden was likely sufficient. But in this day, where we spend far too much time in cubicles or sitting in meetings, exercise becomes essential to our overall well-being. I appreciate Kent Holland's response to people's complaints that they just don't have time to exercise: "We can get more accomplished in far fewer hours when we take care of the spiritual, physical and emotional areas of our lives. Time spent tending to those areas is time well spent. It's like the busy businessman who has said, 'I'm too busy not to pray.' To that I would add that I'm too busy not to exercise at the gym."[15] And I would add to his comments that in recognizing that we all have time limitations, benefit can be gained from even ten-minute segments of exercise. This might include such things as taking the stairs instead of the elevator or walking or riding your bicycle to the store instead of driving.

Now if you subscribe to my dad's theory, then you will probably want to bring up the rare instances when some exercise guru has been found dead of a heart attack. But I would remind you that the overwhelming evidence shows that being physically fit contributes to longevity of life. For example, a study of former Olympians found that they lived from three to six years longer than the general population.[16]

Exercising for as little as two and a half hours per week can enhance sleep, prevent weight gain, reduce the risk of high blood pressure, stroke, type 2 diabetes, and even depression.[17] And while some studies report that the time of day you exercise may augment its benefits, the most important component is to find a time of day that works for you and make that time relatively consistent. Your body will adjust to accommodate.[18]

While I have mentioned exercising at a gym or on a treadmill at home, neither one of those is necessary. Finding something that you enjoy—of your choosing—can help you get started. Perhaps you find it enjoyable to bike, walk, swim, play tennis, or any number of other activities. You might find it helpful to have a friend exercise with you.

My wife is amazingly consistent in walking and being on the treadmill. So it was somewhat of a surprise when, a few months ago, we found ourselves in the ER dealing with some severe leg pain. She learned that she had "patellar tendonitis," which in her case came about because of a lack of stretching. We often think of aerobic activities when we think of huffing and puffing. However, it is important that we remember, especially as we age, that flexibility exercises are essential. "Connective tissues within ligaments and tendons become more rigid and brittle with age."[19] Pilates can be beneficial, but so can simple controlled stretches.

In addition to flexibility exercises, we also need strength training. It is not about becoming buff; it is about keeping our muscles and joints healthy. One study reported that older adults who did strength training twice a week had a 46 percent lower risk of death for any reason over those who did not.[20]

As I mentioned before, this is not a health book. Yet I would be remiss if I did not address, at least in passing, the importance of how we eat, rest, and move. If we begin to make even small changes in these areas, we will feel better and function more efficiently. And I don't know about you, but I want to fulfill my purposes here as long as God desires for me to, and I would like to do it well.

Growth and Success

Touré Roberts tells about an important lesson that he learned regarding "growth" from raising a pet turtle.[21] It seems that his turtle had remained the same size for a number of years, but then one day he noticed that the turtle was much bigger. Being puzzled by this, he consulted his friend who raised turtles. Apparently, Roberts had moved his turtle to a larger tank and, as his friend related, that was all that was needed to stimulate the turtle's growth. "What blew me away was the growth of the turtle was dependent upon the size of his environment," he exclaimed. Embedded in his account is a lesson for all of us.

On a regular basis, I hear clients talk about the fact that they want to grow in their life. They may want to increase their job skills, get a graduate degree, build their business, focus on growing spiritually, or enlarge their circle of friends. Unfortunately, they are not taking any steps to move beyond where they currently are. And if they don't, in five years they will be in the same place having the same conversations. We all know people who talk about making changes, but we know far fewer who have actually done so. Honestly, what is required is that they, like the turtle, get into a larger tank. You might ask yourself, "What box do I need to step out of in order to expand my horizons? Where is God trying to lead me that I am resisting? What comfort zone do I need to be pushed out of if I am to grow?"

I love and find confidence in the encouragement that comes from Romans 8:28: *"And we know that in all things God works for the good of those who love Him, who have been called according to His purpose."* Now don't misunderstand, thinking that the writer is saying that all things are good—because they are not. There are bad things that happen to good people. But this passage indicates that if we love God and have been called according to His purpose, He will make lemonade out of the lemons that come into our lives. He will take all of our circumstances—the loss of a job, a death in the family, a house fire, even a broken-down car—to help us be shaped and conformed in becoming more like His Son (see Rom. 8:29). I can complain and grumble about circumstances I encounter, or I can view them through a prism of "What is God doing? How is He using the events in my life to grow me? For what purpose is He placing me in a bigger tank?" It is important that I choose to view my circumstances as an opportunity for God to work, rather than simply seeing them as some awful thing happening to me again.

We have to ask ourselves, "Do I want to grow?" I am not looking for a "yes" answer because it seems like the appropriate thing to say. I want you to dig deep in asking that question. Are you willing to let God take you out of your comfort zone and grow you so that you are better prepared to live His purposes in your life? If you are, know that spiritual growth doesn't just happen around you. It requires intentionality. "You must want to grow, decide to grow, make an effort to grow, and persist in growing."[22]

~~~

Growing and being successful in that growth often requires thinking, planning, discipline, diligence, and integrity. When we embody these qualities, we certainly stack the deck in our favor. For example, think about your approach to challenging circumstances. If you are able to see them as obstacles that you can overcome, then they have the potential to make you stronger—in much the same way that the wind blowing against a tree causes its roots to grow, in turn strengthening the tree. Or think about the diligence of a steady stream of water and its effect on the rocks in its path. Some of the most amazing and beautiful canyons have been eroded and carved out by the consistent flow of water. Unfortunately, too many of us are more like a single glass of water poured on a rock. When a hole is not immediately bored into the rock, we give up, proclaiming that "I tried but it didn't work." Michael Jordan says, "I've missed more than 9,000 shots in my career. I've lost almost 300 games; 26 times I've been trusted to take the game-winning shot and missed. I failed over and over and over again in my life. And that is why I succeed."[23] Persistence is key.

Author Sue Fitzmaurice observes that there "is an extraordinary truth for those seeking to make a difference: the more positive contribution we make in our daily lives with the people around us right now the greater the contribution we will be called on to make in the lives of more and more people."[24] Jesus said it this way: *"...Well done, good and faithful servant! You have been faithful with a few things; I will put you in charge of many things..."* (Matt. 25:23).

Again, I want to remind you that your success in growing is not dependent on the uncontrollable circumstances that swirl around you in your day-to-day world. Instead, your success has everything "to do with what is going on inside of you and your connection with God, other individuals and your purpose."[25] While the battles inside your head and the discipline of setting yourself up well are critical to your effectiveness, ultimately your success rests with God and your connection to Him. This is expressed so clearly in John 15:5-8, which begins with the words, *"I am the vine; you are the branches. If a man remains in Me and I in him, he will bear much fruit; apart from Me you can do nothing"* (John 15:5).

Life Is Meant to Be Enjoyed

Have you ever wondered if it is OK to enjoy life? While that might seem to be a strange question, I have encountered individuals who wanted to have nothing to do with God because of their view that He is just a cosmic killjoy. They believe that He is just about rules of "Don't do this, and don't do that," and that He is sitting and watching people, just waiting to zap them when they make a mistake. And unfortunately, I'm afraid that they got those ideas from watching the lives of too many believers.

Over the course of my life I have encountered groups of Christians who seemed to equate fun with sin. Life was about being serious all of the time and not enjoying things. As a matter of fact, the more people deprived themselves of enjoyment, the more spiritual they were considered to be. This mind-set has ranged from the Gnosticism[26] of the first century to austere groups of people today. But I think it is important for us to examine whether or not this reflects the desires of the God of the Scriptures.

~~~

Jolee and Bailey are my two dogs that I dearly love. They are loving, playful, curious, and full of life. We live on five acres of land, and needless to say, the dogs enjoy running around the property. And run they do. They love to chase rabbits as well as run along the fence to bark at everything from people to school buses. Even when there is nothing particular to chase, they still love to run. It was one day as I watched them run that the light bulb came on for me. I enjoyed watching them run. I know that doesn't sound too profound, but my point is that I got satisfaction out of watching them enjoy doing what God had created them to do. They were born, in part, to enjoy running.

Similarly, I believe that God derives pleasure from watching us enjoy the things He created us for. You see, I don't believe that He made human life for it to be simply an endurance test of drudgery at every turn. I am convinced that He made us to be artistic, athletic, musical, loving, childlike, amazed, tender, and a host of other qualities. Just as I am pleased at my dogs' being thrilled with life, I believe God finds pleasure as He observes us enjoying life. Just look at some of the things that are mentioned by King Solomon, the wisest man to live: *"A man can do nothing better than to eat and drink and find satisfaction in his work..."* **(Eccles. 2:24).** *"Then I realized that it is good and proper for a man to eat and drink, and to find satisfaction in his toilsome labor under the sun during the few days of life God has given him—for this is his lot. Moreover, when God gives any man wealth and possessions, and enables him to enjoy them, to accept his lot and be happy in his work—this is a gift of God"* **(Eccles. 5:18-19).** *"So I commend the enjoyment of life..."* **(Eccles. 8:15).** *"Go, eat your food with gladness, and* *drink your wine with a joyful heart, for it is now that God favors what you do"* (**Eccles. 9:7**). Solomon clearly paints a picture of a God who delights in seeing us, in essence, run free on the five acres that He created us to run.

While I am a strong proponent of dreaming, planning, and diligently making the most of the opportunities for serving others that God gives us, I am also learning to enjoy life. An important component of that for me is learning to be more present in the moment. As *The God-Powered Life* points out, our existence on this earth "is not about a long life, it is about a full life. You cannot have a full life unless you are fully immersed in what you're doing right now and turning it into an opportunity to lovingly serve and know God."[27]

In the Gospel of John, Jesus talks about His desires for us. He uses words like *sheep, gatekeeper,* and being *saved* from those who wish to destroy us. And it is in that context that He says, *"…I have come that they may have life, and have it to the full"* (John 10:10). Some translations use the word *abundantly* in place of *full*. But the picture is clear—if we are willing to place ourselves in relationship with God, He will give us "life." This is not just eternal life (even though that is a critical part of it), but it is a full and rich life even now. Most of us would not want our children to hide in the house, afraid to venture out. We want them to run and play and have a blast. God also gives us life to enjoy—not in some self-indulgent, drunken, party lifestyle; but it is His desire that we would find meaning and satisfaction in our work, joy in serving people, and gladness in the things He has created for us. As our Father, He wants us to run and play and have a blast.

~~~

In order for us to know how to love others, we have to be able to love ourselves. Taking steps to care for our bodies so that they will work well and last longer, learning to trust God to grow us spiritually and to direct our steps and our successes, and relaxing into the life He designed for our enjoyment are key steps to loving ourselves and others.

Purpose Recapped

1. Two Foundational Truths—

    #1—God is, and He knows what His creation needs.

    #2—The Scriptures are God's written instructions for how to live.

2. Overarching Purpose #1—To love God with all my heart, soul, mind, and strength.

    Sub-purpose #1—To relate to my Creator by: having faith, being obedient, confessing and repenting of my sins, and worshiping God with everything in my life.

    Sub-purpose #2—To walk humbly with God by giving up control and trusting Him.

    Sub-purpose #3—To connect with God through a lifestyle of quiet—praying and listening.

3. Overarching Purpose #2—To love my neighbor.

    Sub-purpose #1—If I am married: committing myself to traveling together with my mate, being united and intimate, developing an interdependent relationship, and making the choice to truly love my spouse.

    Sub-purpose #2—If I have children: viewing my children as a blessing and an opportunity; loving my children by effectively shaping them, honoring my own parents, and empowering my children.

    Sub-purpose #3—Relating to others: relating externally—promoting justice, prohibiting gossip, and providing for the poor; relating internally—guarding my mouth, offering forgiveness, and being a peacemaker;

relating as a community; and relating with the risk of accountability.

Sub-purpose #4—To honor the Lord with my wealth by: serving God, making a difference with my energies, making a difference with my money, becoming trustworthy, and deciding my heart's focus.

4.   Overarching Purpose #3—To love yourself.

Sub-purpose #1—To relate with yourself by:
   a.   Recognizing your uniqueness.
   b.   Guarding your heart.
   c.   Being careful how you live.
   d.   Being intentional with your health.
   e.   Deciding to grow.
   f.   Enjoying life.

Chapter Eleven

What Am I Going To Do When I Grow Up?—God-Given Jobs

"My goal is to build a life I don't need a vacation from."
—ROB HILL SR.[1]

"I can't wait to get my first summer job," exclaims a teenager eager with anticipation. "I can't wait to retire from this lousy job," grumbles the burned-out worker at the end of his career. Most of us entered the work world with some level of expectation and excitement. Unfortunately, most do not end their work journey the same way.

I remember as a kid, everyone seemed interested in asking, "What do you want to do when you grow up?" Some days the answer might have ranged from "fireman" to "superhero" (actually, those may be one and the same), and on other days I was clueless. Yet somewhere between childhood and becoming an independent adult, we hopefully figure it out.

Yesterday, I was sitting in my office having this discussion with a high school senior who is more on the "I don't have a clue" end of the scale. If you have been there, then you know the anxiety and, perhaps, utter fear this can create. We worry about, "What if I'm not good at anything? How will I know where to apply? Will I make enough money to live? What if nobody ever hires me—will I be homeless and starve to death?" And, as a God follower, I might add to the list of questions: "What does God want me to do?"

When my parents were growing up, it was common for someone to get a job with a company and stay there for 30 to 40 years and then retire. Therefore, a person might feel that they had one shot at picking a career, so they had better get it right. However, in the 21st century, individuals are much more likely to have more than one job, and even different types of jobs, over the years than they are to camp out at the same desk for decades. Therefore, it is not just elementary school, high school, and college students trying to figure out what they will spend their lives doing; it is also people entering mid-life—clear up to retirees. They are all asking, "What job should I pursue?" or "What am I going to do when I grow up?"

Employees who find going to work each day complete drudgery is not uncommon. We get to Wednesday, "hump day," and we figure, "OK, I am over the hump; there are only a couple days until the weekend." Then Friday comes and we say, "TGIF!"—the day we have been living for. I recall a friend who was in a very unpleasant job for a year. He so dreaded going to work each day that when it got to Thursday, he would proclaim, "It's Friday eve," as he longed for the weekend.

Most of us have, at one time or another, worked at a job we didn't enjoy. Perhaps it was a fast food job as a teenager that we knew we needed because it was a stepping stone to better things in the future. So, we made the best of it. However, it is discouraging if you find yourself going through a string of jobs, waiting for things to get better, but they never seem to improve.

Michael Strahan, the former NFL star and morning talk show host, commented, "I was always told 'Work hard when you're young so you can enjoy it when you're older.' ...We should really be enjoying it all the way through. We shouldn't just say, "Well, let me be miserable now, and later...then I'll be happy.' You've got to learn to find the joy all the way."[2]

Working at an inner-city high school in central California in the early 90s, I came across a sign in the Career Resource Room that stated, "Find a career that you love and you will never have to work another day in your life." Reflected in that statement is the thought that if I will pursue my dreams and passions, then I will love what I do. I will enjoy it and look forward to it most days. But wait a minute—not everybody can land their dream job...or can they? Perhaps we need to reconsider what that means. Does a job's being "ideal" indicate that it pays great money, or that it is not too strenuous, or that it is just plain fun? I know lots of kids who think that if they could just get paid to play video games, life would be perfect. However, if you were to talk with a video game programmer or tester, you would find out that it is not all fun and games (pardon the pun). They still get bored and have bosses with whom they don't always get along.

How is it that you can have two people doing the same job and one loves it and one hates it? You see, it is not always about the specifics of the job or the money. Most times it is about perspective. I recall a few years ago when Pastor Jimmy Dodd went through a teaching series titled "TGIM." The idea was "Thank God it's Monday," which is certainly an alternate approach to what we are used to using. We think in terms of getting the work week over, but he spoke about looking forward to doing those things that we have been called to do. Now you might say, "Well, I have been called to be a music star in Nashville—I just haven't been discovered yet so I am working this job at Starbucks that is really beneath my talent and abilities." If that is your perspective, you are probably less than happy. But is that because Starbucks is a lousy place to work? In his book *The Starbucks Experience,* Joseph Michelli relates that one of the reasons that Starbucks is so successful is that the employees have created an inviting environment. And as one former Starbucks employee shared, it is inviting and pleasant because "the staff choose to find enjoyment in their jobs."[3] Those employees have found significance and fulfillment in providing great customer service. They have found joy in service.

You see, it is not money that brings happiness. There are many in what some might consider to be low-paying jobs who are exhilarated when they go to their jobs as truck drivers, custodians, school attendance clerks, or yes, Starbucks baristas. Having worked in the past in a high school setting, I have seen the extremes in perspective. I recall one teacher who would cross each day off her calendar, telling everyone how many days were left until she could retire. She did this for years. At the other end was Liz, who always had a smile on her face as she served people. When I asked her what caused her to look forward to her job, she replied, "I get a front row seat to some of God's best work." How cool is that! And that attitude is generational, as she passes it on. When her eight-year-old granddaughter was asked if she was doing anything special one day, her response was, "No, it's just a normal happy day." Now, I will grant you that it is easier when we are eight to have that perspective. But if we will allow God to invade our outlook, a majority of "happy days" could become the norm rather than the exception.

What Does God Want Me to Do?

So—the $64,000 question—how do I know what God wants me to do? If we are honest, we would really like to have a "burning bush" experience like Moses. Wouldn't that be cool? No need to ponder and worry about this topic. No need to take a StrengthsFinder analysis, a Myers-Briggs personality test, or a Strong Interest Inventory assessment. I simply hike up the hill, find a miraculous event—like a bush that is on fire and not being consumed—and God speaks and says, "Hey Barry, listen up, here is what I want you to do." Then it would be crystal clear! But I have to be honest, unless your name is Moses or Samuel, or one of the names of a few other select individuals to whom God gave unique direction, you are probably not going to be the recipient of a message written in the sky directly to you. So, what job are you supposed to do? Does God specify what people are to do?

~~~

While God doesn't provide us a list of all the jobs out there with an asterisk by the one He wants us to have, He does specify tasks that mankind needs to address. For example, in the very first chapter of the Bible, we are told that **we are to rule over the fish of the sea, the birds of the air, the livestock, and everything that moves on the ground (see Gen. 1:26,28); in other words, we are charged with the responsibility of managing all the animals. In verse 29 of the same chapter, God says that He has given us all the plants and trees to care for (see Gen. 1:29). He gets a little more specific when it is written that man is to work and tend to the garden so that he will have food. This is reiterated in Proverbs 12:11. Solomon also points out that** *"a righteous man cares for the needs of his animal..."* **(Prov. 12:10).**

So what do I take away from that? Are the only jobs that God intends for us to have those that involve farming, cattle ranching, zoo keeping, forestry, and the like? Not at all. Those passages are just an indication that God created everything—plants, trees, animals— everything, and He has entrusted us with His "stuff" and asks us to take care of it. With that in mind, we begin to look at all jobs, in one way or another, as caretaking or managing jobs. While that certainly includes professions like farming, it can also be careers that involve managing resources, people, or a host of other kinds of services. The possibilities are limitless, and if they are taking care of God's stuff, then they are all God-ordained jobs.

You Can Achieve Happiness in Your Work, Especially if You Don't Pursue It

You may be thinking, "Did I read that right? Shouldn't I pursue happiness so that I can get it?" While I know my statement may seem counterintuitive, I believe it to be correct. Happiness is rarely achieved by making that our focus. People strive to fill their lives with distractions to keep themselves from feeling sad. But these distractions are fleeting and leave an emptiness in the individual. Conversely, genuine happiness is not dependent on having the newest toy, nor is it on some event. It is an inner state of being, regardless of the possible chaos of circumstances swirling around us. Repeatedly I see individuals who commit their lives to serving others finding happiness and satisfaction as a resulting benefit. As one writer observed, when we allow our lives to be a conduit for God's presence in the world, we find "the secret to profound joy and ultimate fulfillment."[4]

Now some would distinguish between "happiness" and "joy." When they do so, they perhaps describe "happiness" as more momentary while they see "joy" as reflecting a deeper satisfaction that comes from allowing our existence and direction to be rooted in a relationship with God. While I don't disagree with that distinction, my point is that whether we are using the term *happiness*, *joy*, *fulfillment*, or *satisfaction*, those feelings of peace, gratification, and contentment of the soul are the result of our being anchored to our Creator and serving people. Albert Schweitzer summed it up when he said, "I don't know what your destiny will be, but one thing I know: the only ones among you who will be really happy are those who will have sought and found how to serve."[5]

You may be thinking that I have digressed from our discussion about work, jobs, and careers. But actually, I am laying an important foundation. If God's umbrella job description for us is that we take care of His "stuff," and if how we do that usually impacts people, service is a key component. It is my desire to enjoy my week as well as my weekend. If I only live for getting off work on Friday afternoon, my percentages for happiness are slim. I don't know about you, but two out of seven days is not enough for me. I much prefer to enjoy and find fulfillment in seven out of seven days. Beginning my career decision making with a view to my higher calling of service can completely shift my perspective. It injects the life and power of my Creator into my world of work. It changes everything.

Making Career Decisions

So—here we are. Maybe you are young and making choices about college and career fields. Or perhaps you have been in a job that is definitely not a fit for who you are, and you are ready to make significant changes. You understand that whatever you do, God wants you to manage His creation, and most often that entails serving. Now what?

Author and speaker Max Lucado suggests that the first thing you have to do is not "go to God with options and expect Him to choose one of your preferences. Go to Him with empty hands—no hidden agendas, no crossed fingers, nothing behind your back. Go to Him with a willingness to do whatever He says."[6] Martin Luther King Jr. urged people to view where God leads us as our calling: "If a man is called to be a street sweeper, he should sweep streets even as Michelangelo painted, or Beethoven composed music, or Shakespeare wrote poetry. He should sweep streets so well that all the hosts of heaven and earth will pause and say, 'Here lived a great street sweeper who did his job well."[7] I believe that King was making an insightful point here—all jobs are sacred.

I have fond memories of going to summer camp while in high school. The camp was located in Warda, Texas, and a number of churches from Houston, Austin, and a few other cities would send their students there. The weeks that I spent there were enriching and even life changing. One of the weeks of camp was called "Life Recruit Week." This was a special experience that was designed for those students who had made a decision to serve in some type of full-time Christian work. This might include those who felt called to be ministers, missionaries, or a number of other Christian professions. As much as I enjoyed those weeks, I look back and wonder if that created an artificial category of people that were to be viewed differently. I mean, after all, they were going to work in positions of ministry.

Now don't get me wrong, for those who believe that God's calling for them is in ministry, I applaud them. It takes a very special type of person to serve as a pastor, youth director, or overseas missionary. It is not a decision to be made lightly. But I have at times observed an "air" around this. "Oh wow, you're a pastor. I'm just a mechanic at Firestone." Just a mechanic? Really? Do we believe that God is somehow prouder or more pleased with people who have chosen to be pastors? Do they have special seats in Heaven for these individuals, kind of like the head table at a wedding? I am convinced that God is not as focused on *what job we are doing* as much as He is *how we do the job that we are in.* You see, God finds delight in the pastor who faithfully serves his congregation, the teacher who serves her students, the sales representative at the cell phone outlet or the car salesman at the dealership who serve their customers, the pet store employee who serves his animals and their owners, the social worker who serves her at-risk students, the accountant who serves his employer, the school administrator who serves her teachers and parents, the human resources worker who serves the new hires, the receptionist at the medical facility who serves their patients, the artist or musician who creates in a manner that serves and honors both God and people, and the street sweeper who serves us all. Whatever God has called you to do—it is important, it is honorable, and He is pleased when you do it well. As the renowned Scottish athlete and Olympic runner Eric Liddell exclaimed, "God made me fast, and when I run, I feel His pleasure."[8]

I find encouragement in the words, *"Ask and it will be given to you; seek and you will find; knock and the door will be opened to you"* **(Matt. 7:7).** I believe that when we ask, seek, and knock, God opens the doors of opportunity for us. He offers us wisdom, if we will embrace it, to help us make decisions, to help us sort through the possibilities. He uses circumstances in our decision-making process to shape and mature us. But the Bible does not tell us what job we should take. While it would be nice if it were that simple, we would not grow and trust nearly as well. But, as Garry Friesen acknowledges, God's Word does teach us "how to come to a decision that is acceptable to God. It is from Scripture that we learn the necessity of determining those choices that are both moral and wise."[9] He elaborates: "With the wisdom view, the believer may confidently apply common sense to every single decision....The only time common sense is to be set aside is when it contradicts God's revealed (moral) will."[10]

~~~

So, again we ask ourselves, "How do I know what job or career I should pursue?" I would suggest that the following factors are worthy of consideration in your decision making process: 1) priorities that you glean from the Scriptures (the things that convict and convince your heart that you deem most important to give your attention to); 2) your areas of giftedness and abilities (the things that you are naturally good at and that you have, or are willing, to develop); and 3) your circumstances (this might include everything from where you live to available time, finances, family needs, and a host of other considerations). Now, please don't think that as I list these factors, I am excluding the power and work of the Living God. He can do with you whatever He desires. He is not limited by your lack of ability or your complex circumstances. At this same time, I see that He works through those very factors in people's lives. I appreciate the words of Bruce Waltke on this subject:

> The common idea of divining God's will is either a pagan notion that we Christians need to let go of or a mode of administration that God no longer uses. God has given us a program of guidance that involves getting to know Him through His Word and letting Him share our character, our hearts, and our desires. Then as we know the mind of God we can live out His will. He expects us to first draw close to Him, then allows for seeking wise counsel as confirmation, or taking our circumstances into consideration and using our own sound judgment to make a decision. He never calls us in the New Testament to "seek His will," but to seek His kingdom and do His will.[11]

~~~

Whether you are a young person making initial career decisions or a more seasoned adult wanting to chart a different vocational path, I want to offer four general steps to assist you in your journey.

1. Ask Questions

Ask yourself some of the following questions to stimulate your thinking and focus your passions: What drives you? Where do your dreams or interests drift toward? When you were a child, what did you enjoy doing and thinking about? What motivates you? Who do you care about? Has anyone told you that you clearly have a particular gift? What captivates your attention? What needs do you hope to meet? What activity have you engaged in, in the past or present, which caused you to lose track of time? If you had unlimited funds to develop a project that would make the world a better place for humanity, what would that project be?

As you ponder your answers to these questions, realize that throughout your life you have found things that you naturally loved to do and that you gravitated toward. You may feel that there are some things that are crucial to you that you can't live without. And conversely, there are other things that you absolutely wouldn't miss. You might recall being given certain opportunities that triggered an eager anticipation, while others were like pulling teeth. Remember that the God of the universe has designed you and knows everything about you. Wouldn't it make sense that He would place in you the desires to use the gifts, abilities, and longings He has given you? In the words of Bob Shank, "When something so moves your heart and demands your energy that you would do anything to make it happen, you're onto your passion."[12]

2. Seek Wise Counsel

Once you have considered your priorities, abilities, and circumstances and have spent time deeply pondering (thinking and praying through) the questions above, it is time to seek wise counsel. Spend time with trusted individuals who know you in a variety of settings. This could be friends, bosses, parents, church leaders, and even work colleagues. You might talk with them about the particular questions above with which you have been grappling. Share with them your thoughts and feelings as well as where your decisions are leaning. Invite their input into the process as an objective outsider who has observed how you interact with people and your environment. Listen to their wise counsel as a part of your process.

3. Test Drive Your Plan

Like any good problem-solving model might suggest, you need to make and try out your decision. This might involve job shadowing someone who works in your career field of interest in order to gain a clearer perspective on the various aspects of the job, particularly those components that may not be quite so attractive from the outside. It might entail enrolling in a college or vocational training course to see if it stokes or dampens your perceived passion. If I am searching for a new car, I will read about the various makes and models in *Consumer Reports*, I will watch them on the road, and I will see them up close in the showroom. But before I buy it, at some point I am going to get in it and drive it to see if it is really the car that I think it is and the car that I want. My next step in the career process is similar. This is the time to move from talking about it to trying it.

4. Do Something Every Day

After the decision is made as to the direction of your pursuit, follow-through is essential. This begins by directing your daily focus toward that decision. Now granted, if you have determined that you are a talented poet and your desire is to write poetry that will touch and move people to grow and care about others and the world in which they live, but your current job is making burritos as Taco Bell, there is some incongruence. But you can begin to move in a new direction. Sure, you still need to earn money at your job while you plan your college path. But you can continue to serve the needs of your customers in a God-honoring manner while in your off time you are applying to colleges and working on your craft. If you are a poet or writer, I would urge you to write a little each day. I have a colleague who is an author who makes it a point to carve out time to write at least 500 words every day.

Or maybe your passion is in the medical profession. So you might find a time each week when you can volunteer at a hospital, where needs are enormous. If your goal is to become a teacher, schools would welcome assistance in overcrowded classrooms. Perhaps your talents and passions are musical, so as a guitarist you spend time every day practicing. Whatever your area of interest, it is important to do something every day that will hone your craft and feed the fire of your longings.

Trust God with Your Desires

I am sometimes surprised that people don't trust God with their deepest longings. Remember when I said earlier that some have the idea that God is a giant killjoy? Well, along those same lines, some fear that if they are honest with God about the endeavors they wish to pursue, then He will stop them in their tracks and not allow them to have it. As flawed and broken people, we know that we don't deserve anything but death. Therefore, we conclude that God knows this as well so He won't let us have what we want. But how contrary that is to Scripture! Listen to King David's words from Psalms 37:4: *"Delight yourself in the Lord and He will give you the desires of your heart."* In other words, if we will trust Him, find our fulfillment in loving Him and loving people, He graciously will allow us what we desire. How can that be? It seems so simple. We are certainly willing to get the desires of our heart, but it is the "delighting" in Him out of which we opt. Putting Him first and seeking the life He longs to give us involves giving Him control. We talked at length about control in an earlier chapter. We are so resistant to giving up control and depending on Him that we leave ourselves in a position to miss out on the filling of the "desires of our heart."

Oh what foolish creatures we can be! God is not nearly as concerned about the job that we have or the conditions in which we live as He is the focus and attitude of our heart. And if our heart is determined to live as He has purposed us, the desires of our heart are waiting. The fourth century theologian, St. Augustine, phrased it this way: "Love God and do as you please."[13] Television commercials today promise everything from having the perfect body to driving the best car. But of course you want the most competitive price. No problem—the ads promise that you can have it all. Now, if you have watched enough of these commercials, you know how bogus this is—you cannot have it all. Yet, there is a word used in the Hebrew language for representing the presence of God in your life that means "the all." "When you feel you have all, you feel satisfied, full."[14] When you feel that, it is indeed a godly experience.

Purpose Recapped

1. Two Foundational Truths—

    #1—God is, and He knows what His creation needs.

    #2—The Scriptures are God's written instructions for how to live.

2. Overarching Purpose #1—To love God with all my heart, soul, mind, and strength.

    Sub-purpose #1—To relate to my Creator by: having faith, being obedient, confessing and repenting of my sins, and worshiping God with everything in my life.

    Sub-purpose #2—To walk humbly with God by giving up control and trusting Him.

    Sub-purpose #3—To connect with God through a lifestyle of quiet—praying and listening.

3. Overarching Purpose #2—To love my neighbor.

    Sub-purpose #1—If I am married: committing myself to traveling together with my mate, being united and intimate, developing an interdependent relationship, and making the choice to truly love my spouse.

    Sub-purpose #2—If I have children: viewing my children as a blessing and an opportunity; loving my children by effectively shaping them, by honoring my own parents, and by empowering my children.

    Sub-purpose #3—Relating to others: relating externally—promoting justice, prohibiting gossip, and providing for the poor; relating internally—guarding my mouth, offering forgiveness, and being a peacemaker; relating as a community; and relating with the risk of accountability.

Sub-purpose #4—To honor the Lord with my wealth by: serving God, making a difference with my energies and with my money, becoming trustworthy, and deciding my heart's focus.

4. Overarching Purpose #3—To love yourself.

   Sub-purpose #1—To relate with yourself by:
   a. Recognizing your uniqueness.
   b. Guarding your heart.
   c. Being careful how you live.
   d. Being intentional with your health.
   e. Deciding to grow.
   f. Enjoying life.
   g. Achieving happiness in your work by making God-led career decisions.
   h. Trusting God with your desires.

Chapter Twelve

Finally...What Should I Do?—Decision Making Beyond the Known

"God has a plan for your life. The enemy has a plan for your life. Be ready for both. Be wise enough to know which one to battle and which one to embrace."
—UNKNOWN

"What is God's will for my life?" "What college should I attend?" "Where am I supposed to live?" "Whom should I marry?" "Should I buy this house or the other one?" "Help—I don't know what I am supposed to be doing!" These statements, and others like them, are common as people seek direction in life (which has been pretty much everyone).

Life is loaded with choices—lots of them. We may find the magnitude of them to be both confusing and overwhelming. As we attempt to navigate it all, in exasperation we might finally scream, "Someone just tell me what to do!" And for God followers, we would like that "someone" to be God. We want Him to reveal to us His purpose for our lives and His will in all of our decisions. In our quest to unravel the "mysterious will of God," we have seen throughout this book that "God's purposes" are anything but mysterious. God has been pretty clear in teaching us His purposes because He wants us to understand them. *"Be very careful, then, how you live—not as unwise but as wise, making the most of every opportunity, because the days are evil. Therefore do not be foolish, but understand what the Lord's will is"* (**Eph. 5:15-17**). You see, God has never told us in Scripture to go find "God's will," but, as we see here, He does want us to understand His will.

Some approach God's will as fatalists: "Whatever happens, happens." Whether a person is fired from a job, a child is killed by a drunk driver, a husband cheats on his spouse, or a person's unhealthy eating habits lead to diabetes, they say, "Well, that must be God's will." Leslie Weatherhead relates this insightfully:

> Somebody once asked me, when a baby had fallen out of a fifth-story window, whether its death was the will of God. The question shows how important it is that we should get our thinking straight, for the answer is both Yes and No. Yes, it is God's circumstantial will. I mean there that it is God's will that the law of gravity should operate. It is God's will that a baby is made of flesh and blood; and if a baby hits a concrete pavement after falling from such a height, of course it is God's will that the little body should be broken—otherwise God would have

made babies' bodies of something like India rubber. Yet we feel that we must answer the question by an emphatic No and say that the death of the baby was not the will of God, for it was not the will of God that it should be allowed to fall out of the window at all.[1]

Clearly not everything that happens in this life is God's will. Yet there is nothing that can defeat God's ultimate will.

Various authors and theologians refer to different aspects of God's will with a variety of labels—God's "sovereign will," "moral will," "circumstantial will," and, of course, what we tend to perseverate on, His "individual will." We want to know His specific purposes for "me." If we are honest, the thought of studying the Scriptures to learn His purposes does not thrill most of us. We would much prefer Him to leave us a note under our pillow that would spell out "His will for my life." As a matter of fact, we would really appreciate it if He would just write out a plan in detail that would tell us everything in sequence that we are to do—where to go to school, whom to marry, how many kids to have, what job to take, when to retire, and so on. Now of course, as we read those words, we recognize that they sound a bit silly—but we still want them.

As a parent, we want our children to grow into healthy, independent, self-supportive adults. Can you imagine if at age 12 we handed our son or daughter a document that specified step by step what they were to do in life? Of course not. The reality is that a wise parent teaches their child basic life concepts. They teach them right from wrong and the difference in wise versus foolish decisions. The parent endeavors to give their child the tools that prepare them to make good decisions. They don't make the decisions for them. Similarly, God provides for us what we need to address the opportunities and adversities of life. He wants us to know His purposes and how to go about making decisions that assist us in fulfilling our role in His story. I would contend that the individual who invests great time and energy searching for answers to every detail of his individual life in Scripture will be frustrated and disillusioned.

And yet, I have heard people explain decisions they have made using such statements as "I know that God directed me to go to college here," "We prayed and felt that God was telling us to get married," or as one individual related to me years ago, "I knew that this was the house God wanted me to buy because it had more trees on the property." As Charles Swindoll writes, "How many times have you heard someone say, 'The Lord told me to do so and so'? I confess to you, in my unguarded moments I want to ask, 'Was his voice a baritone or a bass? You're telling me you heard His voice?' Of course when people say they have actually heard God's voice, I get even more spooked!"[2]

I apologize if I seem flippant here. That is not my intention. I am in no way discounting the leading of the Holy Spirit or God's ability to move powerfully in an individual's life. I am simply suggesting that just because I may attribute something that happens to God's doing doesn't necessarily make it so. We have seen how that has played out in everything from the 11th-century Crusades to the Salem witch trials of the late 1600s. In history, more often than we care to remember, God has been blamed for events and decisions that He had nothing to do with. I am simply urging caution in this area.

Learning and embracing God's purposes for our lives is not to be taken lightly. As the Ephesians 5 passage in the beginning of this chapter instructs, God's will is serious stuff. **Therefore, we are to carefully and wisely take advantage of every opportunity God gives us to understand His will.** And what a relief it is to realize that we don't have to decode, discover, or decipher His will. We simply have to understand it. He makes it clear to us, and in doing so, He gives us the wisdom and guidance that we need to make future decisions.

How Can I See Where I Am Going?

"Your word is a lamp to my feet and a light for my path" **(Ps. 119:105)**. *"Trust in the Lord with all your heart and lean not on your own understanding; in all your ways acknowledge Him, and He will make your paths straight"* **(Prov. 3:5-6)**. I believe that these are some of the most comforting words in all of the Bible because they tell me, most assuredly, that I am not left on my own with the task of "cracking the code" to God's will.

As kids, we used to go outside and play at night. Whether it was "hide and seek," looking for bugs, or we were just trying to sneak up and scare each other, we enjoyed the games. Sometimes, in an effort to elude each other, we would run down a dark path, only to be smacked in the face with a tree branch. However, if you were lucky enough to have a flashlight, you were able to run faster and farther because you could see where you were going. The psalmist, in the passage above, calms us with those words that bolster us as we are running the dark paths of life, wondering where to turn and not get smacked down (see Ps. 119:105). God's Word brings light and clarity to our journey. King Solomon adds to that thought when he says that trusting God on our path, rather than our own limited insight, will allow Him to make our paths straight (see Prov. 3:5-6).

Going back to my story of playing in the dark—if I am heading down a path that I can barely make out with very limited starlight and my friend, who is ahead of me, calls out and says, "Turn left right here; there is a clear path," but I can't see a thing, what do I do? Keep going my own direction for the simple reason that I can see a couple of feet in front of me, or trust that the one ahead of me has found a better marked path? God is saying, "Listen, if you will trust Me, I will light your path and make it easier to follow." Yet so often we stay on our own course. We figure that even though we can only see a little ways in front of us, it is better than nothing. We discount the fact that our Creator sees the entire road—from the beginning to the end. If we will seek Him and allow Him to light and direct our path, we will find much greater clarity. God's Word is an indispensable light.

Sometimes decisions seem easy—"Should I get a job or go hungry?" But other times they are not so simple—"You have a good job in Southern California, but you're tired of the smog and the traffic-clogged commute. A company in Colorado offers you a similar position at the same income level. Should you move or stay where you are? A number of factors will enter into your decision, but you will not find the answer directly stated in the Scriptures. If you think you do, you're getting weird."[3]

We have determined that while the Bible does not tell us what to do in every situation, it does instruct us how to come to decisions that are acceptable and pleasing to God. We learn from the Scriptures the parameters that lead to decisions that are both moral and wise. But for the Scriptures to be of use, we have to apply them. Are you willing to do that? This is a critical question. If I apply the light of God's moral will and the wisdom of His written Word to my decision, and within that context the decision becomes clear, am I willing to do it? The truth of the matter is that the real problem for many of us is not so much a lack of knowledge as it is a reluctance to follow God in the direction we believe He is leading us. When I find myself at this point, I have to look deep within and ask a truly soul-searching question: "Do I really want God's direction, or do I simply want Him to sanction what already I want to do?"

Jumping back again to playing outside at night, when I use my flashlight on the trail or path, I do so to see what is there. If in doing so I see a large boulder in front of me, I will hopefully stop. Otherwise I will run smack dab into it, and the consequences could range from bruises to broken bones. Now I can already hear my mother as my friends carry me back to my house: "What happened?"

"Well, I ran into a boulder."

"You should have used your flashlight."

"Well, um, I did."

"Didn't you see the boulder?"

"Uh, yeah."

"Then why didn't you stop?"

"Because I didn't want it to be there?"

Now at that point, she probably would drive me to the emergency room convinced that my brains are scrambled—because my response didn't make good sense. Yet so many of us proceed in life in much the same manner.

As I seek God's direction, allowing His Word to illuminate my path, He will open and close doors. If I am not paying attention, I may miss the open doors that He gives me. At the same time, I may be determined to go through one that He has clearly closed. When I do that, I can get pretty skinned up. For example, using the wisdom of Scripture, I know that it is foolish for me as a believer to marry someone who doesn't share my faith in the God of the universe. If I know the warning that the Bible gives in this regard and choose to ignore it, God will not stop me. He has given us free will. But when my marriage begins to come unhinged because we are not on the same path of pursuing the Living God, there shouldn't be a lot of surprise. I have run into a boulder, and I will get hurt. Was it avoidable? Absolutely! Did God's Word provide light for my path? Without a doubt. But if I am not willing to listen, if I am not willing to be obedient, I might as well have continued down the dark path without the flashlight. Whether I run into the boulder because it is dark and I didn't see it or I run into it even though I clearly spotted it with my flashlight but ignored it—the results are the same. God's Word will provide a floodlight on my path. It is up to me whether or not I will choose to allow that to guide my decisions.

~~~

King Solomon is often referred to as the "wisest man" to ever live. And this label comes with good reason. When Solomon followed his father, David, as king of Israel, God told Solomon to ask Him for whatever he wanted. Solomon could readily see that his father had been a great king and that he himself had inherited a great responsibility in leading the nation of Israel, a people he referred to *"as numerous as the dust of the earth"* (2 Chron. 1:9). His response to God is recorded in Second Chronicles 1:10: *"Give me wisdom and knowledge, that I may lead this people, for who is able to govern this great people of Yours?"* Solomon sought the best from God in order to be a worthy king. And notice God's response: *"Since this is your heart's desire and you have not asked for wealth, riches or honor, nor for the death of your enemies, and since you have not asked for a long life but for wisdom and knowledge to govern My people over whom I have made you king, therefore wisdom and knowledge will be given you. And I will also give you wealth, riches, honor, such as no king who was before you ever had and none after you will have"* (2 Chron. 1:11-12).

We repeatedly see throughout Scripture that our purposes are best served when our attention is focused on things that truly matter. Notice Solomon's advice to women: *"Charm is deceptive, and beauty is fleeting; but a woman who fears the Lord is to be praised"* **(Prov. 31:30)**. In other words, it is not the glamorous movie star with the air-brushed makeup and slim figure that should garner our attention. Oh, I know it is what our culture may be drawn to, but God values the person whose priority is a right relationship with Him. This is the one who should be praised. God's Word is a lamp and a light. It enables us to see what is important and to avoid stumbling.

I recently had breakfast with my friend Paul who is a marathon runner. Now, I should explain that while running 26.2 miles is an enormous feat, Paul also has run the Pikes Peak Marathon—not once, but 18 times. Keep in mind that this is 26.2 miles that begins at approximately 7,000-feet elevation and climbs to over 14,000 feet before returning back down. Hundreds of people are a part of this race, with elite runners coming from all over the country. Paul related to me how 12 years ago when he reached the top of the mountain (the halfway point), he was running eleventh. Now I should point out that this is not some paved trail but is a hiking trail with all the perils one would expect—rocks, tree roots, sharp drop-offs, and so on. As he started his decent, just for a moment, something caught his attention, and he took his eyes off the trail. The next thing he knew he had tripped over a root and fallen, breaking a tooth and getting banged up pretty good. While he completed the race, he did not finish anywhere near the top. That accident occurred all because he allowed himself to be distracted, even for a moment.

In his letter to the church at Philippi, Paul (the disciple of Jesus, not the marathon runner) encouraged the people to keep their attention focused on the trail—the things that mattered. He writes, *"Finally, brothers, whatever is true, whatever is noble, whatever is pure, whatever is lovely, whatever is admirable—if anything is excellent or praiseworthy—think about such things"* **(Phil. 4:8).** When we do that, we run much better toward God's purposes for us, making the decisions that will honor God and bring us fulfillment.

~~~

How we focus our attention is critical. If we find ourselves in a perplexing situation, we have choices. Up to now, your view of God may have been that He is sort of a magic genie in a lamp. While I doubt that you looked for a lamp on a beach to rub, hoping that your genie god would pop out and grant your wishes, your efforts may not have been that far off. Some people's method of discerning God's will is to close their eyes, flip open their Bible, and blindly drop their finger on a page, concluding that wherever it lands, this is God's word for them. Others want to give God an "either/or" test. For example, "I don't know whether I should ask Janet to go out with me. So, God, I will walk by her house, and if she is standing out by her mailbox, I will take that as Your sign that You want me to ask her out." It is almost like we give God the kind of "forced answer" test we have taken in school.

As God followers, many have thought this method to be a good one because it worked for Gideon. During the time that various judges ruled the nation of Israel, Gideon was called upon to serve in this capacity. At one point, when several nations had gathered to do battle with Israel, Gideon was afraid. God had told him that He would be with him and give him victory, but Gideon wanted a sign from God. He told God that he would put a wool fleece outside and if the next morning the fleece was wet with dew, but the ground around it was dry, then he would know that God would be with them. God did exactly what Gideon requested. While that should have assured Gideon of God's ability to take care of him, instead he came back, still afraid, and ask for one more sign. This time he would put the fleece out and if the next morning the ground was wet with dew but the fleece was dry, then Gideon would believe that God would take care of him. Once again, God gave him the sign (see Judg. 6:36-40).

Gideon's circumstances were unique and a rare instance of God giving that type of obviously clear sign. Oh sure, if we could all have our "fleeces" that we could just put out with a clear "dew or no dew" sign, it would seem so easy. But it would also rob us of our dependence on, and our relationship with, our Maker. As one writer points out, "'laying out a fleece' is generally the lazy man's way to discern the will of God."[4]

While God can and will speak to us through whatever means He chooses, using Him like a Magic 8-Ball or a genie, with arbitrary "fleeces" that we put out, can often lead to disastrous consequences. While wise counsel is valuable in the discernment process, sometimes we are guilty of seeking the input of others for their approval rather than their candor.

So, we come back to the notion that God's purposes are clearly knowable, and the nuances of those purposes in our lives become more evident the closer we draw to Him. And the more we rely on His Word, the brighter is the light on our particular path. We also have to remind ourselves that God is not driven or restricted by our calendars and clocks. Rather than patiently waiting on God to lead, we are tempted to lurch on ahead without Him. While there is no question that God wants to lead us, bless us, provide us with opportunities, and give us good things, He sometimes has to wait for us to grow up.

If you have grown children, remember when you may have given them their first car. Whether it was at 16, 18, or 21, it was a "rite of passage" kind of experience about which they were thrilled. You, of course, wanted them to have the necessary driving skills as well as some solid successful experiences before you entrusted them with a car. But if your children were anything like I was as a kid, they would have taken the car at age 10 if they could have. By the time they were old enough to drive, they may have been bugging you daily to let them get their license and have the car. Because children mature differently, some may be ready to drive responsibly at 16, while others, some spouses would attest, should never be behind a wheel.

Just as we have to wait, as much as we may hate it, to be given the privilege of driving, we also sometimes have to wait to receive God's opportunities. I honestly believe that most often when I am having to "wait" on God, it is because He is telling me to "grow up." Perhaps I need to grow some spiritual depth before I will be ready for His blessing. Just because I want blessings and clear-cut opportunities *today* is not an indication that I am ready to receive them. We will be much better served when we realize that "the investment in our preparation determines the quality of our performance."[5]

Principles of Decision Making

In our journey deeper and deeper into purpose, we are repeatedly learning that the more connected we are to our Creator—through His Word, through the leading of His Holy Spirit, and through our intimate relationships with other believers—the more freedom and insight we gain. God has given us clear guidelines with regard to His moral will, and within that moral will we have a great deal of latitude in making decisions. But even though we have lots of discretion, we want to be careful to make the most of life's opportunities. So let's examine some helpful steps toward making decisions beyond what we know.

Author Garry Friesen suggests that asking the right questions as we face a decision is essential. He states that several good ones are suggested by Paul's discussion in First Corinthians 10:23–11:1:

- Is there anything wrong with this activity? Is it lawful? (10:23)

- Is it profitable? (10:23)

- Is it edifying? (10:23)

- Is it self-serving at the expense of someone else's benefit? (10:33; Romans 15:1-2)

- Is this something I can thank God for? (10:30; Romans 14:6)

- Is this something that will glorify God? (10:31)

- Is this worth imitating? (11:1)

- Is this following the example of Christ? (11:1; Romans 15:7-8)[6]

One question that I might add to this list is, "What desire has God placed on your heart?" As the prophet Nehemiah embarked on the task of rebuilding Jerusalem, he identified the fact that God had placed it upon his heart to do this. I firmly believe that God can place desires in our heart that He then works through.

As I have indicated before, I don't believe that God has just one possibility for each of us: one job, one person picked to be our mate, one possible geographic region to live in, and so on. I am convinced there are a variety of options that can all be found within the will of God. It is for this very reason that He has given us capable brains with which to navigate decisions, and He expects us to use them. Deciding whether to eat a Big Mac at McDonald's or a Whopper at Burger King probably doesn't make much difference (of course either one may have a negative impact on your weight loss goals). But endeavoring to settle on a career path or make a spouse selection requires us to use those brain cells with which God has provided us. Sometimes we find ourselves faced with two wonderful choices, challenging us to choose the "better" over the "good." I heard it once said that we have to be able to recognize the difference between a "good idea" and a "God idea." While God may be pleased with either choice if it fits in His moral will, He still knows us intimately—how we are wired individually—and therefore He knows which choice might be a better fit for us. A Native American proverb reminds us that "If you chase two rabbits, you will lose them both."[7] We strive to choose the best.

Once you have asked yourself the introspective questions mentioned above and you have begun to sort through "good" and "better" choices, I encourage you to consider the following steps:

1. As you encounter His Word, ponder what priorities jump off the pages of Scripture at you.

2. As you meditate on His truths, listen carefully to the nudgings of the Holy Spirit.

3. Seek counsel and input from individuals who are older and more mature and who have nothing to gain or lose from your decision.

4. Remember to take into account your heartfelt desires.

5. Pay attention to the circumstances that may impact your decision or the circumstances that are impacted by your decision.

6. Carefully sort through impressions and emotions. It is essential that you realize your feelings can come from a multitude of sources: God, satan, past experiences, stress, insomnia, indigestion, and a host of other things. Learn to recognize and sort out the different emotions. When your emotions confirm what the rest of your decision-making process has told you, you can move forward with greater confidence. When your rational thoughts and your feelings are in conflict, step ever so carefully. It is critical that you remember that just because you feel something strongly doesn't make it true. You may become frightened if you mistake a garden hose on the ground for a snake. While you may be petrified, your fear does not change the truth and turn the hose into a snake.

7. Use your God-given common sense and sound judgment.

8. Rather than be in a hurry, wait for God's peace. **Colossians 3:15 reads,** *"Let the peace of Christ rule in your hearts..."* The word that is used for "rule" actually means "to arbitrate like an umpire."[8] Just as a baseball umpire might decide whether a runner is safe or out at first base, you can rely on God's peace to help you "make the call," in conjunction with all of the other steps, as you are faced with decisions.

Purpose Recapped

1. Two Foundational Truths—

    #1—God is, and He knows what His creation needs.

    #2—The Scriptures are God's written instructions for how to live.

2. Overarching Purpose #1—To love God with all my heart, soul, mind, and strength.

    Sub-purpose #1—To relate to my Creator by: having faith, being obedient, confessing and repenting of my sins, and worshiping God with everything in my life.

    Sub-purpose #2—To walk humbly with God by giving up control and trusting Him.

    Sub-purpose #3—To connect with God through a lifestyle of quiet—praying and listening.

3. Overarching Purpose #2—To love my neighbor.

    Sub-purpose #1—If I am married: committing myself to traveling together with my mate, being united and intimate, developing an interdependent relationship, and making the choice to truly love my spouse.

    Sub-purpose #2—If I have children: viewing my children as a blessing and an opportunity; loving my children by effectively shaping them, by honoring my own parents, and by empowering my children.

    Sub-purpose #3—Relating to others: relating externally—promoting justice, prohibiting gossip, and providing for the poor; relating internally—guarding my mouth, offering forgiveness, and being a peacemaker; relating as a community; and relating with the risk of accountability.

Sub-purpose #4—To honor the Lord with my wealth by: serving God, making a difference with my energies and with my money, becoming trustworthy, and deciding my heart's focus.

4.   Overarching Purpose #3—To love yourself.

Sub-purpose #1—To relate with yourself by: recognizing your uniqueness, guarding your heart, and taking care in how you live—including attending to your health, growing, enjoying life, finding fulfillment in work, and trusting God with your desires.

Sub-purpose #2—To make decisions for yourself by:
   a.   Learning to listen and understand God's will.
   b.   Allowing His Word to illuminate your decisions.
   c.   Utilizing wise decision-making principles.

Chapter Thirteen

Let's Go to Wally World— Retirement (Legacy)

"This is the true joy of life, the being used up for a purpose recognized by yourself as a mighty one; being a force of nature instead of a feverish, selfish little clod of ailments and grievances, complaining that the world will not devote itself to making you happy."
—GEORGE BERNARD SHAW[1]

"Retirement!" To read that word conjures up all kinds of thoughts in individuals' imaginations. Perhaps you picture lying on some isolated beach soaking up the sun while an attendant brings you drinks with little umbrellas in them. Or maybe you dream of sleeping until noon every day. Others long to travel and see the sights other locations have to offer. But there are others who look forward to their work and aren't as anxious to retire. You might be thinking, "What kind of weirdos are those people?"

Elena Griffing is just such a person. In 2016, she celebrated 70 years of working at the same San Francisco Bay Area hospital and had no plans to retire. She recently turned 90 and has enjoyed working in a variety of positions at the hospital over the decades. She was quoted as saying, "I can't wait to come to work every day, this is my hospital. I enjoy anything I can do to be of service. Truly, it's the patient that counts. If it's helping someone, it's my bag."[2]

Individuals like Elena have always resonated with me, and I think it is because she operates counter to our American idea of retirement, even perhaps in a manner that is more biblical. As strange as this may sound, I am just not sure that Scripture promotes the concept of "retirement" quite the way that we tend to think about it. I have difficulty finding leaders recorded in the Bible who worked until 62 (or until they were in their 50s if they took early retirement) and then hung up their hats. Take Moses for example; he was tending flocks when God called him and his brother to lead the children of Israel out of Egypt. When he began his new assignment, he was 80 years old, and his brother Aaron was 83 (see Exod. 7:7). Not exactly spring chickens. Joshua, who followed Moses as the nation's leader, appears to have served nearly up to the time of his death, which was at 110 years of age (see Josh. 24:29). And John, the writer of the Book of Revelation, was approximately 92 years old when he completed penning this profound work.[3]

The award-winning actor Anthony Hopkins turned 79 in 2016. When asked in an interview if he ever thinks about retiring, he responded, "No! Once you retire, it's over. My agent calls me: 'Would you like to do this? Would you like to [do] that?' 'Yea, OK.' I'm happy to be working, and I enjoy it. It keeps my brain active, and I enjoy the life."[4]

Celebrating his ninetieth birthday, Byrd Collins Curtis from Ft. Collins, Colorado, begins every day at 7:00 A.M. in the gym.[5] Whether on the track or working out with the weights, Byrd has discovered over the years that his time in the gym keeps him physically fit and, in turn, mentally alert. He may be 90, but he is certainly not done with living.

There have been many noteworthy individuals who were not subscribing to the "time to hang it up" theory as they aged. Benjamin Franklin invented bifocals at 78; Pablo Picasso was producing drawings and engravings at age 90; at 101 Grandma Moses created her most famous work; Albert Schweitzer built a hospital in Africa and oversaw it until he was 89; Michelangelo drafted architectural plans for the Basilica of St. Mary of the Angels and the Martyrs when he was 88; at age 85, Johann Sebastian Bach composed some of his best music; and Arthur Rubinstein gave one of his greatest recitals in Carnegie Hall at 89. Consider what the world would have been deprived of had these individuals given up their pursuits at 62. I can't help but wonder if retirement, as we tend to think of it, isn't a shortsighted goal?

Now, I certainly understand that everyone is not able to jog around a track in their later years. For some, aging-related health concerns can indeed be limiting—even downright devastating. But I have seen far too many people who retire from their jobs and, in doing so, seem to retire from life. Their job ends, and unfortunately their purpose appears to end as well. And with that, as Bob Shank states, many men and women who are otherwise healthy die off in large numbers because "they simply don't have a big enough reason to live."[6]

Too many individuals have retired from their vocation, rolled up their life, stuffed it into an RV, and have proceeded to "leave it all behind," spending the rest of their lives focused on themselves. My fear is that once I make that choice, my usefulness is done. Now please understand that I have nothing against RVs or traveling and seeing life. In fact, I am a whole-hearted advocate of vacationing, relaxing, and recharging one's batteries. But there is a significant difference between renewing myself so that I am able to come back and serve people and vacationing as a way of life, which serves me.

It is not uncommon for retirees to struggle with self-image once they no longer have their work status to give them purpose. But again, this is easily rectified if we have found our meaning in a God who is much bigger than our career. Unfortunately, without an understanding of why God has put us here, there are too many people who die at 30 but aren't buried until they are 70 or 80. It is such a needless waste to live out one's life with meaningless years.

As our bodies grow older, they don't move as quickly as they once did. But there is a difference between "slow down" and "stop." It is essential that we know our best days are ahead. We bring into our "winter" years a plethora of "summer" experiences.

There are times, following a Saturday of working in the yard, when my body hurts. I will comment to my wife, "I am really sore, but I'm not sure why." She will respond with something like, "Well, you did a bunch of work outside today." In denial, I make some profound comment such as, "Yeah, but I didn't feel this way when I was 25." Then, ever so gently and wisely, she will say, "That's true, but you're not 25 anymore." While I know that glaring fact, my mind still thinks like it is 25 (most days).

Would I like for my body to function with greater ease like it did when I was younger? Certainly. Would I want to go back and be 25 again? Absolutely not! While I could do without the aches and pains and creaking bones in the morning when I get up, I wouldn't trade my place in life with all of its experiences. As I live and work in what I would consider the "autumn" of my life, it is the experiences and successes from the "summer" years that allow me influence in this current season. I did not have that at 25. Living in the first half of my 60s is the best place that I have been—and there is still better to come.

~~~

Our culture is preoccupied with recapturing our youth. Youth is treasured, and age is something to be feared. All you have to do is observe the focus of television commercials and magazine ads. And yet, that pursuit leaves us looking silly.

Former presidents Ulysses S. Grant (in 1876) and Theodore Roosevelt (in 1912) attempted to come back and recapture their glory years in the White House. Both their attempts were unsuccessful.[7] While they should have been basking in their presidential contributions and embracing their next stage of life, they instead were grasping for an earlier season. If we will take the skills that we have mastered during our summer years into our autumn years, embracing the new season and its challenges, we can experience some of our greatest fulfillments.

Author Damien Wills shares his experiences from working in a senior citizens home when he was younger. He observed that about half of the residents rejected the fact that they were in the "winter" years of life. These individuals were caught up in a cycle of complaining and grumbling about everything. Needless to say, they were not pleasant to be around. The other half of the population was quite the opposite. They accepted and even embraced their stage in life with a calmness and peace. It is no surprise that this group of people was pleasant to be around, tended to live longer, and still functioned well in their interactions with other people. What made such a big difference was the perspective they chose as to how they approached this stage of life.

We can't avoid age, though many try. In our unsuccessful attempts to out-run age, we only create feelings of anxiety and disappointment at not being able to "measure up." Why chase and try to hold on to what will be lost? In his *Letters to an American Lady*, C.

S. Lewis writes, "As for wrinkles—pshaw! Why shouldn't we have wrinkles? Honorable insignia of long service in this warfare."[8] Each season of life is glorious. Each brings different experiences, and with each stage we have new things to offer. As Touré Roberts states, "But when you get older and you don't embrace who you've become, the world is deprived of the great measure you've evolved to be."[9]

~~~

Retirement? Rather than being a time to "hang it up," I want to suggest that it is a time to "pick it up"—to pick up and begin new opportunities for service. Even as we enter the "winter" season of life, our purpose for being here remains constant. I have known school superintendents who have retired and begun volunteering to read to children in classrooms, former CEOs who have taken on mentoring young business majors, retired doctors who have donated their time and efforts in serving the underprivileged, individuals who in their "autumn" and "winter" years have found "springtime" opportunities in a variety of different but related fields. They know that the "best" is still to come, and they eagerly embrace it.

Rather than clinging to what we think we are going to lose, growing older is valuing what we will gain. The psalmist writes, *"The righteous will flourish like a palm tree, they will grow like a cedar of Lebanon; planted in the house of the Lord, they will flourish in the courts of our God. They will still bear fruit in old age, they will stay fresh and green, proclaiming, 'The Lord is upright...'"* **(Ps. 92:12-15).** What a promise! When we are rooted in the Lord, even when we are in the "winter" we can still experience the freshness and green-ness of springtime opportunities. We need never think that we are too old for the Lord to dramatically do "spring" experiences with us and through us.

We are reminded that God designed us to contribute at every season of our life, not just in the "summer." I resonate with the encouraging words of Richard Blackaby: "Often people fail to thrive because they wish they were somewhere else, in a different season. They're in summer, but they act as if they're in spring. Or winter has come, but they want to hold on to autumn. **The key to maximizing your life is to fervently embrace your current season.**"[10] We need to commit ourselves to thrive where we are.

Mentoring

I once heard the question asked, "How many seeds are in an apple?" "Hmm...I don't know," I responded. "I guess we could cut one open and count them." But the follow-up question was actually the more important one: "How many apples are in a seed?" From one seed comes a tree with an untold number of apples coming from that tree. The countless pies and jars of applesauce that result and the number of lives that are touched because of that one seed are enormous. Likewise, the potential impact of one life is unknown.

There is without a doubt no more powerful way to influence the world than through how we live and how we pass on our values. Modeling our values in a genuine lifestyle for our children and others communicates authenticity in who we are and what we believe. In a more formalized way, we refer to this as mentoring. While the Scriptures don't mention mentoring by name, the concept is certainly encouraged. Consider the following excerpts from **the second chapter of the New Testament Book of Titus:** *"You must teach what is in accord with sound doctrine"* **(Titus 2:1);** *"...encourage the young men to be self-controlled. In everything set them an example by doing what is good. In your teaching show integrity, seriousness and soundness of speech that cannot be condemned"* **(Titus 2:6-8); and** *"...train the younger women to love their husbands and children, to be self-controlled and pure..."* **(Titus 2:4-5).**

Professional sports figures can often be controversial. They are looked up to by many young people, yet it is not uncommon to hear about their run-ins with the law. When this happens and the person is asked in an interview what kind of example they are setting, they have been known to respond with, "I never signed up to be anybody's role model." People watch us. Whether we like it or not, people will learn about God by watching us. "Wait a minute—I didn't tell anybody to look to me for information about Him." It doesn't matter—they will. Is that pressure? Yep. Is that a lot of responsibility? Absolutely! But oh, what an opportunity.

I have a dear friend who lives on a lake in Florida. He retired a few years ago, but nearly every evening he can be found on his deck with another guy, or even a group of guys, doing what he fondly refers to as "deck therapy." A few years ago, I was out visiting him when he was having a group of guys over. These were young men with whom he has developed genuine, transparent relationships. It was a pleasure to be an outsider peeking in on Rob's active intentional pouring out of his life into these men. It was pure mentoring in action. You see, he may be retired from his day job, but he is not retired from his purpose of influencing lives for the Kingdom of God. It is this privilege and opportunity that contributes to his ability to look forward to the next day.

We all need "Robs" in our life. Over the years, whenever possible, I have sought out individuals who were 15 to 20 years further down the road of their lives than I am to spend some regular time with. I figured that I could continue to "learn from my mistakes," doing damage to myself and others around me in the process, or I could learn from the wisdom of others and avoid those "crash and burn" experiences. In my 20s, I wish I had connected with a mentor— perhaps I would have created less chaos. Fortunately, I stumbled onto the wisdom of having a mentor later on and have never regretted those relationships and experiences. As I mentioned earlier, using our "summer" years well gives us wisdom and credibility as we get older. We have great value to offer those coming down the road behind us. And we have a great opportunity to do so in our retirement years.

While it is easy to get caught up in thinking that life is about me, the reality is that it is not. The truth is, my life is really about all those other lives that I will touch. Perhaps part of my purpose is to help someone else discover their purpose and to help them advance their purpose. You and I were placed here to make a contribution. Or as Rick Warren puts it, "You were created to add life on earth, not just take from it."[11]

If you are at all like I am, you may think, "I can't mentor anybody. I have been a train wreck. I mean, I have so many issues that they just call it a 'subscription.' Nobody would want to listen to me. They need a mentor who 'has it together' and has perfected it." Not so! God wants to use us, including all our disasters, to help others. You see, when someone looks at your life or mine, they may observe weaknesses and mistakes that come with being a flawed and broken human being. But with the power of God's grace and forgiveness, they can also see a person redeemed by the Living God. His strength far out-powers my weakness. If we will look inside our internal chaos and extract the lessons that we have learned, we might just find that others can benefit from those same lessons. And wouldn't it be great if they could benefit without falling into the same potholes that we did?

Mentoring comes from a powerful place. If love is a primary purpose of our time here on earth, is it any surprise that we are more fulfilled when we love? Focusing on pampering and entertaining ourselves often causes us to become less effective and less fruitful. You see, when we mentor—we love.

Leaving a Legacy

There is much talk today from parents to presidents about leaving a legacy. It carries with it the idea of both "what do I want to be remembered for?" as well as "what do I want to leave behind and pass on to those coming behind me?"

Most of us probably recall, following the death of a relative or an acquaintance, hearing conversation about that person that was not flattering. Such comments may have consisted of: "He was always complaining about everything." "She didn't like anyone." "He was definitely not generous. I think he still had the first dollar he ever made." "I think she enjoyed being the victim and making everyone miserable." I don't know about you, but that is not how I hope to be remembered.

Whether I am recounting the kindness of my grandmother, reading the insightful words of C. S. Lewis, or seeing the benefits afforded a student because of a scholarship fund established by an individual's will—in all of these instances, it is almost as though the person were still alive because of the ongoing influence and good that continues because of their life. Listen to the words of Dr. Martin Luther King Jr.:

> If any of you are around when I have to meet my day, I don't want a long funeral. And if you get somebody to deliver the eulogy, tell them not to talk too long. And every now and then I wonder what I want them to say. Tell them not to mention that I have a Nobel Peace Prize—that isn't important. Tell them not to mention that I have 300 or 400 other awards—that's not important. Tell them not to mention where I went to school.
>
> I'd like somebody to mention that day that Martin Luther King Jr. tried to love somebody. I want you to say that day that I tried to be right on the war question. I want you to be able to say that day that I did try to feed the hungry. And I want you to be able to say that day that I did try in my life to clothe those who were naked. I want you to say on that day that I did try in my life to visit those who were in prison. I want you to say that I tried to love and serve humanity.[12]

~~~

As the apostle Paul neared the end of his life, he made the following observation: *"...the time has come for my departure. I have fought the good fight, I have finished the race, I have kept the faith. Now there is in store for me the crown of righteousness, which the Lord, the righteous Judge, will award to me on that day..."* **(2 Tim. 4:6-8).** He is encouraging us, in so many words, to **finish well!**

In the last chapter, I mentioned my friend Paul, the marathon runner. While I cannot conceive of running 26.2 miles, Paul has run 76 marathons, with 18 of those being up Pikes Peak. I wanted to know more about how he successfully ran these races and what he learned from them. I left our meeting with some nuggets that are not just applicable to marathons but are insights for all of life. He began with a quote from marathon trainer Juma Ikangaa: "The will to win means nothing without the will to prepare." In other words, lots of people want to stand in the winner's circle holding the ribbon, prize, or trophy. But it is an empty "want" unless they are willing to do the hard and disciplined preparation required to run the race.

I was intrigued as Paul talked about pacing. Those who leave the starting line at a sprint may lead for a while, but they will wind up in the end of the pack, if they finish at all. He said that pacing yourself during those first ten miles is critical, otherwise you wind up with what is referred to as a "negative split." You have to train at the pace that you want to run at. The goal is to run the second half of the race faster than the first half. What an appropriate illustration of how we want to run in the "summer" and "fall" seasons of our lives. We will discuss these stages in more detail in the next chapter.

As Paul discussed the final six miles and what is needed to "finish well," he had these words of advice:

- Hold on.

- Avoid mental mistakes.

- Stay positive.

- Encourage each other.

Talking about "finishing well" may cause some discomfort. It may feel a bit morbid. But living in denial about death is akin to burying our head in the sand, and it does nothing to deter the end of life from coming. Examining how to run all the way to the finish line with the goal of eternity in sight is a much healthier perspective. I do this not to achieve some sort of worth. God's love for me gives me my worth. But it is because of my love for Him that I want to honor Him by finishing well and leaving a legacy. Crossing the finish line need not be a time of dread; it can actually be a celebration of a life fully lived.

Mike Huckabee tells a story about the attitude with which he wants to leave this world:

> George Brett was one of the greatest baseball players of all time. And in his career for the Kansas City Royals, he was asked, when he was nearing the end of his career, how he wanted his last play in the major leagues to go. Well, everyone assumed that he would say that he wanted to hit a grand slam in the bottom of the ninth to win a game, perhaps even a World Series. He surprised all of the sportswriters, because what he said was, "I want my last play at bat to be that I hit an easy [out], just one bounce to the second baseman, and they throw me out at first. But I was running as hard as I could toward the bag when they got me." And he said, "Because I want it to be said of George Brett that, no matter what, he played his best game, he gave his best, all the way to the very end."[13]

I want to give my best to the very end. Yet in that statement, there is an "end." I am reminded of the humorous words of comedian

George Burns, who said, "If you live to be 100, you've got it made. Very few people die past that age."[14] But ultimately, all people die. While we don't particularly like to focus on death, ignoring it won't make it go away. We can certainly choose to spend our energy dreading or trying to cheat and out-run death, but as believers who have been redeemed by the blood of the Lamb we can actually look forward to what lies ahead in the next chapter of eternity. C. S. Lewis compares our bodies to older cars when he states that as we age, "more and more repairs and replacements are necessary. We must just look forward to the fine new machines (latest Resurrection model) which are waiting for us, we hope, in the Divine garage!"[15]

~~~

As I ponder the significance of the legacy that I want to leave behind, I am reminded of a poem that I came across a few years ago by Linda Ellis entitled "The Dash."[16]

I read of a man who stood to speak
at the funeral of a friend.
He referred to the dates on her tombstone
from the beginning...to the end.

He noted that first came the date of her birth
and spoke of the following date with tears,
but he said what mattered most of all
was the dash between those years.

For that dash represents all the time
that she spent alive on earth...
and now only those who loved her
know what that little line is worth.

For it matters not, how much we own;
the cars...the house...the cash.
What matters is how we live and love

and how we spend our dash.

So think about this long and hard...
are there things you'd like to change?
For you never know how much time is left.
(You could be at "dash midrange.")

If we could just slow down enough
to consider what's true and real,
and always try to understand
the way other people feel.

And be less quick to anger,
and show appreciation more
and love the people in our lives
like we've never loved before.

If we treat each other with respect,
and more often wear a smile...
remembering that this special dash
might only last a little while.

So, when your eulogy's being read
with your life's actions to rehash...
would you be proud of the things they
say about how you spend your dash?

Purpose Recapped

1.   Two Foundational Truths—

     #1—God is, and He knows what His creation needs.

     #2—Scriptures are God's written instructions for how
     to live.

2.   Scriptures are God's written instructions for how to live.

3. Overarching Purpose #1—To love God with all my heart, soul, mind, and strength.

    Sub-purpose #1—To relate to my Creator by: having faith, being obedient, confessing and repenting of my sins, and worshiping God with everything in my life.

    Sub-purpose #2—To walk humbly with God by giving up control and trusting Him.

    Sub-purpose #3—To connect with God through a lifestyle of quiet—praying and listening.

4. Overarching Purpose #2—To love my neighbor.

    Sub-purpose #1—If I am married: committing myself to traveling together with my mate, being united and intimate, developing an interdependent relationship, and making the choice to truly love my spouse.

    Sub-purpose #2—If I have children: viewing my children as a blessing and an opportunity; loving my children by effectively shaping them, by honoring my own parents, and by empowering my children.

    Sub-purpose #3—Relating to others: relating externally—promoting justice, prohibiting gossip, and providing for the poor; relating internally—guarding my mouth, offering forgiveness, and being a peacemaker; relating as a community; and relating with the risk of accountability.

    Sub-purpose #4—To honor the Lord with my wealth by: serving God, making a difference with my energies and with my money, becoming trustworthy, and deciding my heart's focus.

5. Overarching Purpose #3—To love yourself.

Sub-purpose #1—To relate with yourself by: recognizing your uniqueness, guarding your heart, and taking care in how you live—including attending to your health, growing, enjoying life, finding fulfillment in work, and trusting God with your desires.

Sub-purpose #2—To make decisions for yourself by: understanding God's will, looking to His Word to illuminate decisions, and using wise decision-making principles.

Sub-purpose #3—To navigate the end of this journey by:

    a. Endeavoring to use all your years to leave the world a better place.

    b. Mentoring those on the road behind you.

    c. Leaving a legacy—finishing well.

Chapter Fourteen

Your Life Is Not An Accident!—Your Purpose and Developing a Plan

"There will be many chapters in your life. Don't get lost in the one you're in now."
—UNKNOWN

"Just because the past didn't turn out like you wanted it to doesn't mean your future can't be better than you ever imagined."
—UNKNOWN

Hopefully, as you have read the chapters of this book, your heart has awakened—awakened to the fact that you are not an accident and that God had specific things in mind when He created you. As we have seen reiterated in the course of our journey through the Scriptures, God has reasons for creating us and purposes to be fulfilled in our lives. My desire has been that you would clearly understand that our existence is driven toward loving God, others, and ourselves. From these three arenas come the purposes of our Creator.

At some time in our lives, most of us have desired to be successful. Unfortunately, we may have confused success with purpose. For example, if I am a football quarterback, I might feel that I have been successful if I have a high pass completion rate. My suspicion is that I could lead the league in completion rates, but if my team winds up 0-16, no one will care, because my purpose is to win games. I can argue with the coach all day about how many passes I have completed and that I have been successful, but I could still be looking for another job in the off-season. It is necessary for us to keep our purposes clearly in our sights.

I resonate with the illustration below used by author Randy Alcorn regarding life and eternity.

The Dot: The Line:
Life on earth   Life in Heaven

He writes, "Our present life on earth is the dot. It begins. It ends. It's brief. But from that dot extends a line that goes on forever." Moreover, he states, "Right now we're living in the dot. But what are we living for? The shortsighted person lives for the dot. The person with perspective lives for the line."[1]

It is my hope that you are becoming a person with perspective.

I will tell you that 30 years ago, I adopted a new approach to how I live life. Certainly, I am aware of the realities of "the dot," life in the here and now. If I tried to deny them, I would be as mistaken as those first-century heretics known as Gnostics who did their best to deny the material world. But because of my awareness of "the line," I live life with a renewed purpose. I live with my eyes directed toward eternity.

In this final chapter, we will look at the benefits of developing a mission statement, regrouping when life hasn't gone according to plan, and some strategies for planning—making the wisest use of our remaining time.

Developing a Mission Statement

"We have to write a mission statement," we were told. At the time, I was working as a counselor in a school district and writing a mission statement was the newest fad, not only in school districts, but in businesses as well. Educators were called upon to write mission statements at the district level, the building level, and even within individual departments. This was a process with specific guidelines that took anywhere from hours to days.

While it seemed like a good idea in theory, people began to dread the process. Every time there was any kind of leadership change, there was a change of vision, and with that came what felt like the "exercise in futility." I believe that one of the reasons for this sentiment was people felt as though they were checking off boxes and just doing something because we were "supposed to do it." While the resulting product might be framed and hung on a wall in some hallway, rarely was it referred to again. In other words, there was no practical use for it. Nothing meaningful came from the multi-hour process. If this has been your experience, I certainly understand your hesitance to want to revisit the topic. But I would ask that you indulge me for a few moments.

While there are a variety of writers who would advocate for some very specific components to be part of a mission statement, I will leave those discussions to them. I want to approach this in more general terms and suggest that a mission statement is a guiding document that is not time dependent. It is more global in nature—unlike a goal, which is more specific and time limited. For example, stating that I want to complete a college degree in the next four years is a goal. If that were my life's purpose, then in four years it would be time for me to be done on this planet because I would have fulfilled my purpose. On the other hand, if a part of my purpose were to feed children in Third World countries, it is unlikely that I will ever exhaust that effort, as there will probably always be hungry children in those places. A goal I can meet, but my purpose will never be fully attained in this life. As Bob Shank states, "A purpose is not measurable....It will only be refined and restated (never replaced) in your lifetime—if it is the right purpose for you."[2] In his book *Working on Purpose,* Kent Holland writes, "A mission statement is a succinct written statement of commitment to fulfill a specific purpose. It has been compared to a compass, an anchor, a map, and a rudder."[3]

It is my heartfelt desire that as you have begun to understand why God put you here, through the lens of loving Him, others, and yourself, that your purpose has started to percolate. Developing the relationship with your Maker for which He designed you and grasping what is involved in loving our fellow human beings and ourselves lays the foundation for knowing how we fit into the story of God's purpose.

Writing your mission statement takes into account first and foremost your understanding of God's purposes and His will for us as people (which this book has endeavored to address), your own hardwiring (how God has made you), your personality (including your strengths and weaknesses), and your passions (the desires God has placed on your heart). This is probably not a quick process that you will whip out in an hour this afternoon. Grappling with charting your course is an important and sacred process. Be prepared to give it the time it deserves. It is a marinating experience, as you ponder, pray, and carefully examine your heart in relation to the truths of God's Word.

As you bring all the components to bear on the process, I would encourage you to put your thoughts on paper (or in this day and age, in a program such as Microsoft Word)—something that you can look at. While you may have a multitude of thoughts bouncing around in your head, putting it on paper makes it real and concrete. It gives you the opportunity to look at it, modify it, and mull it over some more. Be willing to give it some time. Perhaps you might talk about it with those who know you best, getting their feedback on whether or not it appropriately fits you. Bathe it in prayer before God, asking for His wisdom. As King Solomon learned, when you ask God for wisdom, He is faithful to provide it. Read it over and put it away. Pray about it some more. Pull it back out and examine it days later to check for durability—does it still resonate as true?

Once you are confident that you have captured your personal life purpose, what I do *not* want you to do is what we did after those school district meetings, which is to frame it and never look at it again. No, I want you to put it where you will be continually reminded of how you fit into the puzzle—your role in God's narrative. We will talk about how to do this when we discuss planning a little later in this chapter.

While I certainly do not believe that my own personal mission statement is anything grandiose or worthy of imitating, I simply share it here so that you can better visualize the brevity and yet the lifelong guidance that a mission statement can offer: "My purpose is to live a life that grows in intimacy with God that, as a result, reflects Christ's love and servanthood by demonstrating compassion for others and by modeling and educating others in life-changing biblical truth in a manner that will enhance their intimacy with God and their connectedness with others."

As you can see, I will never exhaust this pursuit; I will never run out of opportunities to grow, reflect, model, or educate. And while my purpose will remain constant, specific goals and ways that this may look can and will change. A decade ago, I pursued my purpose with a greater proportion of my time spent doing counseling and teaching. While I am still actively involved in those same efforts, the specifics have modified now to include a good chunk of time spent writing. A decade from now—who knows? My purpose will remain the same, but I can imagine that I might spend more time teaching and actively mentoring. A decade after—while my purpose will be unchanged, how it looks during my "legacy" years will probably be quite different.

So, how does all of this funnel down to you? Taking the known global aspects of God's will and purpose and sifting them down to the applications in your life is an exciting opportunity. I urge you not to pass it up. Anchoring your internal GPS to your life's purpose can radically alter your journey. And in doing so, I believe you will get the chance to experience a level of peace and contentment that transcends the storms and unknowns of this world.

Regrouping

It was the afternoon of Thanksgiving Day, November 23, 1994. I was engaging in the annual holiday tradition that I assume most of us love—watching the Dallas Cowboys game. OK, OK—I know that you may root for another team, but having lived in Dallas during my college years, this is my team. On this particular day, it was ugly. Quarterback Troy Aikman was out with an injury, as was backup quarterback Rodney Peete. This left third string backup Jason Garrett at the helm, and things were not going well. At half-time, Green Bay was up 17 to 6, with no end in sight. Everything that Garrett did seemed, at best, not to work, but proved to be a disaster at worst. By half-time, fans probably wanted to turn off their televisions and go hide in the closet from embarrassment. It was obvious to those watching that while there may have been 30 minutes of play time left, clearly the game was over. Although I recognize that the score did not seem all that lopsided, the tempo of the game certainly did.

But as the second half started, something was different. Garrett was "on"—executing plays, it seemed that he could do no wrong. As the game ended, Green Bay stared in disbelief at the scoreboard, which read, "Dallas 42—Green Bay 31." Thrilled, fans asked themselves, "What happened?" The answer is—half-time.

Dallas certainly had every reason to go into the locker room and groan about the impossible situation they were in, playing with their third string quarterback. They could have been defeated before the second half kick-off even took place. But they weren't. I don't know all of the words that were spoken in the locker room that day, but obviously they recognized the fact that the game was far from over. I am certain that there were discussions about mistakes that had been made and how they needed to play differently. My guess is that new strategies were put in place in order to play the second half of the game more effectively than the first. And more effective they were. Instead of continuing to play the way they had been and making defeat a reality, they regrouped and came out and changed the way the game would end.

~~~

Many of us can relate to the Dallas Cowboys in that Thanksgiving game. We are at half-time, and the game is not going well. Some will choose to crawl into a corner and live out their life just waiting for the game-ending gun to sound. But others will choose to grasp their God-given purpose and live radically different.

Listen to the life-changing words from **Philippians 3:13:** *"... But one thing I do: Forgetting what is behind and straining toward what is ahead, I press on toward the goal to win the prize for which God has called me heavenward in Christ Jesus"* **(Phil. 3:13-14).** In other words (my paraphrase), "I know it is half-time and I have taken a beating so far in this game. It has not gone as I had planned, and now I want to just give up. But I am not going to. Instead, I'm going to forget what has happened and press on in this next half toward the goal of fulfilling God's purposes in my life. I am going to win the prize!"

If you are like I am, then you have made a bucket-load of mistakes, gotten off track, and felt that you were beyond salvaging. God knows that. But the most exciting thing is that He is a God of second chances (or in my case—third, fourth, fifth…). No matter how big of a mess we have made of things, here is the promise—when we take the step of acknowledging the disaster we have created, repent of our sins, and turn and walk the other direction, God, out of His perfect love, is faithful to forgive our sins. If you are still shaking your head, camping on how unworthy you are, then I want you to go back and read the previous sentence. Read it as many times as it takes, because wrapping your head around that simple fact is critical to living the second half of your game.

In the 27th chapter of the Book of Genesis, we read the account of the brothers Jacob and Esau. While they were twins, they extremely different from each other. Esau was the firstborn, and with that status came benefits and blessings. However, because Jacob was his mother's favorite (and Esau his dad's), they conspired, hatching a plan for Jacob to deceive his father and get the blessings of the firstborn. While they successfully pulled off the ruse, it created a fractured relationship between Jacob and Esau that led to threats of murder. This was not Jacob's only incident of dishonesty. While it would be easy to assume that Jacob was beyond rehabilitation, God not only salvaged him but changed his name to "Israel" and created an entire nation from his descendants, whom God blessed and treasured.

You see, God is not limited by our foul-ups. You may falsely believe that you can't change, but God knows you can. Until you accept His grace, your most derailing limitation is you. If you continue to dwell on your first half mistakes, you will never be able to enjoy a second half victory. Again, as the letter to the Philippians said, *"...Forgetting what is behind..."* (Phil. 3:13). Once we repent and move in a new direction, it is imperative that we leave the past in our rear-view mirror. I so appreciate Tim Timberlake's profound statement: "You can't stumble over what's behind you."[4] While that would seem rather obvious, far too many of us continue to trip and fall because we place all our mistakes directly in front of us, cluttering our path. That is clearly not where they belong. So, be intentional about picking them up, repenting and learning from them, and placing them firmly behind you. In the affirming words of St. Augustine of Hippo, "Trust the past to God's mercy, the present to God's love, and the future to God's providence."[5]

Former president George W. Bush relates how his life came to a crossroads and, as a result, experienced a radical change. He and his wife, Laura, had traveled to the Broadmoor Resort in Colorado Springs in 1986 to celebrate their fortieth birthdays. At this time, he was well-known as an extremely heavy drinker. Following a night of too much alcohol and embarrassing behavior, Bush reflected on his life and the continued adverse effects the alcohol played in it. Talking with Laura, he told her that he was giving up alcohol and changing his life. He was at half-time, and he knew that he needed to reinvent himself. That decision was followed by a new season of life, leading to his election as governor of Texas and, a few years later, president of the United States.[6] What a profound turning point! Certainly he could have made the choice to continue living his life as he was, but the game after half-time would have been completely different.

God, in His great love, has given us the freedom to live our lives as we choose. But we have to acknowledge that the choices we make will lead to the consequences we will experience. No one was created outside the purposes of God. We would not have been born if we did not have a place on the stage of life. Now granted, we may have started out life by mangling things pretty badly, but that still doesn't mean that we are a mistake. What it means is that we need to turn and live life differently. We need to lay before the throne of God all our problems, regrets, weaknesses, frailties, bad habits, as well as our future dreams, desires, and ambitions. We need to allow God to redeem our lives from the inside out.

In an interview with author Jim Stovall in 2011, publishing executive Steve Forbes explained that our lives will have setbacks and we have to be prepared for them. "Life never goes in a straight line. There will be tradeoffs. But if you realize that it's not my way or no way, or I didn't succeed therefore I do not try again, you end up being a better person—more seasoned—more mature—and [have] a better chance to achieve that ultimate goal."[7]

Planning for the Future

Back in the first chapter, I talked about how a builder approaches a construction project. They have blueprints, materials, and a timeline. In other words, they have a plan. They would never amass the materials and simply say, "Well, let's begin and see what happens." They would be out of business rather quickly. We also examined **Psalms 90:12:** *"Teach us to number our days aright, that we may gain a heart of wisdom."* With a little more of an intentional eye, I want to spend some time looking at the importance of planning.

While I have completely acknowledged that we are not in control of life—God is—I also recognize that God wants us to fully utilize the time that He has given us on earth. The fact that I may buy an airline ticket for a trip six months from now does not mean that I somehow think I have God over a barrel and He now has to honor my plans. Far from it. Certainly, my life could end two months before the trip is scheduled to take place. But it doesn't mean that I shouldn't buy the ticket—especially if I expect to get a seat at a reasonable price.

I appreciate the example of the apostle Paul in the Book of Acts, where several of his missionary journeys are recorded in great detail. Paul made plans to visit a number of churches in a variety of countries and meet with particular individuals. Sometimes his trips went according to plan—frequently they didn't. At times, there were delays due to weather. On other occasions, such as is recorded in Acts 27 and 28, their sailing was disrupted by a storm and an ensuing shipwreck. But no matter what transpired, Paul would take advantage of whatever opportunity presented itself to interact with people and touch lives. He knew that seeking godly wisdom, he would make long-term plans. But he also knew that if those plans were interrupted, he would make the most of whatever presented itself, very simply, because God is in control. He gives us a healthy model to follow: "numbering"—or examining—"our days," as the psalmist says, making wise plans for our life, but being prepared to live in the moments that God provides us (see Ps. 90:12). As a friend of mine consistently says, "I am going to do [whatever the plans might be] tomorrow, the Lord willing." With God's guidance, I will give thought to my days, and I will carry out those plans, if the Lord is willing.

Living a life without a plan makes us vulnerable to the whims of our emotions, the fads of the day, and reactions to the uncertainties of life. In the words of Kent Holland, "It is a terrible experience to look back on our lives thus far only to find we have diligently climbed the ladder of success but that we leaned the ladder against the wrong building."[8]

~~~

As we approach making the most of our days, the mind-set that we adopt is tremendously important. Famed psychologist Abraham Maslow was fascinated with his research on the effects of purpose in the lives of individuals. While it may come as no surprise that he found that a person's sense of purpose impacted the quality of their lives, he also discovered that their perspective at mid-life directly affected the length of their lives as well. A person who didn't have a picture big enough to fill their life wouldn't live as long as someone who did.[9]

A recent study in Britain determined that individuals who assumed a perspective that they were "old" tended to physically respond differently than those adopting a younger mind-set. Those ages 65 or older who saw themselves as three or more years younger than their actual age were less likely to die in an eight-year period than those who viewed themselves as their age or older.[10] This study also referenced, adding support to Maslow's theories, research published in *Psychological Science* that suggested that people who have a sense of purpose in their life "are less likely to die over a 14-year period."[11]

~~~

So, in examining some thoughts regarding planning, I want to share strategies in looking at the big picture, mid-range planning, as well as tackling life on a weekly and daily basis.

Big Picture Planning

One particular strategy that has been valuable to me in "numbering my days" has been to view my life through the prism of "seasons." Ecclesiastes 3:1 says, *"There is a time for everything, and a season for every activity under heaven."* I like the way Blackaby puts it when he writes, "A seasonal perspective on life gives you a better grid for understanding your unfolding purpose in life—that thrilling sense of knowing where you're going, which in turn motivates you to adequately prepare for that particular journey and destination."[12] From birth to death, our lives in many ways mimic the four seasons. As children, our parents do their best to plant seeds, like fields in the springtime. It becomes a time of beginnings, potential, and possibilities. It is the time to explore opportunities, and it is typically exciting as we do so. During the spring of our lives, we go to school, move away from home, go to college, pursue our vocation, get married, and have a host of other "launching" experiences.

If spring is about "new beginnings," then summer is about maturing. The seeds that were planted in the spring begin to take root and grow. During the summer months, we roll up our sleeves and really get our hands dirty, embracing our tasks with passion and ambition. The person who we are at our core is revealed, and our character is shaped. I am reminded of the words that Paul wrote to the Corinthians regarding maturity: *"When I was a child, I talked like a child, I thought like a child, I reasoned like a child. When I became a man, I put childish ways behind me"* **(1 Cor. 13:11).** It is during this season that we start to get really serious about the work we believe we are called to do and approach it with a focused determination. Now, please don't misunderstand me and think that I am implying that life becomes all serious all the time. That wouldn't be accurate. I encourage you to have fun and play at all stages of life. If you go to Disneyland, you can still act like you're 12 years old (my wife says that I do). I am simply saying that our perspective is more mature as we recognize where in our lifespan we are.

In our plant growing analogy, fall or autumn is a season of harvest. As Galatians 6:7 states, *"...A man reaps what he sows."* Fall is when our summer efforts begin to pay off as we reach the peak of our labors. This can be a deeply rewarding season, particularly if we prepared in the spring and worked diligently in the summer. Fall should be the time when we have mastered our tasks and are at the pinnacle of our skills and influence. This is the season when we may feel as though it has "all come together" and we work to use it all to make a difference.

But just as the warmth of summer gives way to the changing leaves of fall, fall gives way to the cold of winter. And it is during this final season that we will come to the end of our lives. It is a season for winding down and bringing closure to certain roles in life. We in essence say our goodbyes in winter in anticipation of the spring of eternity. While this may bring a tinge of sadness, it is also a time of acknowledging accomplishments and celebrating the life we have lived.

While we are the same person through each stage, the various seasons bring out the texture of different aspects of who we are. Getting the most out of each season requires that we be truly present in our particular season. Those who try to rush ahead or cling to a previous season will miss the possibilities and the joy of the season they are currently in. We are made to thrive in each season.

⁓

Perhaps thinking about your life in seasons is helpful in giving you a different perspective. Being a person who is visual and likes to see the inner workings of a perspective, I am going to share with you what I call the "100 plan" or the "1200 months plan." Now, I will acknowledge up front that there is nothing particularly special or insightful about this plan, other than that it works for me. I offer it here only to stimulate thinking for you.

In my "100 plan," I am planning as though I will live to the ripe old age of 100. While there are more centenarians in this country than ever before, I haven't found a magic pill or fountain of youth causing me to think I will live to be 100. It is simply a big round number that I like the sound of that gives me a lens through which I can view and plan my life. I absolutely recognize that God can call me home at any moment in time. It is just that I would prefer to be living out His purposes and be called home rather than be twiddling my thumbs with nothing to do, waiting for Him to take me. So, acknowledging that my months and technical seasons of the year don't exactly line up neatly, my plan looks something like the chart below. Keep in mind that the activities are simply some suggested descriptors for perspective.

THE 100 PLAN			
Month	**Ages**		**Activities**
January	0 to 8		Nurtured by parents
February	9 to 17		Raised and trained
March	18 to 26		Exploring and launching
April	27 to 34	Nurture, Train & Raise Children	Establish career direction; continue development
May	35 to 42		Make a difference as you build credibility and expertise foundations
June	43 to 50		Produce and contribute best services; make biggest
July	51 to 59		impact and lasting influences on people; make a difference
August	60 to 67		in the world around you
September	68 to 75		Mentor and support those coming into their summer
October	76 to 83		years; continuing to educate and prepare others
November	84 to 92		Volunteer, relax, and nurture family
December	93 to 100		Enjoy being nurtured by family

As I said, this is simply a framework for life planning. You can use it no matter how long you may live. Obviously, if you knew you would only live until 80, then you could modify the months to reflect that age difference and the activities for the stage of life. I just have chosen to create a framework that I am not likely to outlast.

Mid-range Planning

While some may do five- and ten-year planning, for my purposes here, I am going to look at mid-range planning as being a year at a time.

I have a good friend, Mark, who is a worship pastor and who also leads an international ministry that trains worship leaders around the globe. Recently over breakfast, Mark shared with me how he and his wife, Carrie, do mid-range planning. In November of each year, they schedule very intentional time for planning the coming year. This is a process that overtakes their entire living room. They begin with 2" x 2" Post-it notes that each have a heading. Some of their headings include: international ministry travel, "Mark" personal time, "Carrie" personal time, ministry finances, church worship pastor plans, vacation, personal finances, friends, fun, and others. Under each of these headings they include all of the things that could potentially go into their "next year" plan. They then clarify and prioritize each of these items. Ultimately, Carrie will take all their specific plans on which they have decided and put them into a database. From there the plans emerge on a one-year calendar with different types of events color-coded for easy visual recognition. Finally, these are printed out into 12 "bite-size" individual monthly calendars from which they can operate.

Now you may say that this seems arduous and entirely over the top. But I would contend that this actually gives Mark and Carrie a framework that provides them with a much greater chance of accomplishment and success. While we may have lots of ideas bouncing around in our heads, I am convinced that it is when we actually put it on paper that things become concrete and real.

Weekly/Daily Planning

From the big picture we get the mid-range plan, and from there it is much easier to extrapolate what we determine to do on a weekly and daily basis. With our bigger purposes clearly articulated, knowing how that plays out today becomes more manageable. I encourage individuals to consult their monthly goals and plans weekly in order to determine priorities and schedule for the week. Doing this helps ensure that what we do today—whether work or play, family activities or romantic retreats—all fits within the purposes to which God has called us. It enables us to make the most of every opportunity.

~~~

Years ago, in an interview with Paul Bradshaw, Rick Warren was asked, as he had been many times before, "What is the purpose of life?" I want to share here his succinct answer: "In a nutshell, life is preparation for eternity. We were made to last forever, and God wants us to be with Him in Heaven. One day my heart is going to stop, and that will be the end of my body—but not me. I may live 60 to 100 years on earth, but I am going to spend trillions of years in eternity. This is the warm-up act, the dress rehearsal. God wants us to practice on earth what we will do forever in eternity. We were made by God and for God, and until you figure that out, life isn't going to make sense."[13] I hope that as you have journeyed through this book with me, it has begun to make sense.

In 1994, the Academy Award-winning blockbuster movie *Saving Private Ryan* was released. This film takes the viewer from the beaches of Normandy to the kitchen of Mrs. Ryan, who learns that three of her four sons have died in combat. The army determines that in order to make sure she doesn't lose her fourth son, they will send a mission to find Private Ryan and return him home safely. Captain John H. Miller is given that charge and carries out his orders diligently. In the course of the rescue, several of his men lose their lives. Once Ryan is found, Captain Miller is critically wounded before they can return. With his dying breath, Miller says to Ryan, "Earn it. Earn it."

In the final scene of the movie, we see Private Ryan as a senior citizen visiting Captain Miller's grave in Arlington Cemetery. On bended knee at the graveside, Ryan utters these words: "My family is with me today. They wanted to come with me. To be honest with you, I wasn't sure how I would feel coming back here. Every day I think about what you said to me that day on the bridge. I've tried to live my life the best I could. I hope that was enough. I hope at least in your eyes I've earned what all of you have done for me."[14]

You and I can never "earn" what God has done for us. His redemption of our lives through what He has done for us through the sacrifice of His Son is beyond anything that we can repay. However, it does motivate me. It motivates me to live a life that strives to honor God at every turn and every decision; not to serve Him out of obligation, but from a heart of love and gratefulness. My desire is to know His purpose, to love Him accordingly, and to hear at the end of time, *"Well done, good and faithful servant! You have been faithful with a few things; I will put you in charge of many things. Come and share your master's happiness"* (**Matt. 25:21**).

Purpose Recapped

1. Two Foundational Truths—

    #1—God is, and He knows what His creation needs.

    #2—The Scriptures are God's written instructions for how to live.

2. Overarching Purpose #1—To love God with all my heart, soul, mind, and strength.

    Sub-purpose #1—To relate to my Creator by: having faith, being obedient, confessing and repenting of my sins, and worshiping God with everything in my life.

    Sub-purpose #2—To walk humbly with God by giving up control and trusting Him.

Sub-purpose #3—To connect with God through a lifestyle of quiet—praying and listening.

3.   Overarching Purpose #2—To love my neighbor.

Sub-purpose #1—If I am married: committing myself to traveling together with my mate, being united and intimate, developing an interdependent relationship, and making the choice to truly love my spouse.

Sub-purpose #2—If I have children: viewing my children as a blessing and an opportunity; loving my children by effectively shaping them, by honoring my own parents, and by empowering my children.

Sub-purpose #3—Relating to others: relating externally—promoting justice, prohibiting gossip, and providing for the poor; relating internally—guarding my mouth, offering forgiveness, being a peacemaker; relating as a community; and relating with the risk of accountability.

Sub-purpose #4—To honor the Lord with my wealth by: serving God, making a difference with my energies and with my money, becoming trustworthy, and deciding my heart's focus.

4.   Overarching Purpose #3—To love yourself.

Sub-purpose #1—To relate with yourself by: recognizing your uniqueness, guarding your heart, and taking care in how you live—including attending to your health, growing, enjoying life, finding fulfillment in work, and trusting God with your desires.

Sub-purpose #2—To make decisions for yourself by: understanding God's will, looking to His Word to illuminate decisions, and using wise decision-making principles.

Sub-purpose #3—To navigate the end of this journey by:

    a. Endeavoring to use all your years to leave the world a better place.

    b. Mentoring those on the road behind you.

    c. Leaving a legacy—finishing well.

    d. Developing a mission statement.

    e. Regrouping.

    f. Planning your days.

Appendix

Scriptures Related to Purpose

GENESIS

1:26
1:28
9:4
28:15
45:5
49:29
50:25

EXODUS

7:7
9:16
12:14
15:26
19:5
20:3-17
20:3
20:4
20:7
20:8
20:12
20:13
20:14
20:15;20:16
20:17
20:24
22:16
23:2
23:14
23:25
29:36
31:16

LEVITICUS

3:17
5:1
11
16:29-34
19:1
19:11
19:14
19:15
19:16
19:18
19:32
26:14-39
26:42

NUMBERS

15:37-41

DEUTERONOMY

5:10
5:29
6:2
6:5
6:7
10:12
14:22

JOSHUA	8:13-15	3:27
4:6	**PSALMS**	3:29
22:5	1:2	4:7
24:14	4:4	4:13
24:15	15:1-5	4:20
1 SAMUEL	20:3	4:23
15:22	33:1	5:15-20
2 SAMUEL	37:3-4	6:17
12:11	37:5	6:18
1 KINGS	37:6	6:20-23
2:2-3	37:7	8:5
6:12-13	37:8	8:10-11
6:60-61	39:4-7	9:8
19:11-13	55:22	10:4
2 KINGS	90:10	10:27
5:10-14	90:12	11:1
1 CHRONICLES	103:13	11:2
16:28	128:1	11:14
16:34	136:1	12:10
28:9	147	12:16
2 CHRONICLES	148	12:22
6:32-42	149	13:22
33:13	150:1	13:24
NEHEMIAH	**PROVERBS**	14:7
1:8-9	1:8	14:15
ESTHER	1:10	14:21
4:14	3:1	14:26
JOB	3:3	14:31
7:16	3:5	15:21
	3:9	15:29
	3:11	16:3
	3:21	16:9
		16:28

18:13	**ISAIAH**	**DANIEL**
19:11	1:16-17	5:23
19:17	2:22	**HOSEA**
19:18	26:12	4:6
19:21	33:15-16	6:6
20:3	44:8	
20:19	44:19	**MICAH**
21:3	45:5	6:8
21:21	45:9	**HABAKKUK**
22:6	46:9	3:17-19
23:9	48:17-18	
23:13	53	**ZECHARIAH**
23:20	55:8-9	5:3-4
23:22	56:1	8:16
25:9	56:3-7	**MALACHI**
25:21	58:3-8	2:15
28:13		3:10
29:18	**JEREMIAH**	
31:30	5:2	**MATTHEW**
	10:23	5:16
ECCLESIASTES	22:16	5:19
2:11	29:11	5:22
2:24	33:3	5:25
3:1-8	33:11	5:28-29
3:11		5:31-32
3:12	**LAMENTATIONS**	5:37
4:9-12	3:22-23	5:38-42
5:1	3:25	5:44
5:18-19		5:48
8:15	**EZEKIEL**	6:3
9:7	13:18-21	6:6
12:13	20:20	6:14
	33:1-9	6:17
		6:20

6:25	**LUKE**	15:5
6:33	3:11-14	15:12,17
7:1	6:27	Acts
7:7-8	6:31	2:38
7:13	6:36	16:31
10:16	6:37	**ROMANS**
10:32	9:24	6:12
10:37	10:27-28	12:1
10:39	10:41	12:2
11:28	11:9-10	12:9
12:7	11:28	12:10
12:36	12:15	12:12
12:48	12:22-31	12:13
14:23	12:40	13:1
18:5	12:45-48	14:13
18:15-17	13:5	**1 CORINTHIANS**
18:22-35	13:23	5
19:4-6	15:3-32	6:1-4
21:22	16:11-12	6:18
22:37-40	17:3-4	7:3
23:23	Luke	7:10-11
24:44	18:1-5	8:9
25:14-30	21:34	10:31
25:31-46	**JOHN**	13:1-13
28:19	3:36	15:33
MARK	6:27	16:13
2:27	6:29	16:14
4:33	6:40	**2 CORINTHIANS**
7:8	8:24	5:18
8:35	10:10	6:14
10:2-12	13:34	9:7
10:43-45	14:6	
13:34,37	14:15	

GALATIANS

3:11
5:6
5:16-26
6:1

EPHESIANS

4:2
4:15
4:26
4:29
4:31
4:32
5:3
5:4
5:8
5:15
5:16
5:17
5:18
5:19
5:20
5:21
5:22
5:25
5:33
6:1
6:4
6:5
6:9
6:13-17

PHILIPPIANS

1:6

1:21
2:2
2:3
2:12
2:13
2:14
3:1
3:13-14
4:6
4:8
4:11-13

COLOSSIANS

2:7
2:8
3:2
3:5
3:8
3:9
3:12
3:13
3:14
3:15
3:16
3:17
3:18
3:19
3:20
3:21
3:22
3:23
4:1
4:2
4:5

4:6

1 THESSALONIANS

4:3
4:9
4:11
5: 6
5:11
5:14
5:20
5:21
5:22

2 THESSALONIANS

2:15
3:6
3:10

1 TIMOTHY

2:8
2:9
4:8
5:1
5:8

2 TIMOTHY

6:6
6:11
2:16
2:22
4:7

TITUS

2:1-8
3:1
3:2

HEBREWS
10:25
11:6
12:1
12:2
12:7
12:14
13:1
13:2
13:3
13:4
13:5
13:15
13:16;13:17

JAMES
1:2
1:5-6
1:19
1:22
1:26
1:27
2:8-9
2:14-26

4:7
4:10
4:11
5:12
5:13
5:14
5:16

1 PETER
1:13
1:14
1:15
1:22
2:1
2:11
2:12
2:13
2:18
3:1
3:4
3:7
3:8
3:9
3:11

3:15
4:7
4:8
4:9
4:10
5:5
5:6
5:7

2 PETER
1:5
3:14
3:17

1 JOHN
1:9
2:15
3:10-11
3:18
3:23
4:7-12
5:12
5:14

2 JOHN
6

Notes

Chapter One

1. Jerry Leiber and Mike Stoller, "Is That All There Is?" sung by Peggy Lee in *Is That All There Is?*, Capitol Records, 1969.

2. Bernard Haisch, *The Purpose-Guided Universe: Believing in Einstein, Darwin, and God* (Pompton Plains, NJ: The Career Press, 2010), 67.

3. Kenneth Wood, *In Search of Purpose: A Personal Mentoring Guide for Discovering Your Destiny* (Oklahoma City, OK: Deep Water Press, 2000), 17.

4. Josh McDowell, *Evidence That Demands a Verdict* (San Bernardino, CA: Here's Life Publishing, 1979) and *More Evidence That Demands a Verdict* (San Bernardino, CA: Here's Life Publishing, 1981).

5. Josh McDowell, *The New Evidence That Demands a Verdict* (Nashville, TN: Thomas Nelson, 1999).

6. Eric Lyons, "Isaiah and the Deity of Christ," Apologetic Press, 2007, http://www.apologeticspress.org/apcontent.aspx?category=10&article=30.

7. Bruce Waltke, *Finding the Will of God: A Pagan Notion?* (Gresham, OR: Vision House Publishing, 1995), 98.

8. Myles Munroe, *In Pursuit of Purpose: The Key to Personal Fulfillment* (Shippensburg, PA: Destiny Image, 1992), 6.

9. Ibid., 57.

10. Haisch, 135.

11. Bob Shank, *Total Life Management* (Colorado Springs, CO: Multnomah Books, 1990), 72.

12. Touré Roberts, *Purpose Awakening: Discover the Epic Idea That Motivated Your Birth* (New York: FaithWords, 2014), 163.

13. Albert Barnes, *Notes on The Old Testament: Psalms*, vol. 3 (Grand Rapids, MI: Baker Book House, 1971), 9.

14. Ibid., 9.

15. Sir John Templeton and Rebekah Alezander Dunlap, *Why Are We Created?: Increasing our Understanding of Humanity's Purpose on Earth* (Radnor, PA: Templeton Foundation Press, 2003), 59.

16. Misty Edwards, *What Is The Point?: Discovering Life's Deeper Meaning and Purpose* (Lake Mary, FL: Charisma House, 2012), 64.

17. Rick Warren, *The Purpose Driven Life: What on Earth Am I Here For?* (Grand Rapids, MI: 2002), 177.

Chapter Two

1. Matt Heard, *Life with a Capital L: Embracing Your God-Given Humanity* (Colorado Springs, CO: Multnomah Books, 2014), 146.

2. See also Deuteronomy 6:4-5; Matthew 22:37-38; and Luke 10:27.

3. T. C. Stallings, *The Pursuit: 14 Ways in 14 Days to Passionately Seek God's Purpose for Your Life* (Racine, WI: Broadstreet Publishing Group, 2015), 33.

4. "Self-flagellation," *Wikipedia*, last modified March 26, 2017, http://en.wikipedia.org/wiki/Self-flagellation.

5. Charles Swindoll, *The Mystery of God's Will: What Does He Want For Me?* (Nashville, TN: Word Publishing, 1999), 141.

6. Heard, 84.

7. Warren, *Purpose Driven Life*, 54.

8. Ibid., 103.

Chapter Three

1. "Joseph Campbell Quotes," *Goodreads*, http://www.goodreads.com/author/quotes/20105.Joseph_Campbell.

2. Templeton and Dunlap, *Why Are We Created?*, 61.

3. David Aaron, *The God-Powered Life: Awakening to Your Divine Purpose* (Boston, MA: Trumpeter Books, 2009), pg. 17

4. Steven Curtis Chapman, "God Is God," *Declaration*, Sparrow Records, 2001.   Emphases are mine.

5. *Steel Magnolias*, directed by Herbert Ross (1989; Culver City, CA: Sony Pictures Home Entertainment, 2000), DVD.

6. *Days of Thunder*, directed by Tony Scott (1990; Los Angeles, CA: Paramount Pictures, 1999), DVD.

7. C. S. Lewis, *The Weight of Glory* (New York: HarperOne, 1976), 27.

8. Lewis, *Mere Christianity* (New York: HarperOne, 1980), 225.

9. Swindoll, *Mystery of God's Will*, 205.

10. Ibid., 206.

11. Aaron, 101.

12. Wood, *In Search of Purpose*, 196.

Chapter Four

1. Nixeon Civille Handy, "Points to Ponder," *Reader's Digest*, May 1981, 228.

2. Francis Brown, *A Hebrew and English Lexicon of the Old Testament* (London: Oxford University Press, 1972), 991.

3. James Orr, ed., *The International Standard Bible Encyclopaedia*, vol. 4 (Grand Rapids, MI: William B. Eerdmans Publishing Co., 1939), 2631.

4. Jimmy Dodd, Message at Woodmen Valley Chapel in Colorado Springs, CO, August 1, 2010.

5. Thomas Dreier, "Points to Ponder," *Reader's Digest*, February 1982, 24.

6. "Average Hour-Long TV Show is 36% Commercials," *MarketingCharts*, May 7, 2009, http://www. marketingcharts.com/television/average-hour-long-show -is-36-commercials-9002/.

7. "Finding Balance in Your Family and Life, Part 1 of 2," interview on Focus on the Family radio with Lysa TerKeurst, January 13, 2015.

8. *Stop & Think* (Think Inc., 2005), http://vimeo.com/3553705.

9. Roger Launius, "Why Do People Persist in Denying the Moon Landings?," *Smithsonian National Air and Space Museum*, April 1, 2010, http://airandspace.si.edu/stories/editorial/ why-do-people-persist-denying-moon-landings.

10. "Personal Glimpses," *Reader's Digest*, June 1983, 169.

11. "Dream Maker," *Reader's Digest*, August 1994, 108.

12. "Too Busy NOT to Pray," *Christianity Today*, December 7, 2011, http://www.christianitytoday.com/moi/2011/006/ december/too-busy-not-to-pray.html.

13. Warren, *Purpose Driven Life*, 91.

14. Ibid., 190.

14. Templeton and Dunlap, *Why Are We Created?*, 121.

15. The Torah consists of the first five books of the Old Testament.

16. Aaron, *God-Powered Life*, 110.

Chapter Five

1. Wood, *In Search of Purpose*, 176.
2. "Brave New Digs," *Psychology Today*, vol. 49, no. 1 (2016): 9.
3. Wayne Martindale and Jerry Root, eds., *The Quotable Lewis* (Wheaton, IL: Tyndale House Publishers, 1990), 162.
4. Rodney Brooks, "Gray divorce is on the rise," *The Gazette* (Colorado Springs, CO), April 12, 2016), B-3.
5. Chris Cree, "Contracts vs. Covenants—Why the Difference Matters," last updated May 2012, http://newcreeations.org/contracts-vs-covenants-why-the-difference-matters/.
6. "The Talmud is a huge collection of doctrines and laws compiled and written before the 8th Century, A.D., by ancient Jewish teachers." *Come and Hear*, http://www.come-and-hear.com/editor/whatis.html.
7. Aaron, *God-Powered Life*, 37.
8. Roberts, *Purpose Awakening*, 174.
9. Helen Reddy and Ray Burton, "I Am Woman," sung by Reddy in *I Am Woman*, Capitol Records, 1972.
10. Shank, *Total Life Management*, 92.
11. Martindale and Root, 412.

Chapter Six

1. "Peggy O'Mara," *Goodreads*, http://www.goodreads.com/author/quotes/30657.Peggy_O_Mara.
2. *Worldometers*, accessed April 21, 2017, http://www.worldometers.info/world-population/.
3. Tara Bahrampour, "For millennials, living with mom and dad is the norm." *The Gazette* (Colorado Springs, CO), May 25, 2016, 1.
4. Erik Rees, *S.H.A.P.E.: Finding & Fulfilling Your Unique Purpose in Life* (Grand Rapids, MI: Zondervan, 2006), 199.

5. Carol Kuykendall, *Give Them Wings: Preparing for the Time Your Teens Leave Home* (Colorado Springs, CO: Focus on the Family Publishing, 1994), 41-52.

6. "Discipline," *Dictionary.com*, http://www.dictionary.com/browse/discipline?s=t.

7. "Disciple," *Dictionary.com*, http://www.dictionary.com/browse/disciple?s=t.

8. C. F. Keil and Franz Delitzsch, *Commentary on the Old Testament in Ten Volumes*, vol. 6 (Grand Rapids, MI: Eerdmans Publishing Co., 1981), 30.

9. Ibid., 287.

10. Ibid., 87.

11. Gary Chapman, *The Marriage You've Always Wanted* (Chicago, IL: Moody Publishers, 2009), 121.

12. Richard Blackaby, *The Seasons of God: How the Shifting Patterns of Your Life Reveal His Purposes for You* (Colorado Springs, CO: Multnomah Books, 2012), 161.

Chapter Seven

1. Aaron, *God-Powered Life*, 74.

2. Swindoll, *Mystery of God's Will*, 106.

3. Martindale and Root, *Quotable Lewis*, 221.

4. Ted Haggard, *Your Primary Purpose: How to Reach Your Community and World for Christ* (Lake Mary, FL: Charisma House, 2006), 116.

5. Warren, *Purpose Driven Life*, 163.

6. Ibid., 277.

7. Ibid., 277.

8. Tim Timberlake, *Abandon: Laying Aside Your Plan for God's Purpose* (Shippensburg, PA: Destiny Image, 2015), 105.

9. Waltke, *Finding the Will of God*, 118.

10. Edwards, *What Is The Point?*, 153.

11. Warren, 147-48.

Chapter Eight

1. Randy Alcorn, *The Treasure Principle: Discovering the Secret of Joyful Giving* (Sisters, OR: Multnomah Publishers, 2001), 77-78.

2. "Wealth," *Dictionary.com*, http://www.dictionary.com/browse/wealth?.

3. *Joy*, directed by David O. Russell (2015; Los Angeles, CA: 20th Century Fox, 2016), DVD.

4. "Tragic end to a Canadian lottery winner who just wanted to be liked," *Euro-Millions.org*, http://www.euro-millions.org/stories/567/.

5. *MotherTeresa.org*, http://www.motherteresa.org/layout.html.

6. "Mel Gray to Retire," *The New York Times*, December 7, 1982, http://www.nytimes.com/1982/12/07/sports/sports-people-mel-gray-to-retire.html.

7. Kerry A. Dolan and Luisa Kroll, "Inside The 2015 Forbes Billionaires List: Facts And Figures," *Forbes*, March 2, 2015, http://www.forbes.com/sites/kerryadolan/2015/03/02/inside-the-2015-forbes-billionaires-list-facts-and-figures/#5ec4cee76cec.

8. "Warren Buffett, Billionaire, Still Lives in Modest Omaha Home Which Cost $31,500 in 1958," *The Huffington Post*, January 18, 2013, http://www.huffingtonpost.com/entry/warren-buffett-home_n_2507179.

9. Wood, *In Search of Purpose*, 91.

10. Garry Friesen, *Decision Making and the Will of God: A Biblical Alternative to the Traditional View* (Sisters, OR: Multnomah Press, 1980), 364.

11. Ibid., 369.

12. Ibid., 369.
13. Damien Wills, *The Three Desires: Discovering Your Spiritual Purpose* (Damien Wills, 2015), 68.
14. Warren, *Purpose Driven Life*, 267.
15. Martindale and Root, *Quotable Lewis*, 245.
16. Warren Buffett, "My philanthropic pledge," *Fortune*, June 16, 2010, archive.fortune.com/2010/06/15/news/newsmakers/Warren_Buffett_Pledge_Letter.fortune/index.htm?iid=sr-link1.

Chapter Nine

1. *Ripe 'N Ready*, http://www.ripenready.com/rnrfruit/faq.html.
2. Martindale and Root, *Quotable Lewis*, 308.
3. Swindoll, *Mystery of God's Will*, 22.
4. Munroe, *In Pursuit of Purpose*, 122.
5. Roberts, *Purpose Awakening*, 113.
6. Ibid., 113.
7. Wills, *Three Desires*, 128.
8. Templeton and Dunlap, *Why Are We Created?*, 69.
9. Jimmy Dodd, *Survive or Thrive: 6 Relationships Every Pastor Needs* (Colorado Springs, CO: David C. Cook, 2015), 24-26.
10. Viktor Frankl, *Man's Search for Meaning: An Introduction to Logotherapy* (New York: Simon & Schuster, 1984), 27.
11. Warren, *Purpose Driven Life*, 97.

Chapter Ten

1. "Heavy people might die up to 3 years early," *The Gazette* (Colorado Springs, CO), July 14, 2016, A-9.
2. John Tozzi, "Worldwide, obesity rises at an unprecedented rate," *The Gazette* (Colorado Springs, CO), April 2, 2016, A-1, A-13.

3. Teresa Dumain, "Secrets Your Body's Trying to Tell You," *Reader's Digest*, May 2016, 62.

4. Emily Laber-Warren, "You Are When You Eat," *Reader's Digest*, May 2016, 44-45.

5. Ibid., 45.

6. Ibid., 45.

7. Joyce and Gene Daoust, *40-30-30 Fat Burning Nutrition: The Dietary Hormonal Connection to Permanent Weight Loss and Better Health* (Del Mar, CA: Wharton Publishing, 1997).

8. S. I. McMillen, *None of These Diseases* (Old Tappan, NJ: Fleming H. Revell Company, 2000).

9. *Foods That Harm, Foods That Heal* (Pleasantville, NY: Reader's Digest Books, 2012).

10. Hara Estroff Marano, "Seeing the Light on Vitamin D," *Psychology Today*, vol. 116, no. 1 (January 2016): 30.

11. Rees, *S.H.A.P.E.*, 213.

12. "Kid's sleep guidelines spell out shut-eye requirements by age," *The Gazette* (Colorado Springs, CO), June 13, 2016, A-11.

13. "How Much Sleep Do We Really Need?" *Sleep.org*, https://sleepfoundation.org/how-sleep-works/how-much -sleep-do-we-really-need.

14. Dumain, 62.

15. Kent Holland, *Working on Purpose* (Vienna, VA: Ardent Publications, 2011), 93.

16. David Brown, "Can exercise kill you?" *The Gazette* (Colorado Springs, CO), March 22, 2016), D-2.

17. Heidi Tyline King, "The Lifelong Benefits of Exercise," *Everyday Health*, www.everydayhealth.com/fitness.basics.get -fit-for-life.aspx

18. Hallie Gould, "When should you work out?" *The Gazette* (Colorado Springs, CO), April 14, 2016, D-3.

19. Dumain, 62.
20. Penn State Milton S. Hershey Medical Center, "Strength training helps older adults live longer," *Science Daily*, April 20, 2016, www.sciencedaily.com/releases/2016/04/160420090406 .html.
21. Roberts, *Purpose Awakening*, 30-31.
22. Warren, *Purpose Driven Life*, 179.
23. Rob Link, *Become* (Reformed Church Press, 2013), 75.
24. Sue Fitzmaurice, *Purpose* (Sue Fitzmaurice, 2014), 46-47.
25. Wills, *Three Desires*, 53.
26. Gnosticism refers to ancient religions that shunned the material world, which they viewed as evil, and embraced only things that they considered spiritual.
27. Aaron, *God-Powered Life*, 97.

Chapter Eleven

1. "5 Wise Quotes from Rob Hill Sr. You Need to See," *Travel Quotes*, http://www.lovetravelquotes.com/2015/01/my-goal-is -to-build-life-i-dont-need.html.
2. Michael Strahan, *Wake Up Happy: The Dream Big, Win Big Guide to Transforming Your Life* (New York: Simon & Schuster, 2015), 174.
3. Joseph Michelli, *The Starbucks Experience: 5 Principles for Turning Ordinary into Extraordinary* (New York: McGraw Hill, 2007), 13.
4. Aaron, *God-Powered Life*, 107.
5. Templeton and Dunlap, *Why Are We Created?*, 107.
6. Rees, *S.H.A.P.E.*, 118-19.
7. Ibid., 138.
8. "Eric Liddell," *Goodreads*, http://www.goodreads.com/ quotes/209349-god-made-me-fast-and-when-i-run-i-feel.

9. Friesen, *Decision Making*, 265.

10. Ibid., 267.

11. Waltke, *Finding the Will of God*, 177.

12. Shank, *Total Life Management*, 57.

13. John MacArthur, "Delight Yourself in the Lord (and Do Whatever You Want!)," *Grace to You*, December 21, 2010, http://www.gty.org/blog/B101221/delight-yourself-in-the-lord-and-do-whatever-you-want.

14. Aaron, 101.

Chapter Twelve

1. Leslie Weatherhead, *The Will of God* (Nashville, TN: Abingdon Press, 1972), 27.

2. Swindoll, *Mystery of God's Will*, 33.

3. Ibid., 40.

4. Waltke, *Finding the Will of God*, 68.

5. Timberlake, *Abandon*, 87.

6. Friesen, *Decision Making*, 386.

7. "Quotable Quotes," *Reader's Digest*, September 2015, 148.

8. Martin R. Vincent, *Word Studies in the New Testament*, vol. 3 (Grand Rapids, MI: William B. Eerdmans Publishing Co., 1975), 505.

Chapter Thirteen

1. Michelli, *Starbucks Experience*, 19.

2. "What's trending," *The Gazette* (Colorado Springs, CO), April 12, 2016, A-2.

3. "Introduction—Book of Revelation," *BibleProbe*, http://www.bibleprobe.com/revelation.htm.

4. Walter Scott, "Personality," *Parade Magazine*, May 22, 2016, 2.

5. "Even at age 90, this Byrd remains 100 percent fit," *The Gazette* (Colorado Springs, CO), April 10, 2016, A-10.

6. Shank, *Total Life Management*, 31.

7. Blackaby, *Seasons of God*, 201.

8. Martindale and Root, *Quotable Lewis*, 40.

9. Roberts, *Purpose Awakening*, 193.

10. Blackaby, 230.

11. Warren, *Purpose Driven*, 227.

12. Roberts, 59.

13. Huckabee, pg. 279

14. Blackaby, 208.

15. Martindale and Root, 40.

16. Linda Ellis, "The Dash," *Linda-Ellis.com*, http://www.linda -ellis.com/the-dash-the-dash-poem-by-linda-ellis-.html.

Chapter Fourteen

1. Alcorn, *Treasure Principle*, 48.

2. Shank, *Total Life Management*, 27.

3. Holland, *Working on Purpose*, 93.

4. Timberlake, *Abandon*, 75.

5. "Augustine of Hippo," *Goodreads*, http://www.goodreads.com/ quotes/994001-trust-the-past-to-god-s-mercy-the-present-to -god-s.

6. George W. Bush, *Decision Points* (New York: Crown Publishers, 2010), 2.

7. Steve Forbes, interview by Jim Stovall, *The Lamp*, March 6, 2012, http://youtu.be/pxCIlzSXkic.

8. Holland, 76.

9. Shank, 30.

10. Alyssa Jung, "Science-Backed Signs You Could Live to 100," *Reader's Digest*, July/August 2016, 48.

11. Ibid., 50.

12. Blackaby, *Seasons of God*, 42.

13. Rick Warren, interview by Paul Bradshaw, http://markconner
    .typepad.com/catch_the_wind/2009/05/an-interview-with
    -rick-warren.html.

14. *Saving Private Ryan*, directed by Steven Spielberg (1998;
    Glendale, CA: Dream Works Entertainment, 1999), DVD.

About The Author

Dr. Barry Ham is an educator in a variety of forms—as a college professor, a marriage and family therapist practicing in Colorado Springs, as well as an author and speaker.

He received his BA and BS degrees in Ministry and Music from Dallas Christian College. His first graduate degree was an MS in Psychology from Abilene Christian University, followed by a MS in Marriage and Family Counseling from California State University. Finally, he received his PhD in Clinical Psychology from Southern California University.

He was born in Tulsa, Oklahoma, and was raised there and in Houston, Texas. He currently lives in the Colorado Springs area with his wife and two goldendoodles. He and his wife have grown children who, with their families, live inside and outside of Colorado.

Dr. Ham is available to speak at your church or gathering and also is available for weekend seminars.

For booking and additional information, he can be contacted at:

Dr. Barry D. Ham
c/o Integrative Family/Individual Therapy
P.O. Box 63241
Colorado Springs, CO 80962
drbdham@msn.com
www.livingonpurpose.net